AVID

READER

PRESS

PROFILES *in* IGNORANCE

How America's Politicians
Got Dumb *and* Dumber

ANDY BOROWITZ

AVID READER PRESS

New York   London   Toronto   Sydney   New Delhi

AVID READER PRESS
An Imprint of Simon & Schuster, Inc.
1230 Avenue of the Americas
New York, NY 10020

First Avid Reader Press hardcover edition September 2022

AVID READER PRESS and colophon are trademarks of Simon & Schuster, Inc.
For information about special discounts for bulk purchases, please contact Simon &
Schuster Special Sales at 1-866-506-1949 or business@simonandschuster.com.

The Simon & Schuster Speakers Bureau can bring authors to your live event. For
more information or to book an event, contact the Simon & Schuster Speakers
Bureau at 1-866-248-3049 or visit our website at www.simonspeakers.com.

Interior design by Ruth Lee-Mui

Manufactured in Malaysia

1 3 5 7 9 10 8 6 4 2

Library of Congress Cataloging-in-Publication Data has been applied for.

ISBN 978-1-6680-0388-6
ISBN 978-1-6680-0390-9 (ebook)

To my family, with all my love:
Livy,
Lexi, Max, Maddie,
and Niko

Being dumb's just about the worst thing there is when it comes to holding high office.
—HARRY S. TRUMAN

The worst thing a man can do is go bald.
—DONALD J. TRUMP

Contents

THE THREE STAGES
OF IGNORANCE

Imagine a hypothetical job applicant. He can't spell the simplest words, such as "heal" and "tap." Confused by geography, he thinks there's an African country called "Nambia." As for American history, he's under the impression that Andrew Jackson, who died in 1845, was angry about the Civil War, and that Frederick Douglass, who died in 1895, is still alive.

Given the alarming state of his knowledge, you might wonder what job he could get. Unfortunately, he's not hypothetical, and the job he got, in 2016, was president of the United States.

People sometimes call our nation "the American experiment." Recently, though, we've been lab rats in another, perverse American experiment, seemingly designed to answer this question: Who's the most ignorant person the United States is willing to elect?

Over the past fifty years, what some of our most prominent politicians didn't know could fill a book. This is that book.

This book will also examine what brought our country to such a stupid place. We'll retrace the steps of the vacuous pioneers who turned ignorance from a liability into a virtue. By relentlessly lowering the bar, they made it possible for today's politicians to wear their dunce caps with pride. Gone are the days when leaders had to hide how much they didn't know. Now cluelessness is an electoral asset and smart politicians must play dumb, or risk voters' wrath. Welcome to the survival of the dimmest.

Maybe you're thinking, "So what? We've always had dumb politicians." That's undeniably true; as the political satirist Will Rogers said, "It's easy being a humorist when you've got the whole government working for you." When I was growing up in Cleveland, Ohio, I struggled to find a politician I could take seriously. In 1972, our mayor, Ralph J. Perk (his actual name), presided over a trade expo for the American Society for Metals. There was a metals-themed opening ceremony, requiring the mayor to cut a titanium ribbon with a welding torch. As Perk held the fire-spewing tool, sparks flew skyward and set his hair ablaze. The incident, which, thankfully, is available on YouTube, inspired mocking headlines around the world. It also reinforced Cleveland's unfortunate reputation for flammability: three years earlier, our polluted Cuyahoga River had spontaneously combusted.

Perhaps the hair-on-fire incident was Ralph J. Perk's version of the Icarus myth, a cautionary tale about what happens when a politician flies too close to a welding torch. Like Icarus, Perk came crashing to Earth. In 1974, Ohio's voters rejected his bid for the U.S. Senate and chose someone less likely to be flummoxed by technology: the astronaut John Glenn. Perk received hair transplants at the Cleveland Clinic in 1976 to repair the bald spot the torch had created, but by then his political career had been singed beyond repair. He did have one other notable achievement as mayor: Richard Eberling, a man he hired in 1973 to redecorate Cleveland's city hall, was later convicted of homicide and linked to another murder—the one that inspired the TV series and movie *The Fugitive*. Perk's historic role as a job creator for suspected serial killers hasn't gotten the attention it deserves. I hope I've fixed that.

Perk's political career collapsed in 1977 with a humiliating third-place finish in Cleveland's nonpartisan mayoral primary, a result I found reassuring. I believed his downfall proved democracy had a braking system. If a politician was too big a doofus, the brakes would keep us from hurtling off a cliff. But on Election Night 2016, it felt like the brakes were shot.

As the Trump nightmare unfolded, well-meaning people tried to soothe a rattled nation by arguing that he was no dumber than some of our previous dumb presidents. In this valiant attempt to pretend the hellscape enveloping us was nothing new, they cited a bygone commander in chief reputed to be one of our densest: Warren G. Harding. It's true that our twenty-ninth president would never have been put in charge of designing the next generation of supercolliders. After Harding's inaugural address in 1921, H. L. Mencken wrote, "No other such complete and dreadful nitwit is to be found in the pages of American history." Mencken should've added, ". . . so far."

People have pilloried Harding's campaign slogan, "A Return to Normalcy," for which he allegedly coined the word "normalcy" when a perfectly good actual word, "normality," already existed. But, according to *Merriam-Webster*, "normalcy" first appeared a decade before Harding was born, in a mathematical dictionary published in 1855. Now, it's true that Harding did our language no favors by popularizing "normalcy," a word almost as annoying as "impactful," but he was a slacker compared to Trump, whose mutilation of English could fill a non-word-a-day calendar. Out of fairness, I'll exclude from discussion the much-mocked "covfefe," which was probably just a late-night typo, and draw your attention to remarks he made at the Pentagon in 2019, when he seemed to invent a new military term, "infantroopen." Based on my research, there are no prior appearances of "infantroopen" in any dictionary, mathematical or otherwise.

Of course, Harding's bad reputation stems from more than one iffy word. His presidency birthed a profusion of controversies, most notoriously the Teapot Dome corruption scandal, long considered second only to Watergate in its infamy. (Proof that Watergate was worse: "dome" never became a suffix.) But how much blame Harding should shoulder for Teapot Dome has been debated. In 2004, Watergate celeb John Dean published a biography in which he argued that Harding "had done nothing wrong and had not been involved in any criminal activities." Whether you agree with that verdict or not, it's hard to get too worked up over Teapot Dome once you've seen a president urge a mob wearing fur pelts and face paint to storm the Capitol.

When you review some of Harding's presidential initiatives, comparisons to Trump seem even less apt. Harding supported a federal anti-lynching law and proposed a commission to investigate not only lynching but the disenfranchisement of Black voters. On October 26, 1921, he advocated racial equality in a major civil rights speech in Birmingham, Alabama. "Whether you like it or not, our democracy is a lie unless you stand for that equality," he declared. For a guy Mencken called a nitwit, he was far more enlightened than the person who, in the aftermath of the deadly Unite the Right rally in Charlottesville, said that there were "very fine people on both sides." (It's also possible that Mencken didn't think one's support for racial equality was desirable, since his posthumously published diary revealed him to be racist, anti-Semitic, and pro-Nazi. In other words, a very fine person.)

One quality Harding and Trump have in common: neither excelled at monogamy. But, even here, Harding wins. In 2014, the

Library of Congress released letters he wrote to his lover, Carrie Fulton Phillips, containing florid passages such as this: "I love you more than all the world and have no hope of reward on earth or hereafter so precious as that in your dear arms, in your thrilling lips, in your matchless breasts, in your incomparable embrace." It's hard to imagine Trump writing something so heartfelt to Stormy Daniels, or a sentence that long.

I've saved the best about Harding for last: unlike our forty-fifth president, he knew his limitations. He once lamented, "I am not fit for this office and should never have been here." Though this comment would be a far more accurate assessment of Trump than "stable genius," I can't picture the Donald engaging in such introspection—or, as he might say, introspectroopen.

Although Harding has the dubious distinction of being smarter than Trump—pretty much the dictionary definition of faint praise—both belong to a tradition that we Americans shouldn't be proud of: our habit of installing dim bulbs in the White House. There's a long history of anti-intellectualism in American life, a point that the historian Richard Hofstadter seemed to be making in his 1963 book, *Anti-Intellectualism in American Life*. It wasn't a good sign when the eloquent abolitionist John Quincy Adams lost the 1828 presidential election to the homicidal maniac Andrew Jackson. ("Old Hickory," who was neither stable nor a genius, challenged more than a hundred men to duels. He killed only one, but still.) Over the next thirty years, the nation endured a presidential clown parade. In 1856, ex-president Millard Fillmore ran for the White House under the banner of a new, nativist party, the exquisitely named Know-Nothings. Fillmore and his running mate, Andrew Jackson Donelson (the homicidal maniac's nephew), believed that there was nothing wrong with America that persecuting all its German, Irish, and Catholic immigrants couldn't fix. As dumb as Fillmore sounds, the winner on

Election Day might have been even dumber: James "Old Buck" Buchanan. Though Buchanan failed to avert the Civil War, he sprang into action to defuse a military confrontation with the British over the shooting of a solitary pig in Canada. (This skirmish actually happened; google "Pig War.") The following year, the American people seemed to say, "Enough of this bullshit," and elected Abraham Lincoln.

Yes, our Statue of Stupidity has held her torch high over the years. But she's held it even higher over the past fifty, during the so-called Information Age. By elevating candidates who can entertain over those who can think, mass media have made the election of dunces more likely. Fact-free and nuance-intolerant, these human sound-bite machines have reduced our most complex problems to binary oppositions: us versus communists; us versus terrorists; and that latest crowd-pleaser, us versus scientists. Interestingly, Hofstadter thought that the first televised presidential debates, in 1960, were a positive development, because they benefited John F. Kennedy, who, he believed, combined intelligence with on-screen command. But the historian didn't live to see how TV, tag-teaming with its demented henchman the internet, could boost candidates who were geniuses about those media and dopes about everything else. What happens when you combine ignorance with performing talent? A president who tells the country to inject bleach.

Hofstadter thought things started going downhill for us in the 1720s, when the preachers of the Great Awakening upstaged the learned clergy of the Puritans with bizarre theatrics: "fits and seizures . . . shrieks and groans and grovelings." Neil Postman, in his book *Amusing Ourselves to Death: Public Discourse in the Age of Show Business*, argued that this dumbing-down process exploded during the nineteenth century, when we started reading fewer books because we were going bonkers over two wild new inventions: photography and the telegraph. Clearly, ignorance in America has had kind of a running start. Since this trend has been centuries in the making, why am I even bothering to single out a few dimwits from our recent past? I'm writing this book as a concerned citizen, reporting a ghastly multicar pileup to other concerned citizens. Just as a Stephen King novel might inspire you to bolt your doors, perhaps these political horror stories will rouse you to action. Alternatively, if someday alien scientists are picking through the rubble of our fallen civilization and happen upon a tattered copy of this book, maybe it'll help them piece together what went wrong.

Since I'll be arguing that politicians' ignorance has been surging over the past five decades, I should clarify what I mean by ignorance. The dictionary defines it as "the lack of knowledge, education or awareness." That works for me, only I might add "the refusal to look things up in the dictionary." When discussing a politician, I'll refrain from using words such as *idiot*, *imbecile*, *cretin*, or any other equally tempting term that impugns mental capacity rather than knowledge. I might say "dunce," because that connotes a failure to do one's homework, a problem that has plagued a few recent presidents. I also like "ignoramus," which the dictionary defines as "an utterly ignorant person." Ignoramus is a word you don't hear much these days, which is too bad because it applies so well to so many. If, in writing this book, I somehow bring the word ignoramus back into vogue, I'll consider my work on this planet done. (A caveat: If other people have called a politician an idiot, imbecile, cretin, etc., I'll be obliged to quote them. The historical record must be preserved.)

I'll resist the urge to speculate about a politician's IQ or cognitive health. I might be dazzled by a person's ability to remember the nouns "person, woman, man, camera, TV" and repeat them on command, but, as a non-neurologist, I'm not qualified to say what this monumental achievement says about one's acuity. Neither will I try to assess a politician's mental stability, since I think it's safe to assume that most people who run for president are, to some extent, out of their fucking minds. Instead, I'll ask: During their time in public life, what did these politicians know? Did they have sufficient mastery of math, science, history, geography—and, since I'm being picky, the English language—necessary to govern? When briefed, could they learn? At the very least, did they know not to stare at a solar eclipse?

My preference that politicians be educated probably brands me as an elitist. I'm fine with that. I consider myself the Ted Nugent of elitism. But being an elitist doesn't make me a snob—hear me out, there's a difference. When I say "educated," I want politicians to have the knowledge required to do their jobs well, or at least not to get us all killed. I don't care where, or even whether, a politician went to college. Harry Truman wasn't a college graduate, and he probably took some solace in knowing that a predecessor of his, George Washington, wasn't, either. It's possible to become a great president with no more than twelve months of grade school—an educational background that Abraham Lincoln, being honest and all, would have had to disclose on LinkedIn.

I don't care much about the grades a politician got in school because they're not a reliable predicter of governing ability. Franklin Delano Roosevelt somehow managed to lead the nation out of the Great Depression and to victory in World War II despite his C average, a GPA that today would keep him from getting an interview at McKinsey.* What made Roosevelt a successful president, among other gifts, was his intellectual curiosity, which enabled him to absorb vast amounts of information necessary to resolve unprecedented

---

*The website of the FDR Foundation points out that, when adjusted for grade inflation, his marks would translate to "high B's by today's standards." This assessment of FDR's transcript would have more credibility coming from an organization that didn't have FDR in its name.

crises. When severe drought created the Dust Bowl, he had a lot to learn; he couldn't fall back on his high school experience at Model Dust Bowl. I want the president of the United States to be intellectually curious for a simple reason: I think the person running the country should be smarter than I am. We've just lived through the alternative, and it was only good for the liquor industry.

How can we tell if a politician is intellectually curious? Reading habits are a good place to start. Truman might not have gone to college, but as a kid he tried to devour every library book in Independence, Missouri. As I profile presidents, I'll examine how much they enjoyed, or even tolerated, the act of reading. Why? Well, there's something called the President's Daily Brief (PDB), an intelligence summary that, true to its name, lands on the president's desk every day. It's true to its name in another way: It's literally brief, often just a page or two. Yet to some recent recipients it seemed like *War and Peace*.

To believe that Trump's presidency came out of nowhere, without warning, is the political version of creationism. I, on the other hand, believe in devolution. The election of a serially bankrupt, functionally illiterate reality TV host was the logical consequence of the five decades preceding it, which, with apologies to Edith Wharton, I'll call the Age of Ignorance. How did the bar for our political figures fall so far? To better understand this heinous half century, I've divided it into the **Three Stages of Ignorance: Ridicule, Acceptance, and Celebration.**

During the **Ridicule** stage, ignorance was a magnet for mockery, a serious flaw that could kill a political career. Consequently, dumb politicians had to pretend to be smart. I'll profile two politicians who navigated this perilous stage with radically different outcomes: Ronald Reagan, whose gift as a TV performer helped hide his cluelessness, and Dan Quayle, who shared Reagan's cluelessness but not his knack for hiding it.

During the **Acceptance** stage, ignorance mutated into something more agreeable: a sign that a politician was authentic, down-to-earth, and a "normal person." Consequently, dumb politicians felt free to appear dumb. In this stage, I'll profile George W. Bush, who made ignorance his brand, and Sarah Palin, who made it her business model.

Finally, during the **Celebration** stage—the ordeal we're enduring right now—ignorance has become preferable to knowledge, dunces are exalted over experts, and a candidate can win a seat in Congress after blaming wildfires on Jewish space lasers. Being ill-informed is now a litmus test; consequently, smart politicians must pretend to be dumb. I'll profile the ultimate embodiment of this stage, Donald J. Trump, and Trump wannabes such as Ted Cruz and Ron DeSantis—who, despite being graduates of our nation's finest universities, strenuously try to outdumb him.

The solidly Republican cast of this tragicomedy might prompt you to ask (especially if you're a Republican): Haven't Democrats done a lot of dumb crap? Yes, bucketloads. Democrats have been caught on tape smoking crack (Marion Barry) and trying to sell a U.S. Senate seat (Rod Blagojevich). And we shan't forget the Four Horndogs of the Apocalypse—John Edwards, Eliot Spitzer, Anthony Weiner, and Andrew Cuomo—who, though seemingly endowed with functioning brains, let a different body part do their thinking. But while Democratic dopes have wreaked their share of havoc, the scale of their destruction doesn't equal that of their Republican counterparts. Once Democrats gin up a two-trillion-dollar war to find nonexistent weapons of mass destruction, ignore and then politicize a virus that causes nearly a million needless deaths, and attempt a violent overthrow of the U.S. government, I'll get cracking on a book about them. Until then, I'll recognize them for what they are: supporting players in our national pageant of stupidity, but not towering icons like George W. Bush or Donald J. Trump.

After reading these profiles in ignorance, you might decide that the bar couldn't possibly go lower. Well, sorry. The bar can always go lower. On the plus side, history doesn't move in a straight line. After the glory that was Greece and the grandeur that was Rome, the Dark Ages must've seemed pretty bleak—but, before you knew it, it was the Renaissance, and everyone was singing madrigals and painting frescoes. The lesson is clear: while the bar can always go lower, it can also go higher, as long as you're willing to wait a few centuries.

But I'm not recommending that we sit around waiting for our present Dark Ages to pass. Given what's at stake—things I've grown partial to, like a habitable planet—we need to find an off-ramp from this idiotic highway before it's too late. In my last chapter, I'll explore a possible route.

One final point. For the past twenty years or so, I've written a column in which I've made up news stories for the purpose of satire. In this book, I've made nothing up. All the events I'm about to describe actually happened. They're a part of American history. Unfortunately.

1

THE FIRST STAGE:
RIDICULE

Not so long ago, it was less than ideal for an American politician to seem like a dumbass. If a candidate's stupidity became too glaring, the consequences could be dire: derision, contempt, and electoral oblivion. In this chapter, we'll meet two men who traversed this minefield with wildly different results: the Goofus and Gallant of the Ridicule stage. Gallant is Ronald Reagan, whose talents distracted us from his ignorance. Goofus is Dan Quayle, whose ignorance distracted us from his talents. To this day, those talents remain unknown.

In the mid-1960s, a candidate clip-clopped into town and, though possessing a puny saddlebag of knowledge, stuck to a script that fooled enough of the people enough of the time. It helped that he'd spent years on Hollywood soundstages memorizing lines and performing them with spectacular sincerity, even when acting opposite a chimp. His name was Ronald Reagan, and it's in no small part thanks to him that today we can say: It's Moronic in America.

Reagan was more responsible for the rise of ignorance than for the fall of communism. Like Chuck Yeager shattering the sound barrier, Reagan tested the outer limits of vacuity; the dullards he inspired all stand on his denim-clad shoulders. Today, more than four decades after he entered the White House and took his first nap, his disciples worship him like a prophet, an oracle, the Yoda of cluelessness.

Reagan's devotees have lavished him with the sort of hagiographies usually reserved for the Dalai Lama or LeBron James. His longtime pollster Dick Wirthlin apparently felt that calling his former boss the Great Communicator wasn't effusive enough; he titled his Reagan book *The Greatest Communicator*. Central to these gushy narratives is the claim that Ronnie single-handedly caused the Soviet Union to crumble. I understand why Reaganites would want to cast him as the leading man in the story of communism's disintegration, but I'd argue that he deserves as much credit for the demise of disco—that is, not very much, even though it gurgled its death rattle on his watch.* Praising Reagan for vanquishing communism contradicts his own assertion that the Soviet Union was an inherently flawed enterprise, doomed to fail. Based on that logic, the credit for the Evil Empire's demolition must go to Vladimir Lenin himself, for coming up with such a crappy idea for a society to begin with. I'm in the awkward position of agreeing with Richard Nixon, who observed, "Communism would have collapsed anyway."

Reagan's mythologizers haven't been content to knight him as a commie-slayer. In an audacious leap of imagination, they've tried to recast him as a deep thinker. In 2018, an author named David T. Byrne (an adjunct professor at California Baptist University—not

---

*The man who deserves the most credit for hastening disco's downfall might be the film producer Allan Carr, who, in 1980, unleashed the apocalyptic Village People vehicle *Can't Stop the Music*, which won the first-ever Golden Raspberry Award for Worst Picture, and is easily one of Steve Guttenberg's ten worst films.

the singer of "Burning Down the House") published a book called *Ronald Reagan: An Intellectual Biography*. I couldn't resist buying a book with such a funny title. Astonishingly, it somehow manages to be two hundred pages.

Even before you open his book, you can tell Byrne means business. Unlike many Reagan hagiographies, which feature a cover photo of their grinning, Stetson-crowned hero clearing brush or miming some other rancher-like chore, this one boasts a severe black-and-white image of a bespectacled Ronnie at a desk, intently reading a serious-looking piece of paper. In his introduction, Byrne cites several injurious examples of disrespect aimed at Reagan's mind, including a comment by an adviser to four presidents, Clark Clifford, who rated him an "amiable dunce." Somewhat undermining Byrne's authority on intellectual matters, he misspells Clifford's first name as "Clarke." Explaining why he wrote the book, Byrne says that he became frustrated by the widespread recognition Barack Obama received for his intellect, while Reagan's big brain remained ignored. This slight was particularly galling, he argues, because Reagan was a far more original thinker than Obama. That's true, in the way Dr. Oz is a far more original thinker than Dr. Stephen Hawking.

As the book drags on, Byrne apes his namesake and stops making sense. In one particularly unfortunate illustration of Reagan's brilliance, he quotes one of his most famous pieces of oratory, a 1964 address called "A Time for Choosing" that Reaganites cultishly refer to as "The Speech." "We're spending 45 billion dollars on welfare," Reagan said. "Now do a little arithmetic, and you'll find that if we divided the 45 billion dollars up equally among those 9 million poor families, we'd be able to give each family 4,600 dollars a year." Although 4,600 might be a highly original answer to that division problem, if you do a little arithmetic, the correct answer is 5,000. When George H. W. Bush, Reagan's chief rival for the 1980 Republican nomination, accused him of "voodoo economics," he might have been exaggerating. Maybe Reagan just sucked at math.

It's fun to imagine what Reagan would have made of Byrne's nervy attempt to remake him as an intellectual. Appraising him more sensibly, Hollywood producers often cast him as a man of action— a soldier or a gunslinger—and as a professor only twice: in 1951's *Bedtime for Bonzo*, in which he acted opposite a simian, and in the following year's *She's Working Her Way Through College*, in which, in an unlikely turn for the future icon of the Moral Majority, he mentored an exotic dancer. "Intellectual," in fact, was one of Reagan's favorite put-downs. In a radio address in 1963, he heaped scorn on the theory "that we can do without a few freedoms in order to enjoy government by an intellectual elite which obviously knows what is best for us." A year later, he declared that voters must decide "whether we abandon the American Revolution and confess that a little intellectual elite in a far-distant capital can plan our lives for us better than we can plan them ourselves." By the time Reagan became governor of California, in 1967, intellectuals were his piñatas of choice, with the students and faculty at UC Berkeley a regular target for bashing. In his most damning broadside, he said that California's taxpayers shouldn't be "subsidizing intellectual curiosity." Harsh!

Let's consider an opposing view to the revisionist portrait of Reagan as chin-stroking sage. Christopher Hitchens wrote, "The fox, as has been pointed out by more than one philosopher, knows many small things, whereas the hedgehog knows one big thing. Ronald Reagan was neither a fox nor a hedgehog. He was as dumb as a stump." The humorist Molly Ivins offered, "The charm of Ronald Reagan is not just that he kept telling us screwy things, it was that he believed them all. . . . His stubbornness, even defiance, in the face of facts . . . was nothing short of splendid. . . . This is the man who proved that ignorance is no handicap to the presidency." The columnist David S. Broder remarked, "The task of watering the arid desert between Reagan's ears is a challenging one for his aides." And, continuing with the water imagery, a California legislator said, "You could walk through Ronald Reagan's deepest thoughts and not get your ankles wet." A dunce, a stump, a desert, a mental wading pool. Were these people underestimating him? Or were they, despite the vaunting claims of David T. Byrne, estimating him? To answer that, let's ask another question, which arose repeatedly during the Iran-Contra scandal that plagued his second term: What did Ronald Reagan know?

"He was not intellectually curious, not deeply read," the journalist Haynes Johnson wrote. Reagan's brother Neil recalled one of Ronnie's professors at Eureka College, in Illinois, grousing that he "never opened a book." Once he got to Hollywood, he went a little crazy and decided to open one. That book, *The Law*, by the nineteenth-century French economist Frédéric Bastiat, might not have been as random a choice as it sounds: the author had already been championed by another Hollywood luminary, then-screenwriter and former movie extra Ayn Rand.* Interestingly, though Reagan and Rand were both fans of Bastiat, Rand was no fan of Reagan. In a 1975 letter, she wrote, "I urge you, as emphatically as I can, *not* to support the candidacy of Ronald Reagan. I urge you not to work for or advocate his nomination, and not to vote for him. . . . [M]ost Republican politicians . . . preserve some respect for the rights of the individual. Mr. Reagan does not: He opposes the right to abortion."

Though presidential photo ops tended to show Reagan clearing

---

*The woman who'd influence the economic "philosophies" of Republicans from Alan Greenspan to Paul Ryan made her film debut in Cecil B. DeMille's 1927 Jesus epic, *The King of Kings*. Looking at a still from that flick, in which the young, wide-eyed Rand is lost in a sea of biblically garbed extras, you'd never guess that, eighty years later, her ideas would help spark a global financial meltdown.

brush at his ranch, his hagiographers would have us believe that, the second the TV cameras left, he ditched his chain saw and grabbed a book. Longtime aide Michael Deaver called Reagan a "voracious reader"; unfortunately, he couldn't name a single book his boss voraciously read. As for Reagan's favorite authors, his mythologizers keep citing the same one: Bastiat. *The Reagan Revolution*, published in 1981, might have inspired the trend by quoting Reagan himself: "Bastiat has dominated my reading so much—ideas of that kind." Of what kind? He doesn't say. Steven F. Hayward, the author of the unironically titled *Greatness: Reagan, Churchill, and the Making of Extraordinary Leaders*, said of those two alleged equals, "[T]hey are the only two chief executives in history that I am aware of who quoted the obscure French economist Frédéric Bastiat." Adding his voice to the chorus, the ever-dependable David T. Byrne notes that Bastiat "was part of Reagan's private library." Always good to have Bastiat in your private library, in case that pesky Ayn Rand already checked it out from the public one.

If Reagan was such a voracious reader of Bastiat, that would make the Frenchman the rare economist he didn't disdain. "An economist is a person with a Phi Beta Kappa key on one end of his watch chain and no watch on the other," he liked to say. One book about economics he probably didn't crack was *The Triumph of Politics: Why the Reagan Revolution Failed*, in which his former budget director, David Stockman, exposed Reaganomics as a fraud.

During Reagan's presidency, White House reporters described his reading habits in less lofty terms than his hagiographers have. *Time* reported that he was "a voracious reader of newspapers and magazines." More specifically, Gary Schuster, of the *Detroit News*, said, "I know Reagan likes to read the funnies." Unfortunately, he found the printed matter necessary to do his job less appealing than *Beetle Bailey* or *Garfield*. One of his biographers, Lou Cannon, recounted that, on the eve of an economic summit in 1983, Reagan's chief of staff, James Baker, left him a briefing book that remained untouched the following morning. When Baker asked why he hadn't perused it, Reagan replied, "Well, Jim, *The Sound of Music* was on last night." Once he became the most powerful man in the world, his television-watching habits were, by all accounts, voracious.

Having reviewed Reagan's reading, what can we say about his writing? Hoping to convince us that he wasn't just a scripted robot, Reagan's hagiographers tell us he wrote hundreds of weekly radio addresses between 1975 and 1979. After reading these monologues, though, it's hard to imagine why someone else would claim authorship. During his 1980 White House run, his campaign wisely blocked their release. Here he is in 1978: "There were two Vietnams, north and south. They had been separate nations for centuries." (More like since 1954.) Also in 1978: "Swarms of locusts and grasshoppers; a plague of crickets, cutworms, and ants; and swarms of mosquitoes are making life miserable and even impossible in some parts of the world. . . . Some experts are treating this as an unexplainable mystery. Actually, there is no mystery about it. . . . The most effective pesticide, DDT, was outlawed . . . on the theoretical grounds that it might, under some circumstances, some day, harm some one or some thing." This unhinged rant reads like something out of the Bible, if God had been in the pocket of the pesticide industry. And here he is in 1979, revealing that the greatest environmental hazard isn't man-made at all: "Eighty percent of air pollution comes not from chimneys and auto exhaust pipes, but from plants and trees." When he reprised his theory about these toxic emissions during the 1980 campaign, students at California's Claremont College affixed this sign to a tree: "Chop Me Down Before I Kill Again."

But it would take more than mockery to shake Reagan's anti-tree convictions, which went back decades. "A tree's a tree," he said in 1966, while addressing a logging trade group. "How many do you need to look at?" As president, Reagan would continue his War on Flora by naming the tree-hating James Watt secretary of the interior. Watt called himself the nation's "number one environmentalist," which was like Napoleon calling himself Europe's "number one pacifist." Watt's dream of turning America's forests into one big lumberyard met its Waterloo after he made this career-ending boast about diversity on one of his department's panels: "I have a black, a woman, two Jews, and a cripple."

Trees weren't the only form of vegetation that Reagan deemed a menace. "Leading medical researchers," he said in 1980, "are coming to the conclusion that marijuana, pot, grass, whatever you want to call it, is probably the most dangerous drug in the United States, and we haven't begun to find out all of the ill effects, but they are permanent ill effects. The loss of memory, for example." Clearly, we'd all be better off inhaling something that's been proven safe, such as DDT.

Reagan's knack for making up facts became the gold standard for American politicians. Byrne claims Reagan's "greatest intellectual gift" was "his imagination." No argument there. Byrne recounts an oft-repeated tale about how young Ronnie, auditioning to be a sports broadcaster in Iowa, had to do play-by-play for an imaginary game. As the story goes, he somehow kept his fictitious patter going for an astounding fifteen minutes. What Byrne doesn't mention is that, years later, Reagan revealed that the game he narrated wasn't imaginary at all, but was his recollection of one he'd played in college. Furthermore, the guy who auditioned him said that this incredible performance lasted only three or four minutes. Reagan was such a fabulist that even a story about him making something up turned out to be made-up.

As president, Reagan found another use for his imagination: attributing suspiciously on-point quotations to historical figures who never said them. When he cited this Oliver Wendell Holmes maxim, "Keep the government poor and remain free," the White House had to acknowledge that Reagan "came up with that one himself." His favorite mouth to put words into was Winston Churchill's. In 1982, he offered this Churchillian quote: "The idea that a nation can tax itself into prosperity is one of the crudest delusions which has ever befuddled the human mind." (Never said it.) In 1984, Reagan declared, "Winston Churchill . . . once said that Americans did not cross the ocean, cross the mountains, and cross the prairies because we're made of sugar candy." This time, Reagan came closer to quoting something Churchill actually said; unfortunately, he said it to Canadians.

Reagan's habit of inventing quotations proved contagious. While he was attributing fake quotes to Churchill, his White House press secretary, Larry Speakes, was attributing fake quotes to him. In his 1988 memoir, *Speaking Out*, Speakes admitted that, when quoting Reagan, he "did a little improvising." During Reagan's 1985 summit in Geneva with Mikhail Gorbachev, Speakes announced that Reagan had told the Soviet premier, "There is much that divides us, but I believe the world breathes easier because we are here talking together." When he informed Reagan about this fabrication, Speakes said that his boss "really didn't say much, he didn't have any specific reaction." Weirdly, Speakes didn't invent one for him.

One of the more suspicious fake quotes that Reagan spewed was a self-incriminating rant by one of his favorite evildoers, Vladimir Lenin: "We will take Eastern Europe. We will organize the hordes of Asia. And then we will move into Latin America and we won't have to take the United States; it will fall into our outstretched hands like overripe fruit." It would have been strange for Lenin to spell out his whole evil plan in such detail, like a Bond villain briefing 007 before aiming a laser at his crotch. Vlad, however, wasn't the source of this

unhinged monologue. The quote appeared in the demented manifesto of a prolific paranoiac named Robert W. Welch Jr.

In 1958, Welch, a former executive at the candy company responsible for Junior Mints, founded the John Birch Society, a
conspiracy-theory factory and the QAnon of its day. (His cofounder
was Fred C. Koch, who, having also sired the Koch brothers, has a lot
to answer for.) The Birchers were a community of crackpots who believed, among other wigged-out fantasies, that President Dwight D.
Eisenhower was a Soviet agent. One commie plot keeping Welch up
at night was a demonic scheme to drug the entire U.S. population
by fluoridating the water supply.* Though he was known mainly for
finding a Bolshevik under every rock, the right-wing Willy Wonka
shared other febrile anxieties in his manifesto *The Blue Book of the
John Birch Society*. One of his more inventive theories was that the
United States was being devoured from within not only by communism and fluoride but by the steamy, youth-corrupting novel *Peyton
Place*. By finding the fake Lenin quote in Welch's loony book, Reagan demonstrated that his voracious reading encompassed not only
nineteenth-century French economists but also twentieth-century
American whack jobs.

When Reagan didn't have an apocryphal quote at the ready, he
could be counted on to uncork a suspiciously apropos anecdote.
George P. Shultz, who served as his secretary of state, wrote, "Reagan's talents as a storyteller are legendary." Unfortunately, many of
the stories he told were themselves legendary. David Gergen, Reagan's communications director, defended Reagan's stories as "a form
of moral instruction," while admitting that some of them "weren't
quite true." Reagan liked to tell stories of wartime heroism into

---

*On some level, this was an understandable position for a former confectioner to
take, since, dentally speaking, candy and fluoride are ideological foes.

which he photoshopped himself as the star. He told the Holocaust survivor Simon Wiesenthal about his role in liberating Nazi concentration camps, a feat made even more impressive by his having spent the entire war on soundstages in California. In 1982, the *New York Times* deconstructed one of his favorite anecdotes designed to demonize those on public assistance, in which a man used food stamps to buy an orange and the change to buy a bottle of vodka. As the *Times* pointed out, "Change for food stamps is given in other food stamps. Only if the change is for less than a dollar does one get back coins, and that is not enough, in any case, to buy vodka." As moral instruction, the Fable of the Orange and the Vodka wouldn't have made the cut with Aesop.

We're confronted, then, with two opposing views of the man: Reagan as sage and Reagan as stump. I believe the truth lies somewhere in between, though its precise location is a good deal closer to stump. Reagan had every opportunity to become well-informed, but his extraordinary talent for closed-mindedness shielded him from unwanted enlightenment. The ideas inside his head were as immovable as the Brylcreemed hair on top of it. Once he'd collected those ideas—in the 1950s—he didn't feel compelled to add any more. He had only three: (1) Communism = Bad; (2) Government = Bad; (3) Capitalism = Good. (Trees = Bad deserves an honorable mention.)

In the docuseries *The Reagans*, Ronald Reagan Jr. described his father's imperviousness to information that contradicted his worldview. "I used to get into arguments sometimes with my father and you would think, 'Well, I'm going to now introduce him to a new set of facts,'" he said. "He would listen, somewhat reluctantly, to what I would think are, you know, incontrovertible facts, and then you would get to that point where he would throw up his hands and say, 'Well, all I know is . . . ,' and he'd sort of push away like this with his hands, which was really 'Keep that reality away from me. I do not want that near me now. It's upsetting my whole picture of America, myself,' whatever it might be." The Great Communicator wasn't a Great Listener.

Although Reagan's learning curve flattened in the 1950s, his incuriosity was a political asset. By his 1980 presidential campaign, he was just repeating ideas that had ossified a quarter century earlier. Like his fellow thespian Rex Harrison, who starred in both the 1956 Broadway hit *My Fair Lady* and its 1981 revival, Reagan performed his old lines as if saying them for the first time. This tendency irked one reporter, who carped to Reagan's campaign manager that the candidate hadn't said anything new in months. "I certainly hope he hasn't" came the blithe reply. To his followers, the endless repetition of Reagan's retrograde message was reassuring. They shared his fear of newness, eager to return to his version of a 1950s America that never was.

But long before Reagan could become the star of his own White House infomercial, he faced a challenge that tested his acting skills: how to navigate the Ridicule stage of ignorance while possessing a mind that even his doting speechwriter, Peggy Noonan, described as "barren terrain." Hiding that mental tundra required a transformation that, like many other miraculous makeovers, happened in Hollywood.

Reagan's worshippers and detractors mostly agree on one point: he made the world a better place when he stopped making movies. His filmography is a cavalcade of B-movie detritus: *Brother Rat*, *Cattle Queen of Montana*, and *The Voice of the Turtle*, to cite just three titles in which an animal's name got higher billing than his. The perception of Reagan's second-tier status was so rampant that, when rumors of his California gubernatorial ambitions spread in the mid-1960s, the studio boss, Jack Warner, cracked, "Ronnie for governor? No. Jimmy Stewart for governor. Ronnie for best friend."

As mediocre as his film career may have been, I differ with those who say that Reagan was a bad actor. Acting talent is relative. Compared to Jimmy Stewart or Humphrey Bogart, or even Peggy (the chimp who portrayed Bonzo), Reagan was a journeyman. But compared to his fellow right-wing extremists, he was Meryl Streep. Consider the 1964 GOP presidential nominee, Barry Goldwater, who professed his love of nukes by declaring, "I want to lob one into the men's room of the Kremlin and make sure I hit it." Reagan, though drinking from the same well of commie-hating zealotry, used his Ward Cleaver–ish geniality to give an Oscar-worthy performance as a man with no immediate plans to blow up the world. (Every now and then, though, he let his mask of moderation slip, as when he declared, "It's silly talking about how many years we will have to spend in the jungles of Vietnam when we could pave the whole country and put parking stripes on it and still be home by Christmas," or when he proposed this pithy solution to student unrest at UC Berkeley: "If it takes a bloodbath, let's get it over with.")

In the 1950s, when his fading film career yielded such celluloid gems as *Hellcats of the Navy*, Warner Bros. let his contract expire. Unemployed, Reagan secured a new gig via a scheme that, in its deviousness, was like a prequel to Iran-Contra. At the time, the Screen Actors Guild forbade talent agencies from producing television shows featuring their own clients. Reagan used his position as guild president to grant a "blanket waiver" to his own agency, MCA, allowing it to circumvent that rule. One of MCA's first post-waiver TV productions starred a formerly unemployed actor named Ronald Reagan.

In addition to hosting that series, *General Electric Theater*, Reagan became a paid shill for GE, glad-handing his way through a national tour of the company's factories and research facilities. At every stop, he workshopped a string of increasingly right-wing messages that would become "The Speech." His audiences' ovations emboldened him to consider a new gig: governor of California. When asked, during his first campaign, what sort of governor he'd be, Reagan responded with what would become his trademark, a joke that wasn't entirely a joke: "I don't know, I've never played a governor."

"There once was a time when the idea of Ronald Reagan in politics provoked ridicule and scorn," Gerard DeGroot writes in his absorbing study of the 1966 California gubernatorial race, *Selling Ronald Reagan: The Emergence of a President.* Compounding the problem of his dumb-actor image was the tendency of his "greatest intellectual gift," his imagination, to generate bizarre fact-free riffs. Brimming with uncheckable trivia and "statistics," the following passage from "The Speech" is a typical Reagan tone poem: "We set out to help 19 countries. We're helping 107. We've spent 146 billion dollars. With that money, we bought a 2 million dollar yacht for Haile Selassie. We bought dress suits for Greek undertakers, extra wives for Kenyan government officials. We bought a thousand TV sets for a place where they have no electricity." Though Reagan failed to identify the mysterious "place" we sent all those TVs, he showed amazing prescience in recognizing the value of anti-Kenyan rhetoric to a Republican politician.

With the perils of the Ridicule stage all too palpable, the coterie of California millionaires backing Reagan's gubernatorial bid worried about their well-financed horse being laughed out of the race. They turned to two campaign managers, Stu Spencer and Bill Roberts, innovators in the use of advertising and PR to make candidates more presentable. Spencer posted this motto on his office wall: "If you can't dazzle 'em with brilliance, baffle 'em with bull." This approach would be tested with Reagan, who lacked the former but abounded with the latter.*

Once on board, Spencer and Roberts had to teach the man who wanted to be governor of California the most elementary facts about: (a) being a governor, and (b) California. Though Reagan could unspool lengthy sermons about his two favorite topics, the twin evils of communism and the federal government, his campaign managers had to break it to him gently that, as governor, he'd lack the power to slay either giant. They also worried about the potential destruction that Reagan's muscular imagination could wreak if he answered a factual question with a fanciful reply. To fill this grinning but vacuous vessel, Reagan's campaign managers called in reinforcements.

In *Bedtime for Bonzo*, Reagan played a psychology professor tasked with educating a chimp; in a role reversal, Spencer and Roberts hired clinical psychologists to educate Reagan, who was now a kind of Bonzo. The shrinks were Stanley Plog and Kenneth Holden, UCLA psychologists and founders of the sinister-sounding Behavior Science Corporation (BASICO). While this arrangement conjures sci-fi images of *A Clockwork Orange*–like reprogramming, Plog and Holden's contribution was disappointingly old-school. DeGroot writes, "They asked Reagan what sources of information he was using to prepare himself for speeches and press conferences. Without replying, Reagan got up and left the room. About a minute later, he returned with a shoebox stuffed with newspaper clippings. He explained how he would cut stories that piqued his interest out of newspapers and would store them in the box. As he spoke, bits of

---

* In addition to his prodigious ignorance, Reagan presented other challenges. An associate of Reagan's warned Spencer to get used to firing people because "Ron . . . has never fired anybody in his life." Ron seemingly overcame this personal failing by 1981, when he canned eleven thousand striking air traffic controllers in one day.

paper fell to the floor. For Plog and Holden, that little box seemed ominously symbolic, an indication of just how much needed to be done to brief Reagan on the issues in this campaign." The high-tech innovation that BASICO wound up employing to reboot Reagan was something he'd already used for years while hosting *General Electric Theater*: cue cards. According to DeGroot, "They used 5 x 8 index cards printed front and back. These were ordered according to topic, keyhole punched and inserted into binders." By memorizing BASICO's cue cards, Reagan was soon sufficiently rehearsed to star in a film that might be called *The Man Who Knew Just Barely Enough*.

He didn't fool everyone. Commenting on Reagan's appearance at a voters' forum, Richard Wilson of the *Los Angeles Times* wrote, "He left behind the impression that if he does not know what he is talking about, he has at least got his script down letter perfect." A *New York Times* editorial pronounced, "Mr. Reagan . . . is innocent of experience in government, and his speeches suggest he is equally innocent of knowledge." But Reagan's talent as a television performer, in an electoral process increasingly dominated by that medium, papered over his ignorance beyond Spencer's wildest dreams: he thumped the incumbent governor, Pat Brown, by an astounding million votes. This should have been cause for jubilation, since it meant the definitive end of Reagan's acting career, but some saw it as ominous. *Newsweek*'s Emmet Hughes wrote that Reagan's win "dramatizes the virtual bankruptcy, politically and intellectually, of a national party." Such scolding couldn't have mattered less to Spencer. If he could make Reagan look knowledgeable enough to be elected governor, he would be the go-to Svengali for dumb candidates everywhere. According to Spencer, he wound up managing more than four hundred Republican campaigns.

The victorious Gipper offered Californians a vision of their state that was as lyrical as it was incoherent: "A wind is blowing across this state of ours. And it is not only wind; it will grow into a tidal wave. And there will be a government with men as tall as mountains." He didn't explain how he planned to retrofit government buildings to accommodate such gigantic civil servants.

And though he nailed the audition, California's new governor was unprepared for the role. Lou Cannon wrote, "He did not know how budgets were prepared, how bills were passed, or who it was in state government who checked the backgrounds of prospective appointees. . . . [H]e didn't know what he was supposed to be doing, or how he was supposed to spend his time." Cannon recalled an early press conference where a reporter asked Reagan about his legislative program: "The novice governor did not have a clue. Turning plaintively to aides who were attending the news conference, he said, 'I could take some coaching from the sidelines if anyone can recall my legislative program.' Aides piped up and told Reagan some of the items in 'his' program."

Thanks to those trusty 5 x 8 cards, Reagan convinced voters he was well-informed enough to govern, but not a pointy-headed know-it-all like those intellectually curious hippies at UC Berkeley. The former TV pitchman infantilized the electorate by selling it simplistic solutions. "For many years now, you and I have been shushed like children and told there are no simple answers to the complex problems which are beyond our comprehension," he said. "Well, the truth is, there are simple answers." Reagan could deliver this anti-intellectual message with compelling sincerity because he believed it. The man who never cracked a book in college preferred solutions that didn't require any homework, and so, apparently, did millions of Californians. According to his longtime adviser Ed Meese, "Reagan wanted to be known as a person of the people, not like an Adlai Stevenson."

Ah, Adlai Stevenson. We'll hear that name a lot as we explore the Age of Ignorance. But before we meet Adlai, let's consider what his party, the Democrats, were up to during the Ridicule stage. If the Republicans have been conducting a perverse experiment seemingly designed to answer this question—Who's the most ignorant politician the U.S. is willing to elect?—in the 1950s, the Democrats started asking a perverse question of their own: Who's the most flagrantly cerebral politician we can nominate?

Adlai Stevenson II, the grandson of Grover Cleveland's vice president, Adlai Stevenson I, was governor of Illinois when, in 1952, Harry Truman urged him to run for president. Unlike the plainspoken Truman, Stevenson was a fire hose of lofty rhetoric. In actuality, he was probably less intellectual than Truman, who read a ton and amassed a large personal library. Stevenson, on the other hand, died with only one book on his nightstand: the *Social Register*. He wasn't much of a scholar, either: he had to leave Harvard Law School after failing several courses. But no one *appeared* more intellectual than Adlai. Throughout his political career, he cultivated the image of an egghead. In fact, the journalist Stewart Alsop coined the term "egghead" to describe him. Although political adversaries such as Richard Nixon soon adopted that word as a term of derision, Stevenson took pride in it. "Eggheads of the world, unite: you have nothing to lose but your yolks!" he declared.* His personal motto was "*Via ovicapitum dura est*"—The way of the egghead is hard. Yes, Adlai was not averse to inventing Latin quotations in his effort to pander to the highest common denominator.

All this eggheadedness was catnip for Democrats, as were his dizzying flights of oratory. It was no accident that Stevenson's speeches were distinctive, since his stable of speechwriters included John

---

* It's unclear why Adlai thought combining an egg pun with a quote from *The Communist Manifesto* would be electoral gold at the height of the Cold War.

Kenneth Galbraith, Archibald MacLeish, John Hersey, and Arthur Schlesinger Jr. They crafted high-minded if overwrought pronouncements such as this: "[T]he victory to be won in the twentieth century, this portal to the Golden Age, mocks the pretensions of individual acumen and ingenuity, for it is a citadel guarded by thick walls of ignorance and of mistrust which do not fall before the trumpets' blast or the politicians' imprecations or even a general's baton." Such verbal gusts make one suspect that Stevenson paid his speechwriters by the word, but his Democratic audiences ate this stuff up. During one speech, a woman shouted, "Governor Stevenson, you have the vote of all the thinking people." His response: "That's not enough, madam. I need a majority."

Stevenson's rueful comment reflected an awareness of his low electoral ceiling, a concern that delegates at the 1952 Democratic National Convention didn't share. They nominated him for president, despite his weakness for vocab words like "imprecation." In the general election, he lost by a landslide—442 electoral votes to 89—to Dwight D. Eisenhower, who, in spite of a spell in the groves of academe as president of Columbia University, kept his speeches Latin-free. "The knuckleheads have beaten the eggheads," the columnist Murray Kempton declared. As president, Ike would be a role model for future anti-intellectuals like Reagan and George W. Bush, with comments like this: "I heard a definition of an intellectual that I thought was very interesting—a man who takes more words than are necessary to tell more than he knows." He disdained "wise-cracking so called intellectuals going around and showing how wrong was everybody who didn't happen to agree with them." But Eisenhower, whom his secretary called "deathly afraid of being considered highbrow," was more of an egghead than he let on. While he projected the image of a man who preferred golfing to reading, he often stayed up until 11:00 p.m. poring over government reports and other documents. This was just the kind of subterfuge that the John Birch Society expected from a commie spy like Ike.

Stevenson's defeat didn't cool the Democrats' ardor. They nominated him again in 1956—and this time, when the general election rolled around, he did even worse. By then, Adlai's original booster, Truman, had decided that he was too eggheaded to win. "I was trying as gently as I could, to tell this man—so gifted in speech and intellect, and yet apparently so uncertain of himself and remote from people—that he had to learn how to communicate with the man in the street," Truman wrote. "I had the feeling that I had failed." Surely, after two electoral thrashings, it was time for Stevenson to abandon his futile effort to connect with voters. Nope: he gave the nomination a *third* shot, in 1960. This time, however, possibly having looked up the definition of insanity, Democrats put Stevenson out of his misery (*miseria*, in Latin) and chose John F. Kennedy.

In 1968, another egghead set Democratic hearts aflame and left the rest of the country cold: former college professor Eugene McCarthy, a U.S. Senator from Minnesota. Gene had next-level egghead cred: in addition to delivering fancy speeches, he wrote poetry. (Sample lines from his poem "The Camera": "My eye is everywhere / I am Tom, peeping.") In 1968, McCarthy rocked President Lyndon Johnson's reelection campaign with a strong showing in New Hampshire's Democratic primary. Gene ultimately lost the nomination to Vice President Hubert Horatio Humphrey, a fellow egghead who'd aspired to be a college professor before straying into politics. In the general election, against Nixon, Humphrey wound up losing, too—but the Democrats' egghead addiction persisted. In 1972, they passed the nerd-torch to Humphrey's onetime next-door neighbor, the South Dakota senator George McGovern, another former college professor. McGovern was such an Adlai Stevenson fan that he named his only son, Steven, after him; the senator's four-year-old daughter,

Terry, proclaimed that her three favorite people were "God, Jesus, and Adlai Stevenson." (Consistent with Adlai's losing record, even in this ranking he placed third.) Unfortunately, as the party's nominee, McGovern wound up doing even worse than Adlai, losing all but Massachusetts and the District of Columbia to Nixon. The way of the egghead was indeed hard.

The Democrats' erudition should have served them well in the Ridicule stage, when voters expected politicians to seem knowledgeable. But their professorial rhetoric couldn't woo an electorate increasingly hooked on TV, where short and simple messages—the kind that fit on cue cards—prevailed. Given the failure of the Democrats' egghead strategy, no wonder Reagan didn't want to be seen as an intellectual. It was a fate he masterfully averted.

Two years after he was elected governor, Reagan was already jonesing for another role he'd never played before: president of the United States. Reagan's eleventh-hour challenge to Richard Nixon for the 1968 Republican nomination fizzled, but television's burgeoning impact on politics augured well for the former prime-time host. Nixon had appeared sweaty and unshaven in his 1960 debate with John F. Kennedy, but in 1968 a savvy TV producer gave Dick a media makeover. "This is the beginning of a whole new concept," the producer said. "This is it. This is the way they'll be elected forevermore. The next guys up will have to be performers." This prophet was Roger Ailes, decades away from his career as a serial sexual harasser at Fox News.

By 1973, Reagan's White House ambitions seemed to have cooled. "The thought of being president frightens me and I do not think I want the job," he said, causing millions of Americans to exhale. Sadly, that was a head fake. In 1976, having miraculously vanquished his fear of the presidency, he challenged the incumbent,

Gerald R. Ford, for the GOP nomination. This time, he came much closer, but failed again—possibly because Stu Spencer was now working for the opposition. Spencer's former partner, Bill Roberts, explained Stu's defection from Reagan to Ford. "He feels he's been poorly treated by the people around Reagan, although not so much by Reagan himself," Roberts told the *New York Times*. "He also shares my feeling that Ron is not so qualified to be President." Without Spencer as his minder, signs of Reagan's cluelessness started popping up again like a stubborn STD. He delivered an address about the Third World in which he declared, "The United States has much to offer the Third World War." Reagan went on to use this Freudian turn of phrase nine times in the speech.

Gerald Ford was in some ways Reagan's opposite: a well-informed man who could come across as a big, lumbering dope. "Jerry Ford is so dumb that he can't fart and chew gum at the same time," Lyndon Johnson cracked, thus adding Ford to the list of people he grossly underestimated, which included Eugene McCarthy and Ho Chi Minh. At the University of Michigan, Ford's classmates considered him such a good student that an academically woeful fraternity, Delta Kappa Epsilon (DKE), recruited him to help raise its GPA. Once initiated as a Deke, as DKE members proudly call themselves, Ford, an economics major, seized control of the fraternity's ledger and balanced its books. Upon graduation, he attended Yale Law School, where, in a totally not-Deke move, he finished in the top third of his class.

However, television, which showed Reagan such love, often made Jerry appear tongue-tied and slow-witted. Even more unfairly, it made him look like an oaf. Ford was one of our most athletically gifted presidents, a linebacker who led the Michigan Wolverines to two back-to-back championship seasons and received offers to play for both the Detroit Lions and the Green Bay Packers. When he was vice president, though, cameras captured him maiming spectators with errant golf balls; as president, he tripped down the steps of Air Force One. By contrast, Reagan's famous turn as George "The Gipper" Gipp, in the 1940 biopic *Knute Rockne: All American*, created the impression that he'd been a football star. In reality, the coach of his Eureka College Red Devils football squad remembered him as "just a fellow who wanted to play football but didn't have too much talent."

While TV often made Ford look clumsier, mentally and physically, than he was, he did have one genuine flaw that helped foster his image as a goofball: a Pollyannaish optimism that sometimes veered into magical thinking. The most glaring example of this tendency might have been his apparent belief, upon becoming president in 1974, that everything would turn out okay if he just pardoned Richard Nixon. His naivete attracted more mockery later that year when he attempted to tame an inflationary spiral by launching a deranged PR campaign called "Whip Inflation Now." This mainly consisted of distributing buttons bearing the initials "WIN" in red, white, and blue. Ford even commissioned a "Whip Inflation Now" fight song, possibly reasoning that, if rousing music could spur the Wolverines to two undefeated gridiron seasons, it could also subdue soaring petroleum prices. In a year when the Steve Miller Band and Grand Funk Railroad topped the charts, Ford tapped a different hitmaker for his song, bringing the mothballed Meredith Willson, the composer of the 1957 Broadway smash *The Music Man*, out of retirement. Despite colorful buttons and a jaunty jingle, inflation went unwhipped.

One might wonder why, given the challenges that a client like Ford presented, Spencer decided to take him on. The truth is that, as a political consultant, Spencer didn't exactly play hard to get. His open-mindedness about his clientele enabled him, in 1985, to accept $25,000 a month to help improve the image of the Panamanian general and dictator Manuel Noriega, whose image up to that point had been tarnished by his tendency to rig elections and plot military coups. Spencer's attempted makeover of the general was insufficient to dissuade another of his clients, George H. W. Bush, from invading Panama in 1989.*

Spencer's survival plan for Gerald Ford in 1976 was not altogether different from Noriega's in 1989: go into hiding. With the incumbent president trailing the Democratic challenger, Jimmy Carter, by a whopping thirty points in the polls, Spencer insisted that Ford employ a "Rose Garden strategy" that would keep him in the White House, safe from public inspection. Offering his rationale, Spencer told Ford, "Forgive me, Mr. President, but as much as you love it—you're a [expletive] campaigner." With Reagan, Spencer had faced the challenge of making an ignorant man look smart; now, with Ford, he had to keep a smart man from looking ignorant. Regrettably, Spencer's plan imploded when Ford emerged for televised debates.

Ford's debate opponent, Jimmy Carter, was guaranteed to have done his homework. Sometimes, it seemed, all Carter did was homework. His reputation for possessing vast stores of arcane knowledge later inspired an *SNL* sketch, "Ask President Carter," in which Jimmy (Dan Aykroyd) answered unscreened phone calls and demonstrated surprising expertise about everything from a letter-sorting machine called the Marvex 3000 to the exact kind of acid a freaked-out

---

*When the dictator fled to the Vatican embassy in Panama City, American forces blasted music at the compound to hasten his exit, deploying a playlist that pushed the limits of the Geneva Convention. Despite my earlier claim that disco died on Reagan's watch, "Give It Up" by KC and the Sunshine Band played a key role in this mission. (So did Rick Astley's "Never Gonna Give You Up." Predating the advent of Rickrolling by two decades, this is the first known instance of Astley's song being weaponized.)

seventeen-year-old caller had ingested. (Carter: "Peter, what did the acid look like?" Caller: "Um, they were these little orange pills." Carter: "Were they barrel-shaped?" Caller: "Uh, yes." Carter: "Okay, right, you did some orange sunshine, Peter.") In a debate with an opponent this well-informed, appearing ignorant was not an option—which made what happened to Ford on October 6, 1976, all the more unfortunate.

That night, Ford and Carter faced off at San Francisco's Palace of Fine Arts. When Max Frankel of the *New York Times* asked Ford about America's seeming passivity toward a hegemonic Soviet Union, he gave such a long-winded and boring response that it might've gone unnoticed had it not ended with this startling crescendo: "[T]here is no Soviet domination of Eastern Europe, and there never will be under a Ford administration."

The audience gasped. Frankel, so incredulous he sputtered, offered Ford a chance to retract his statement, but Jerry kept trudging toward new horizons of inanity: "I don't believe, uh, Mr. Frankel, that, uh, the Yugoslavians consider themselves dominated by the Soviet Union. I don't believe that the Romanians consider themselves dominated by the Soviet Union. I don't believe that the Poles consider themselves dominated by the Soviet Union." Had he been permitted to continue, it was only a matter of time before he questioned whether the Soviets considered themselves dominated by the Soviet Union. Ford's later attempt to clarify his position didn't help much. "We are going to make certain to the best of our ability that any allegation of domination is not a fact," he said.

In the decades since, there have been two myths about Ford's gaffe. The first is that it was an off-the-cuff riff gone wrong. But in 1986, Francis L. Loewenheim, a history professor at Rice University, revealed that, astoundingly, Ford meant what he'd said. After combing through notes that Ford wrote before the debate, Loewenheim reported, "Page after page of material I found in the Ford Library in Ann Arbor shows this is exactly what he believed." Ford's jaw-dropping statement might have been yet another manifestation of his cockeyed optimism run amok. He was, after all, a man who thought the composer of "Seventy-Six Trombones" could somehow whip inflation.

The second myth is that Ford's goofy aria cost him the election. The media's overblown postmortem about his flub might have made it seem more consequential than it was. Thanks to Spencer's shrewd decision to sequester Ford in the Rose Garden, the president had started to narrow the gap with Carter before the debate and continued to do so afterward. While the gaffe didn't help, it probably wasn't the reason Ford lost. A bigger factor might have been his pardoning of Nixon. Oh, and inflation.

But the "no Soviet domination" flap is important because of what it indicates about the Ridicule stage of ignorance. In 1976, it wasn't acceptable for a politician to look misinformed. Facts still mattered. For Ford's detour from the facts to be so widely mocked, there had to be at least some shared understanding about what the facts were. Looking back on it now, when no such consensus exists, Ford's gaffe seems a quaint 1970s relic, like an 8-track tape or a Pet Rock.

After Ford lost, Spencer, showing the flexibility of mind that was his hallmark, somehow overcame his grave misgivings about Reagan's presidential timbre and joined his 1980 campaign. With Reagan set to debate Carter on October 28 at Cleveland's Music Hall, Spencer was determined to prevent a repeat of Ford's flameout. Seeking an advantage over the sitting president, the Reagan campaign did something that Manuel Noriega surely would have endorsed: it illicitly obtained Carter's debate briefing book.

Under those circumstances, it wasn't a huge surprise that Reagan showed up to the debate well prepared. The most famous moment in the face-off came after Carter accused him of opposing Medicare. As Carter attacked, the camera caught Reagan smiling beatifically, perhaps remembering his opponent's words, verbatim, from the pilfered briefing materials. After waiting for Carter to finish, he responded with his now immortal comeback: "There you go again."

Interestingly, despite possessing Carter's briefing book, Reagan hadn't spent much time boning up on facts to blunt his opponent's attacks. Instead, as Lou Cannon reported, he rehearsed "one-liners in the belief that viewers would be more apt to remember a deft phrase than a technical argument." The zinger he composed wasn't exactly Wildean; rhetorically, it was a not-very-distant cousin of "I know you are, but what am I?" But Reagan's instincts as an entertainer were spot-on. From the moment he cocked his head and said those four words, you could stick a fork in Carter.

When you watch the debate today, what's striking is that everything Carter said right before Reagan's legendary burn was a hundred percent true. And yet, as Reagan had predicted, the facts were forgettable. All anyone remembered from the night were four sarcastic words that made Carter look like a grumpy crank. Unlike Ford, who tripped over facts, Reagan avoided the annoying problem of facts altogether. When, in 1988, Reagan misquoted John Adams's aphorism "Facts are stubborn things" as "Facts are stupid things," it sounded as if he'd stumbled on the perfect title for his memoirs.

Reagan's zinger had the unintended consequence of making premeditated wisecracks an obligatory feature of future presidential debates. In 1984, former vice president Walter "Fritz" Mondale belittled Senator Gary Hart's "new ideas" campaign theme by weaponizing the catchphrase of a then popular Wendy's commercial, "Where's the beef?" Mondale might have congratulated himself for being the first presidential aspirant to repurpose the rhetoric of a hamburger chain, but he couldn't rest on his laurels as an insult comic for long: the master of the art form, Ronald Reagan, would best him in their eventual fall matchup. After a wobbly performance in their first debate, where Reagan's muddled answers raised concerns about the seventy-three-year-old's mental acuity, he came out zinging in their second contest. "I will not make age an issue of this campaign," he deadpanned. "I am not going to exploit, for political purposes, my opponent's youth and inexperience." As Neil Postman wrote, "The following day, several newspapers indicated that Ron had KO'd Fritz with his joke. Thus, the leader of the free world is chosen by the people in the Age of Television."

Reagan demonstrated that, in the hands of a talented TV performer, one joke could sink a thousand facts. But he had enjoyed another advantage as he cruised to victory in 1980: an all-star roster of morally dubious advisers. His gang of goons included Roy Cohn, the disgraced former aide to Senator Joseph McCarthy, and three hard-charging political consultants, Roger Ailes, Roger Stone, and Paul Manafort. It was hard to imagine another Republican presidential candidate assembling such a team, or coming up with a campaign slogan as winning as Reagan's: "Let's Make America Great Again."

By Inauguration Day, 1981, Reagan had been performing versions of "The Speech" for sixteen years—as long as Celine Dion's residency, more than two decades later, at Caesars Palace. Like Celine, who only had to sing "My Heart Will Go On" to get a standing ovation, Reagan didn't feel pressured to learn new songs. "Politics is just like show business," he said. "You have a hell of an opening, coast for a while, and then have a hell of a close." If his first gubernatorial campaign was a hell of an opening, Reagan's White House years would provide him with ample opportunity for coasting—before he achieved a hell of a close, with Iran-Contra.

It's commonplace for commanders in chief to age visibly from the burdens of the office, but not the Gipper. As Cannon noted, "Reagan may have been the one president in the history of the republic who saw his election as a chance to get some rest." He could've used all that downtime to acquire the knowledge necessary to fulfill his constitutional duties, but his laziness and incuriosity put the kibosh on that. At press conferences early in his presidency, he sounded like an actor who hadn't bothered to learn his lines. When asked about the placement of U.S. missiles, the best he could ad-lib was "I don't know but what maybe you haven't gotten into the area that I'm going to turn over to the secretary of defense."

As the *Sound of Music* incident suggests, Reagan's interest in briefing materials might have peaked when he acquired Jimmy Carter's debate prep. Frustrated by his aversion to reading, cabinet members resorted to bringing him up to speed—or, more accurately, half speed—by showing him videos and cartoons about the subjects at hand. But even these Oval Office versions of *Schoolhouse Rock!* bored Reagan, who spent briefings doodling.

Though a team of psychologists gave him a semblance of sentience when he ran for governor, by the time he became president his semi-informed veneer was wearing thin. The journalist Elizabeth Drew, who covered him during the 1980 campaign, observed, "Reagan's mind appears to be a grab bag of clippings and 'facts' and anecdotes and scraps of ideas." Embarrassingly, he often appeared stupidest when talking with or about foreign leaders. In a 1979 interview, Reagan told NBC's Tom Brokaw, "If I become president, other than perhaps Margaret Thatcher I will probably be younger than almost all the heads of state I will have to do business with." When

Brokaw noted that he'd be considerably older than French president Giscard d'Estaing, Reagan replied, "Who?" (After Reagan was elected, Brokaw, demonstrating a gift for understatement, called him "a gravely under-informed president.") After a half-hour briefing by the Lebanese foreign minister about his nation's factional conflicts, Reagan's only contribution was "You know, your nose looks just like Danny Thomas's." (The former star of the sitcom *Make Room for Daddy* might have been the only other person of Lebanese descent he'd ever met.) In a photo op with the Liberian ruler, Samuel K. Doe, Reagan called him "Chairman Moe." Welcoming the prime minister of Singapore, Lee Kuan Yew, to the White House, he said, "It gives me great pleasure to welcome Prime Minister Lee Kuan Yew and Mrs. Lee to Singapore." During a meeting with Pope John Paul II, at least, he didn't mangle the pontiff's name; he just fell asleep.

Reagan sometimes seemed like Voltaire's Candide, an innocent in a constant state of wonder about the world around him. He called a 1982 trip to Latin America "real fruitful," having gleaned this mind-boggling insight: "They're all individual countries." Reporting on this tour, Lou Cannon wrote, "Over and over again along the way, he expressed enthusiasm in what he was seeing for the first time, and his aides found it appealing and naive." A foreign ministry official in Brazil was less enchanted by his wide-eyed ingenuousness. After Reagan suggested that Brazil could be "a bridge" for the U.S. in South America, the official noted, "If you look at a map, you will see that we cannot be detached from the South American continent. We are not a bridge from South America; we are in South America." It's possible the Brazilian was still sore after Reagan, raising a glass at a state dinner in Brasília, offered a toast to "the people of Bolivia." Belatedly recognizing his goof, he tried to explain it away by saying that Bolivia was where he was headed next. His next stop was Colombia; Bolivia wasn't on his itinerary.

But the Brazilians shouldn't have felt singled out. Reagan's ignorance spanned the globe. He demonstrated unquestioning devotion to the government of apartheid South Africa, possibly because he rarely asked questions about the place. When he did, the question was rhetorical, as in "Can we abandon this country that has stood beside us in every war we've ever fought?" It's true that South Africa had been steadfast in its support, but not of us: many of its officials had ties to a party that supported the Nazis, and John Vorster, who led the country for thirteen years, had been jailed for cozying up to Hitler. Incredibly, Reagan claimed in a radio address that South Africa was a bastion of racial equality: "[T]hey have eliminated the segregation that we once had in our own country—the type of thing where hotels and restaurants and places of entertaining and so forth were segregated. That has all been eliminated." This would have been welcome news to Nelson Mandela, had it reached his prison cell. Turning to a country he presumably knew more about because he despised it so much, Reagan said, "I'm no linguist but I have been told that in the Russian language there isn't even a word for freedom." Reagan was half right: he was no linguist. The Russian word for freedom is *svoboda*.

Reagan might be best remembered for saying, "Mr. Gorbachev, tear down this wall," but many other quotable nuggets emerged from his piehole: "Nuclear war would be the greatest tragedy, I think, ever experienced by mankind in the history of mankind"; "All the waste in a year from a nuclear power plant can be stored under a desk"; and the admirably candid "We are trying to get unemployment to go up, and I think we're going to succeed." As the gaffes piled up like banana peels in Bonzo's dressing room, it was time to call in the man who had disguised Reagan's obliviousness before: Stu Spencer. Summoned to the White House, the Gipper's trusty cornerman revealed his agenda to a reporter: "I'm here to see old foot-in-the-mouth."

Reagan's mythologizers have worked hard to bury this image of him as an object of ridicule, but early in his presidency that's what he often was. Their preferred narrative—that his White House tenure went from strength to strength—is false. Two years after he first entered the Oval Office, perhaps checking under the desk for nuclear waste, Reagan was struggling. As the economy proved obstinately resistant to the miracle of Reaganomics, his approval rating sank to a woeful 35 percent, barely higher than what most of his films would have notched on Rotten Tomatoes.

Reagan's refusal to take responsibility for his failures frustrated Pat Schroeder, a Democratic congresswoman from Colorado. In August 1983, she took to the floor of the House and coined a political cliché: "Mr. Speaker, after carefully watching Ronald Reagan, he is attempting a great breakthrough in political technology—he has been perfecting the Teflon-coated Presidency." Her remark proved tragically prescient. Two months later, 241 U.S. military personnel stationed in Beirut as part of Reagan's confused Lebanon policy died in the bombings of their marine barracks. He changed the subject. In what should have been called Operation Expedient Distraction, he ordered the invasion of the minuscule Caribbean island nation of Grenada, a mission roughly as challenging as the conquest of a Sandals resort. His approval rating soared.

As his popularity grew, the press cowered. In *On Bended Knee: The Press and the Reagan Presidency*, Mark Hertsgaard documents the Fourth Estate's wariness about roughing up Reagan. "We have been kinder to President Reagan than any president that I can remember since I've been at the *Post*," said Ben Bradlee, the executive editor of the *Washington Post*. His colleague at the paper William Greider theorized that the press, in its obsequiousness to Reagan, was compensating for being blindsided by his election: "It was a sense of 'My God, they've elected this guy who nine months ago we thought was a hopeless clown.'" Reagan's burgeoning status as Teflon Ron owed much to the media's decision to handle him like a glass unicorn. "I think a lot of the Teflon came because the press was holding back," his communications director, David Gergen, said. "I don't think they wanted to go after him that toughly."

"Teflon" became an overused label for politicians, as journalists employed it to describe not only Reagan but every president since. Fearing the damage this practice could inflict on its trademark, in 1985 the manufacturer of Teflon, DuPont, pushed back. "DuPont simply wants users of Teflon to add a little circle with an R inside to denote that Teflon is a registered trademark," the *New York Times* reported. "A printed message being sent to reporters all over the capital adds, 'It is not, alas, a verb or an adjective, not even when applied to the President of the United States!'" Despite this stern warning, Teflon® Ron never caught on.

Given the press's reluctance to fact-check Reagan, it's no surprise that the public gradually stopped caring whether anything he said was, well, factual. In 1983, the *New York Times* devoted an entire article to this chicken-or-egg mystery, titled, "Reagan Misstatements Getting Less Attention." "[T]he President continues to make debatable assertions of fact, but news accounts do not deal with them as extensively as they once did," the *Times* reported. "In the view of White House officials, the declining news coverage mirrors a decline in interest by the general public." No one seemed to care when Reagan indulged in one of his favorite vices: attributing fake quotations to Lenin. "Mr. Reagan said at a news conference three weeks ago that 'just the other day' he had read an article quoting 'the Ten Commandments of Nikolai Lenin' to the effect that Soviet leaders reserved the right to lie and cheat to advance the cause of socialism," the *Times* noted. "After the statement, the White House acknowledged that Lenin did not issue 'Ten Commandments' as such. Lyndon K. Allin, a deputy White House press secretary, said Mr. Reagan got the reference from a clipping sent by a friend citing 10 different 'Leninisms.'" The *Times* didn't point out that Reagan, while arguing that the Soviets reserved the right to lie, was reserving the right to lie about the Soviets.

As journalistic oversight shriveled, Reagan's childlike solutions to the nation's problems went virtually unchallenged. His decades-old binary oppositions, *us versus government* and *us versus communists*, yielded made-for-TV catchphrases. "Government is the problem" and "The Evil Empire" became as ubiquitous as "I pity the fool" and "Watchu talkin' 'bout, Willis?"* He added another rhetorical empty calorie in 1984, when his reelection campaign inanely declared that it was "Morning in America." Speaking to business leaders in 1985, he'd apparently run out of catchphrases of his own and borrowed one from Clint Eastwood: "Go ahead, make my day." The quote had an interesting provenance: Clint's cop character, Dirty Harry, had said it while pointing his gun at a Black man. It earned Reagan a thunderous ovation from his largely white audience.

But there were bumps on the road to Reagan's Hollywood ending. His approval rating plunged twenty points after news of the Iran-Contra scandal broke. Wisely, Reagan didn't try to brand this illegal arms deal as Morning in Nicaragua. He deployed a potent alibi instead: his ignorance. When he swore that he had no idea what had been going on at the White House, right under his nose, millions found the explanation plausible. His numbers ticked back up.

After Iran-Contra, some in the media wondered whether their decision to coat Reagan with Teflon® had done the country a disservice.

---

* In a collision of catchphrases, Nancy Reagan dispensed one during a 1983 appearance on the sitcom *Diff'rent Strokes*: her anti-drug mantra "Just Say No." Naturally, the episode also required Arnold, the character portrayed by Gary Coleman, to say, "Watchu talkin' 'bout, Mrs. Reagan?"

Newsweek's Robert Parry groused that the press corps "seemed to be a little fearful that if it wrote stories that were perceived as tough on this president, the public would not like them." The media's unilateral disarmament during Reagan's presidency didn't mean the Ridicule stage of ignorance was over, however. Just as Ronnie the actor had granted a "blanket waiver" only to his own talent agency, the media issued a free pass only to him.

Reagan's ignorance defense during Iran-Contra was the rare instance when he highlighted his obliviousness instead of trying to hide it. Another of his glaring flaws, however—his laziness—became his favorite topic for self-roasting. He owned his sloth and, with his trademark grin 'n' nod, let the nation know that he was in on the joke. Reagan managed to be both a bumbling sitcom dad and his own laugh track. "It's true hard work never killed anybody, but I figure why take the chance?" he jested. After four years of Carter, that annoying grind who always did his homework, Americans seemed to enjoy having a president who didn't even bring his homework home. "I am concerned about what is happening in government," he said, "and it's caused me many a sleepless afternoon." Returning to this seemingly bottomless well of hilarity, he cracked, "When I leave the White House, they will put on my chair in the Cabinet Room 'Ronald Reagan slept here.'" What a kidder!

Even with the president napping, doodling, and watching Julie Andrews, the White House was in no danger of becoming rudderless: the ship of state was being guided by the stars. His wife Nancy's belief in astrology—specifically in a San Francisco–based astrologist named Joan Quigley—filled the leadership vacuum. In his memoir, *For the Record*, Donald Regan, who served as both Reagan's chief of staff and treasury secretary, made palpable the trauma of working in an administration under Quigley's cosmological control. In

1985, arrangements for the crucial first summit between Reagan and the Soviet leader, Mikhail Gorbachev, in Geneva, couldn't be solidified until Quigley had done her planetary due diligence. "As usual, Mrs. Reagan insisted on being consulted on the timing of every presidential appearance and action so that she could consult her Friend in San Francisco about the astrological factor," Regan wrote. "The large number of details involved must have placed a heavy burden on the poor woman, who was called upon not only to choose auspicious moments for meetings between the two most powerful men on our planet, but also to draw up horoscopes that presumably provided clues to the character and probable behavior of Gorbachev."

But Quigley wasn't the only one pondering the heavens during the Geneva summit. According to Gorbachev, at one point Reagan turned to him and said, in all seriousness, "What would you do if the United States were attacked by someone from outer space? Would you help us?" This scenario, lifted from the 1951 sci-fi flick *The Day the Earth Stood Still*, was an obsession of Reagan's. In an appearance before the National Strategy Forum, in Chicago, he was asked to name "the most important need in international relations." He replied, "I've often wondered, what if all of us in the world discovered that we were threatened by a power from outer space—from another planet. Wouldn't we all of a sudden find that we didn't have any differences between us at all—we were all human beings, citizens of the world—and wouldn't we come together to fight that particular threat?" Got it: *The most important need in international relations is an attack from outer space.* These extraterrestrial musings were so frequent that, whenever Reagan uncorked one, his national security adviser, Colin Powell, would roll his eyes and say, "Here come the little green men again."

As Reagan was busy securing the Soviets' help in blasting aliens out of the sky, he was, somewhat ungratefully, searching for new and expensive ways to blast the Soviets out of the sky. The Gipper, whom Hollywood never called upon to play inventors such as Thomas Edison or Alexander Graham Bell (those parts went to Spencer Tracy and Don Ameche, respectively), decided he'd create a high-tech solution to the annoying problem of incoming Soviet missiles: the Strategic Defense Initiative, which became better known as Star Wars.* In a televised address on March 23, 1983, he momentarily shelved the little green men and focused on the big red menace: "What if free people could live secure in the knowledge that their security did not rest upon the threat of instant U.S. retaliation to deter a Soviet attack, that we could intercept and destroy strategic ballistic missiles before they reached our own soil or that of our allies?" He might have been tempted to add, as in the opening sequence of the TV show *The Six Million Dollar Man*, "We have the technology." Only, we didn't, and the whole shebang would cost way more than six mill.

You might wonder how creating a crazily expensive new weapons system squared with Reagan's inaugural pronouncement "Government is not the solution to our problem; government is the problem." Once Reagan got to the White House, he decided government was the solution to a shit ton of problems: big ones, like how to monstrously increase the military arsenal of the United States, and small ones, like how to illegally increase the military arsenal of the Nicaraguan Contras. Despite his reputation as a deficit hawk, he added more to the national debt than all previous presidents combined: it soared from $900 billion to $2.7 trillion on his watch.

---

*Rather than bristling at this derisive nickname, Reagan embraced it, seizing the opportunity to repurpose yet another Hollywood catchphrase. While touting the costly weapons system, he declared, with a straight face, "The Force is with us."

(Math is yet another stupid thing.) As for the Strategic Defense Initiative, it cost American taxpayers $30 billion before the government figured out it didn't work; in sci-fi movie terms, it was less *Star Wars* than *Battlefield Earth*. At least taxpayers could be assured that no future U.S. president would dare blow their precious taxes on an idiotic space force.

As much as Reagan celebrated his own laziness, that moral generosity did not extend to one of his favorite political straw men: the poor, with special emphasis on welfare recipients. During a campaign appearance in 1976, Reagan claimed, "If you are a slum dweller, you can get an apartment with 11-foot ceilings, with a 20-foot balcony, a swimming pool and gymnasium, laundry room and play room, and the rent begins at $113.20 and that includes utilities." The actual residents of this housing project would have had trouble recognizing it from Reagan's fanciful description, which made it sound posher than Haile Selassie's yacht. Another favorite target was the mythical unemployed person who avoided work despite being showered with job opportunities. At a news conference on January 19, 1982, a reporter asked Reagan about Black unemployment, which had soared from 12.4 to 17 percent during his first year in office. His response was typical: "Well, one of the things that's needed, I think, was illustrated in the local paper on Sunday. I made it a point to count the pages of help-wanted ads in this time of great unemployment. There were 24 full pages of classified ads of employers looking for employees." This story seems far-fetched, since it asks us to picture Reagan counting to twenty-four.

Reagan reserved his most scathing commentary about the laziness of others for a woman he made famous as the "welfare queen." At almost every stop during his 1976 campaign, he told his reliably all-white audiences, "There's a woman in Chicago. She has

80 names, 30 addresses, 12 Social Security cards, and is collecting veterans' benefits on four nonexisting [*sic*] deceased husbands. . . . And she's collecting Social Security on her cards. She's got Medicaid, getting food stamps, and she is collecting welfare under each of her names. Her tax-free cash income alone is over $150,000." (Perhaps fearing that his story lacked sufficient punch, he later upgraded the number of her aliases from 80 to 127.) His invocation of the welfare queen became so relentless that the humorist Calvin Trillin wrote, "If a cherry tree in the White House Rose Garden got chopped down and all the evidence pointed to Ronald Reagan, he would say, 'I cannot tell a lie; there's a lady in California who picks up her welfare check every week in a Cadillac.'"

Reagan never explicitly said that the welfare queen was Black, but he didn't have to. By referring to a welfare cheat in Chicago, a city with a large African American population, he was sending a message his white audience would have no trouble decoding. (Never mind that the vast majority of welfare recipients were, and still are, white.) Reagan used the fable of the welfare queen to show that laziness, when it wasn't his, was reprehensible. But his effort to fact-check his story about the queen, whose actual name was Linda Taylor, was, as you might expect from Reagan, lazy. As the *New York Times* reported on February 15, 1976, "Miss Taylor is now charged with using not 80 aliases but four. The amount the state is charging that she received from her alleged fraud is not $150,000 but $3,000." Josh Levin, an investigative journalist who has become the preeminent expert on the welfare queen, later unearthed another inconvenient truth about Taylor: in the 1930 census, her race was listed as white.

Reagan's mythologizers claim that, despite his frequent use of such dog whistles, he wasn't racist. Often their evidence is his admiration of Jackie Robinson; overachievers in this line of defense note that he also liked the entertainer Sammy Davis Jr. But Reagan's Morning in

America was really only a morning for white people. The soft-focus 1984 campaign ad establishing that reelection theme featured only one fleeting glimpse of someone who might be Black (a little girl). This commercial was an accurate representation of the America the Reagans preferred. At a New Hampshire campaign event in 1980, Ronnie had Nancy call in from an event of her own, in Illinois. Over the PA system, Nancy could be heard lamenting that her husband couldn't be with her to see "all these beautiful white people." Those who argue that the economic hardship suffered by people of color under Reagan's presidency was just a nutty coincidence rather than the inevitable result of racist policies should turn their attention to a 1971 phone conversation between him and then president Richard Nixon, who, always so helpful to historians, taped just about everything.

After the United Nations voted to recognize the People's Republic of China, on October 25, 1971, members of the Tanzanian delegation danced in celebration. The confluence of a communist state attaining prestige and Africans being happy was too much for Reagan, who, in a rage, rang up Nixon. "Last night, I tell you, to watch that thing on television as I did," Reagan said. "To see those, those monkeys from those African countries—damn them, they're still uncomfortable wearing shoes!" Ever the performer, the Gipper knew his audience; Nixon can be heard laughing uproariously. Confronted with this recording, Reagan apologists can at least console themselves that he finally uttered a quotation worthy of Winston Churchill.

In his 1990 autobiography, *An American Life*, Reagan wrote, "Whatever the reasons for the myth that I'm a racist, I blow my top every time I hear it." Let us count the reasons. His "monkeys" remark is of a piece with his disparagement of allegedly polygamous Kenyans, his full-throated praise of South Africa's apartheid regime, and his 1965 comment about recently independent African nations: "When they have a man for lunch, they really have him for lunch." Reagan also had a knack for surrounding himself with bigots. There was his secretary of the interior, James Watt, of "a black, a woman, two Jews, and a cripple" fame. And there was Marianne Mele Hall, whom Reagan appointed in 1985 as the chair of the Copyright Royalty Tribunal. It emerged that she had coauthored a book claiming that African Americans "insist on preserving their jungle freedoms, their women, their avoidance of personal responsibility and their abhorrence of the work ethic." She was forced to resign for sentiments that, translated into the right code words, could have been applause lines in a Reagan stump speech. In 2005, Reagan's former secretary of education, Bill Bennett, dispensed with code words altogether when he told a caller to his radio show, "I do know that it's true that if you wanted to reduce crime, you could—if that were your sole purpose—you could abort every black baby in this country, and your crime rate would go down." The name of Bennett's show was *Morning in America.*

Reagan's "monkeys" tape didn't surface until 2019, but his racism was hardly a secret before then. He kicked off his 1980 general election campaign near Philadelphia, Mississippi, the site of the Mississippi Burning murders of the civil rights activists James Chaney, Andrew Goodman, and Michael Schwerner. As in his welfare queen tirades, he made sure his speech at the Neshoba County Fair, to an all-white audience waving Confederate flags, included a time-tested racist dog whistle: "I believe in states' rights." There he went again.

Five months later, when he became president, his cabinet was as white as his reelection commercial would be, with only one Black person in a peripheral role: Housing and Urban Development Secretary Samuel Pierce. Remarkably, considering Pierce was the only non-Caucasian in the group, Reagan had trouble recognizing him. In 1981, Reagan was hosting a group of mayors at the White House when he came upon his HUD secretary. "How are you, Mr. Mayor?" he said. "I'm glad to meet you. How are things in your city?" In the years ahead, Reagan didn't show much interest in becoming more familiar with Pierce's face; the entire time he was president, he didn't visit the HUD offices once. (I'm not sure this mitigates his offense, but he had a history of failing to recognize people he deemed insignificant. In 1964, while visiting a Scottsdale, Arizona, boarding school as its commencement speaker, he said to a student, "My name is Ronald Reagan. What's yours?" The boy replied, "I'm your son, Mike.")

Given his lack of interest in HUD, it's no surprise that Morning in America was also Twilight of Housing. Thanks to Reagan's draconian housing cuts, homelessness, which had historically been a temporary problem during economic calamities, became chronic. According to Peter Dreier, the director of the Urban and Environmental Policy Department at Occidental College, "Every park bench in America—everywhere a homeless person sleeps—should have Ronald Reagan's name on it." The Gipper's analysis of the homeless epidemic was vintage Reagan: the homeless wanted to be homeless. "They make it their own choice for staying out there," he told ABC's David Brinkley. "There are shelters in virtually every city, and shelters here, and those people still prefer out there on the grates or the lawn to going into one of those shelters." In Reaganland, the homeless didn't want homes, the unemployed didn't want jobs, and, in possibly his nerviest claim, the hungry didn't want food. "We were told four years ago that 17 million people went to bed hungry each night," Reagan said in 1964. "Well, that was probably true. They were all on a diet." Later, when his image as governor was tarnished by a huge crowd of poor people jostling for free food at a distribution site, he suggested this novel solution to the hunger problem: "It's just too bad we can't have an epidemic of botulism."*

Though Reagan might have wished for a deadly epidemic while governor, when one arrived during his presidency, he did his best to ignore it. He refused even to utter the word AIDS until 1985, after thousands of Americans had perished. Even more shockingly, he permitted his press secretary, Larry Speakes, to treat the virus as one big joke. In 1982, after it had already claimed a thousand lives in the U.S., Speakes parried a reporter's questions about AIDS with anti-gay wisecracks:

> REPORTER: Does the president have any reaction to the
> announcement by the Centers for Disease Control
> in Atlanta that AIDS is now an epidemic in over
> 600 cases?
>
> SPEAKES: AIDS? I haven't got anything on it.
>
> REPORTER: Over a third of them have died. It's known as "gay
> plague." [Press pool laughter.] No, it is. It's a pretty
> serious thing. One in every three people that get this
> have died. And I wonder if the president was aware
> of this.
>
> SPEAKES: I don't have it. [Press pool laughter.] Do you?

---

*The Hearst Corporation had donated $2 million in food to satisfy a ransom demand of the Symbionese Liberation Army, the kidnappers of Patricia Hearst, William Randolph Hearst's granddaughter. The elder Hearst, of course, inspired Orson Welles's title character in *Citizen Kane*, who unsuccessfully runs for governor of New York. In 1982, Welles suggested that he found the fictitious candidate Kane a more compelling character than the real-life President Reagan, about whom he said, "There's not enough there for a feature movie."

As I write, the number of Americans killed by a newer virus, COVID-19, approaches a million. Reagan's negligent AIDS "response" could have been a cautionary tale for Donald J. Trump, but instead he followed it almost to the letter. In 1987, with AIDS raging around the world and the United States its epicenter, the U.S. defaulted on its obligation to the World Health Organization for the first time since its inception. Reagan reversed this disgraceful decision in the last year of his presidency, for a reason befitting a former actor: he was scheduled to make his farewell speech to the United Nations, and he didn't want to be booed.

When Reagan took his final bow in the White House, though, none of his failures mattered to Republicans, who gave him an approval rating in the eighties. Reagan's performing talent had mitigated the scorn that greeted him when he entered politics, but that achievement was deceptive: the Ridicule stage was still in effect, ready to devour an unsuspecting victim. Eight years after the Gipper won the presidency, our perverse American experiment was about to pose a new question: What if a candidate had all of Reagan's ignorance but none of his talent?

In 1988, an overconfident, underinformed senator who thought himself the Great Communicator's rightful heir thrust his rosy-cheeked mug into the American psyche. Five years later, after being relentlessly mocked as an intellectual gerbil, he was finished in politics. If no one emerged from the Ridicule stage with a sunnier smile than Ronald Reagan, no one suffered its humiliations more spectacularly than Dan Quayle.

The man who would become George H. W. Bush's running mate was born James Danforth Quayle in 1947, the grandson of the Midwestern newspaper magnate Eugene C. Pulliam. "Life has been very good to me," Quayle said. "I never had to worry about where I was going to go." One place young Danny Quayle never seemed worried about going to was class. Years later, he revealed that *Ferris Bueller's Day Off* was his favorite movie because "it reminded me of my time in school."*

To the extent that Quayle was physically present in the classroom, he seemed impervious to what transpired there. A third-generation legacy at Indiana's DePauw University, he followed in the footsteps of his dad and grandpa by joining the Delta Kappa Epsilon fraternity. Unlike Jerry Ford, whose induction into the Michigan DKE chapter raised the frat's GPA, Quayle had the worst grades in the DePauw branch. One of his professors, William Cavanaugh, was astounded by Danny's mental vacancy: "I looked into those blue eyes, and I might as well have been looking out the window." Another, Robert Calvert, remembered Danny as "vapid, indifferent to his studies, lazy, given to following the path of least resistance."[†] Amazingly, as poor as his grades were, faculty members suspected that Quayle plagiarized in order to lift them to those lofty heights. Although a smoking gun was never found, one professor said that "rumors of plagiarism have been around for so long, and we have taken them so seriously, because they fit into the view we had of him, a view of him as a corner-cutter, a manipulator, an apple-polisher, a kid who tried to get by on looks and family connections." In other words, an egregious kiss-ass who'd shine a path forward for another toadying vice president from Indiana, Mike Pence.

If Danny Quayle didn't get much out of school (*Homeroom teacher: "Quayle? . . . Quayle?"*), what did make a mark on this blank

---

*According to Quayle's sister, Martha, "None of us growing up were A students. Our parents just said, Do what you can and do it good," a family motto with appropriately Quaylian grammar.

[†] Perhaps influencing this assessment, Quayle dropped Calvert's course before exam time.

slate of a boy? One beacon of knowledge was Robert W. Welch Jr., the cuckoo-for-Cocoa-Puffs founder of the John Birch Society and the source of one of Ronald Reagan's favorite fake Lenin quotations. Dan's father, Jim "Big Jim" Quayle, was in awe of the Junior Mints mogul turned commie hunter: "He was a brilliant man with a tremendous IQ. He was, in a way, a Nostradamus, a man whose vision has come true in some sense today." In contrast, Big Jim said that his son Danny "doesn't have the greatest smarts in the world." One of the Bush campaign's first tasks after Quayle's selection was getting Dad to shut up. This gag order was a shame, because Big Jim had the potential to become an even more reliable source of hilarious utterances than his son, who, as we'll see, set that bar high. Commenting on Danny's major in college, for example, Big Jim observed, "If he's anything like his old man, it was probably booze and broads."

Armed with such fatherly wisdom, a wicked golf game, and vacant blue eyes, Dan Quayle won his first House race in 1976, at the age of twenty-nine; four years later, he ran for the U.S. Senate. To prep for that campaign, Quayle received training from a media consultant, Don Ringe, who recorded the callow candidate's responses to a series of questions. A transcript of this tape begins with Quayle warming up: "I'm Dan Quayle. I'm Dan Quayle. I'm Dan Quayle. I am Dan Quayle. The real Dan Quayle. The real Dan Quayle stand up. I'm Dan Quayle. I'm Dan Quayle."

That is by far his best answer. When Ringe asks why he had gone to public school, Quayle replies, "Because there were no private schools around." Asked why he'd worked in the Republican attorney general's consumer protection office, he says, "Actually it was a job. It wasn't any special interest in the consumer affairs." Ringe offers him another crack at the question, and, improbably, he does even worse: "I needed a paycheck and the attorney general said that I would be the best to go down there because he knew that I was anti-consumer." After a series of such gems, Ringe says, "I'm going to have this tape bronzed."

When you inventory Quayle's negligible gifts, his placement on the 1988 Republican ticket starts to seem like a prank. He topped a VP shortlist on which every other candidate was more qualified, including the revered trickle-down-economics evangelist Jack Kemp and both Bob and Elizabeth Dole.* So let's ask a question that in 1988 baffled millions: Why Dan Quayle?

Bush, sixty-four, sought to add youth to the ticket with Quayle, a dewy forty-one.† More important, Bush was unpopular with women, while Quayle, in Bush's infinite wisdom, was catnip for the ladies. This generous assessment of Quayle's magnetism was widespread among Republican insiders, nearly all of whom, it's worth noting, were men. Richard F. Fenno Jr., author of *The Making of a Senator: Dan Quayle* (yes, such a book exists), quoted an Indiana Republican bigwig who backed Quayle's first congressional bid: "I told the fellas that I thought he could win because every woman in the district would want to make love to him." It's unclear why Bush, who was responsible for the gender gap in the first place, considered himself the best arbiter of what women liked, but he, too, seemed convinced that whatever Quayle lacked in seasoning he would more than compensate for with his unbridled sex appeal. It's debatable whether women melted under Quayle's spell, but Bush and the fellas who advised him undeniably did. Among them was the Nixon

* Bob Dole may have lost points for his gaffe during the VP debate in 1976, when he referred to the four U.S. wars of the twentieth century up to that point as "Democrat wars," seemingly ignoring the key contributions of Hitler and Hirohito, among others.
† If only pandering to Quayle's generation were that simple: right before the election, a *Washington Post*/ABC News poll revealed that boomers loathed him even more than the general public did.

makeover artist Roger Ailes, who'd worked on Quayle's 1986 Senate campaign. Ailes floated the idea of a stunt in which Quayle would appear in a convertible and frenzied women would tear off his cuff links. The Bush brain trust convinced themselves that their boy wasn't just handsome: he was a dead ringer for Robert Redford. This might have been true had there been a film in which Redford played a startled deer.

Remarkably, Quayle shared the delusion that he and the Sundance Kid were separated at birth. "Danny thinks he has more nearly perfect features than Robert Redford," said a law school friend, Frank Pope.* ("More nearly perfect" sounds like the kind of English usage one might lapse into after spending too much time hanging out with Danny.) In 1972, Quayle and Pope caught a matinee of *The Candidate*, in which Redford played a blond, bland, empty husk of a politician whom a cabal of savvy and amoral media advisers propel into office. Enthralled by the movie, the two buds spent the next eleven hours imagining how Danny might follow the Redford character's blueprint. In 1988, Jeremy Larner, the film's screenwriter, wrote, "I am amazed to have inspired Dan Quayle. . . . [I]t seems he didn't understand the movie."

Indeed, a thirty-second TV spot from Quayle's Senate campaign in 1980 plays like a low-budget trailer for *The Candidate*. Viewing it, you might detect a slight resemblance to Redford, as long as you squint hard and ignore the absence of charisma; Quayle does appear to have yellow hair. He's shown shaking hands, smiling, and walking upright, while a disembodied voice intones, "Every so often a young man comes along who's special." Noticeably missing from the ad is any footage of Quayle speaking. It's possible that the producers of

---

* Chutzpah fans will admire this (actual) early campaign slogan of Quayle's: "Here's a guy who's better-looking than Robert Redford."

the ad already knew something about this special young man that the rest of the country had yet to discover.

Still, it might have been Quayle's resemblance not to Redford but to Bush himself that best explains his anointment. In a novel approach to ticket-balancing, a white male scion of a wealthy family in Connecticut chose a white male scion of a wealthy family in Indiana. Quayle was George Bush 2.0, sharing not just the original model's privileged upbringing but also his hapless steel-cage match with the English language—two qualities the Texas state treasurer (and later governor) Ann Richards combined in her immortal quip at the 1988 Democratic National Convention: "Poor George, he can't help it. He was born with a silver foot in his mouth."

Bush showed some self-awareness when he acknowledged, "I'm not the most articulate emotionalist," but that was one of his more decipherable utterances. He created word mazes worthy of M. C. Escher from which his audiences had no easy escape: "And let me say in conclusion, thanks for the kids. I learned an awful lot about bathtub toys—about how to work the telephone. One guy knows—several of them know their own phone numbers—preparation to go to the dentist. A lot of things that I'd forgotten. So it's been a good day." Sometimes his pronouncements veered into surrealism: "If a frog had wings, he wouldn't hit his tail on the ground. Too hypothetical"; "When I need a little free advice about Saddam Hussein, I turn to country music." Even the most hackneyed bromide couldn't escape his mutilation: "Please just don't look at part of the glass, the part that is only less than half full." Dipping his toe into punditry, he said, "It's no exaggeration to say the undecideds could go one way or another." He could state the obvious and somehow make it shocking, as when he visited Auschwitz and observed, "Boy, they were big on crematoriums, weren't they?" Sometimes his slips were unmistakably Freudian: "For seven and a half years I've worked alongside President

Reagan. We've had triumphs. Made some mistakes. We've had some sex—uh—setbacks." And what could a media adviser do with a politician who, in an attempt to praise dogs and his wife, managed to insult both: "It has been said by some cynic, maybe it was a former president, 'If you want a friend in Washington, get a dog.' We took them literally—that advice—as you know. But I didn't need that because I have Barbara Bush."

Even when his handlers tried to make a speech goof-proof, Bush managed to snatch incoherence from the jaws of clarity. During his reelection campaign, when polls suggested, with some justification, that he lacked empathy, his speechwriters fed the stage direction (*message: I care*) into the teleprompter to remind him to read the next line with something approximating human emotion. Instead, he read the stage direction aloud, robotically emitting the non sequitur MESSAGE I CARE to a confused audience.

But if Bush was prone to gaffes, Quayle spewed nonsense worthy of Lewis Carroll on opium. To document all of Quayle's bloopers, you'd need an entire magazine dedicated to the task—and, in fact, just such a periodical, *The Quayle Quarterly*, was published four times a year between 1989 and 1992. His most famous gaffe occurred during an address to the United Negro College Fund, when, just as Bush struggled to retrieve the correct cliché about a half-empty glass, Quayle tried to pry loose from his tangled synapses the organization's famous slogan, "A mind is a terrible thing to waste": "You take the United Negro College Fund model that what a waste it is to lose one's mind or not to have a mind is being very wasteful. How true that is."

Turning his attention to the cosmos, he declared, "For NASA, space is still a high priority" and "[It's] time for the human race to enter the solar system." Of special interest was the Red Planet; he observed, "Mars is essentially in the same orbit. Mars is somewhat the same distance from the Sun, which is very important. We have seen pictures where there are canals, we believe, and water. If there is water, that means there is oxygen. If oxygen, that means we can breathe."

When he spoke about his home planet, he remained a stranger in a strange land. After a reporter asked him, in 1988, where his campaign was headed next (Pennsylvania), he replied, "The western part of Pennsylvania is very, uh, Midwestern. Midwestern. And the eastern part is more . . . east. Uh, the Midwest, uh, Pennsylvania is a very important state, a big state; we've done well there in the past. The western part is—Pennsylvania is a divided state, like Tennessee is divided into three parts. Pennsylvania is divided into two parts. You have western Pennsylvania and then you have eastern Pennsylvania. And that's the way you campaign there. And we're going to— I think we're going mostly to the eastern part."

Though Quayle correctly deduced that the eastern part of Pennsylvania was more east than the western part, his grasp of geography elsewhere was less secure. "We have a firm commitment to Europe," he said. "We are a part of Europe." And: "I love California. I practically grew up in Phoenix." And, sublimely: "It's wonderful to be here in the great state of Chicago." He found the Aloha State even more confusing than the state of Chicago. "Hawaii is a unique state," he said. "It is a small state. It is a state that is by itself. It is a—it is different than the other 49 states. Well, all states are different, but it's got a particularly unique situation." One of the particularly unique things about Hawaii's situation was where it was situated. "Hawaii has always been a very pivotal role in the Pacific," he said. "It is in the Pacific. It is a part of the United States that is an island that is right here." (Actually, Hawaii consists of eight major islands, but, in the spirit of generosity, I'll award him partial credit—something his stingy professors at DePauw seemed loath to do.) Though Quayle's geography skills were meager, he promised the next generation would fare better: "We're going to have the best-educated American people in the world."

His most glorious gaffes were mind-bending adventures that challenged the linear nature of time: "I have made good judgments in the past. I have made good judgments in the future"; "The future will be better tomorrow"; "The real question for 1988 is whether we're going to go forward to tomorrow or past to the . . . to the back"; and "The Holocaust was an obscene period in our nation's history. I mean in this century's history. But we all lived in this century. I didn't live in this century." Quayle's verbal contortions would have killed a lesser man, but he remained unbowed. "I stand by all the misstatements that I've made," he declared.

On August 16, 1988, full of misplaced confidence that he'd selected an outstanding running mate, George H. W. Bush was ready to unleash Dan Quayle on an unsuspecting public. Quayle's product launch took place during a riverfront rally at Spanish Plaza, in New Orleans, which was hosting the Republican National Convention. To kick off the festivities, a Dixieland jazz band played and, although the music didn't whip inflation, it inspired an array of middle-aged white Republican dignitaries onstage to treat the audience to a vigorous display of arrhythmic dancing. Then Bush, sweating through a short-sleeved white oxford shirt—a garment that seemed to cry, *Message: I'm square*—introduced his protégé. True to his self-description as "not the most articulate emotionalist," Bush extolled his ticket partner for being "born in the middle of this century, and from the middle of America." Yes, reaching for a word that would capture the young man in whom his campaign had invested such hope, the best Bush could do was "middle." At least he couldn't be accused of hype.

Now it was Quayle's turn. Wearing a blue blazer, white shirt, and red tie, he seized the podium and started with a joke: "Actually, I was just in the area and decided to stop by." (Quayle had yet to learn that the biggest laughs he'd get would always be unintentional.*) It's not clear from the video whether Quayle was dripping with flop sweat or just sweat, but in any case, after this gambit, he decided to lose the blazer. Shifting from comedy to straight-up shouting, Quayle declaimed several forgettable platitudes about "George Bush's America" before grasping the shoulder of George Bush himself, who seemed alarmed by the unexpected invasion of his personal space. "I can't remember with any degree of recollection what I said," Quayle later commented, in a mixture of modesty and redundancy. As Bob Woodward and David S. Broder wrote in their terrifyingly titled book, *The Man Who Would Be President: Dan Quayle*, "News media coverage of the event compared Quayle to a cheerleader or a game show contestant who had just won the Oldsmobile."

People watching his hyperkinetic unveiling were understandably concerned that Quayle, if elected, would be one botched colonoscopy away from the presidency.† But Bush's campaign manager, Lee Atwater, knew who could help: Stu Spencer. Having masked Ronald Reagan's ignorance, Spencer was now the go-to concealer in the Republican makeup kit. He assumed the unenviable role of Quayle's "mother hen," doing everything in his power to make this empty

---

*Another typical comedy attempt by Quayle came at an appearance at John Henry Neff Elementary School, in Lancaster, Pennsylvania, where he told the assembled kids, "Think about your education. But have fun. I want you to take the weekend off." Silence.

†One person who didn't doubt Dan Quayle's fitness to be president was Dan Quayle. In a stunning example of his hubris, before Bush tapped him as VP, Quayle had considered making his own bid for the presidency. A GOP primary debate between Bush and Quayle would have required an English simulcast.

glass of a candidate appear at least half full. That wouldn't be easy. One TV anchor who interviewed Quayle at the convention had a reaction similar to that of his professor at DePauw: "When I looked into his eyes I could see to the back of his head."

The morning after the unfortunate shoulder-grabbing incident, it seemed as though every journalist in George Bush's America was searching for evidence of Quayle's unfitness. At a joint press conference with Bush, Quayle, who'd never faced a hostile press in his congressional races in Indiana, now saw how unpleasant it was to be covered by newspapers not owned by his grandfather. Reporters peppered him with questions about two issues that would dog him in the weeks ahead: his reputedly execrable academic record and his alleged use of family connections to avoid serving in Vietnam.* Asked about the latter, he gave what might have been the worst possible answer: "I did not know in 1969 that I would be in this room today, I'll confess." His performance at this presser was so shaky that it freaked out the usually unflappable Roger Ailes. "I thought, 'Oh shit, we'd better get a hold of this thing,'" he later said.[†]

In the days ahead, the nation's reporters were also trying to get a hold of something: Quayle's grades. The Bush campaign's refusal to release his academic transcripts, which had been given the kind of deep burial usually accorded nuclear waste, made journalists suspect he didn't have a Phi Beta Kappa key jingling in his sock drawer. The columnist Anthony Lewis asked in the *New York Times*, "Why is Dan

---

* A potential third Quayle controversy, a rumored romp with a former lobbyist (and later *Playboy* model) named Paula Parkinson, was expertly quashed by his wife, Marilyn, who told the press, "Anybody who knows Dan Quayle knows he would rather play golf than have sex any day." As Second Lady, she'd adopt an appropriate cause for someone married to Dan Quayle: "disaster preparedness."
[†] Quayle offers a different (and typically clueless) version of events in his memoir, *Standing Firm*: "Quite frankly, I didn't think the press conference went that badly."

Quayle refusing to let the public know what he did at college and law school? Why won't he allow those schools to state the facts? Why does he fear the truth? . . . What is he hiding?"

Well, for starters: as a prelude to his career in politics, he'd failed his final exam in political science. And then there was the fishy way he got into law school. The Cleveland *Plain Dealer* reported that Quayle, a fire-breathing congressional opponent of affirmative action, had taken advantage of a special admissions program designed to favor minority applicants. No one could figure out which minority group he belonged to, other than "blond newspaper heirs." Concurrent with Quayle's acceptance to the University of Indiana Law School, his press-baron grandpa made substantial donations to the very same institution of higher learning.* In September 1988, revelations about how Quayle oozed his way into law school so outraged some of Indiana University's student leaders that they demanded he disclose the precise dollar amount of his family's benevolence.

I won't dwell too long on the controversy over Quayle's academic career because, as I said earlier, politicians' grades aren't as important as their intellectual curiosity. (We'll discuss Quayle's intellectual curiosity later. It won't take long.) It's worth wondering, though, whether he could have avoided the entire brouhaha over his transcripts if he had just released them, admitted he was a lousy student, and moved on. He could even have invoked the example of FDR, who, as we saw, was a mediocre student but became a stellar commander in chief. Given Quayle's later penchant for comparing himself to a beloved dead president, this should have been like rolling off a log for him.

On the campaign trail, Stu Spencer worked overtime to keep Quayle from revealing his glaring cluelessness. That meant putting

---

* He thus blazed a trail for the convicted felon Charles Kushner, whose $2.5 million donation to Harvard eerily predated his son Jared's admission.

him in front of friendly audiences—"friendly" being a delicate way of saying "white." "Dan Quayle doesn't know about cities," Spencer told the *Los Angeles Times*. "He doesn't know who lives there, ghettos, traffic, race, crime, housing, all of that stuff, but we'll teach him."* In deeming Quayle educable, Spencer seemed to believe he'd succeed where the DePauw faculty had failed. Despite his best efforts, Spencer couldn't stop his pupil from asserting that Republicans "understand the importance of bondage between parent and child," or that "[t]his election is about who's going to be the next president of the United States." Traveling with Quayle, Molly Ivins wasn't wowed. "I found him dumber than advertised," she said. "If you put that man's brain in a bumblebee, it would fly backwards."

With so few tangible accomplishments to Quayle's credit, Bush took a unique approach to boosting his VP pick: he started praising him for all the things he *didn't* do. Addressing the Veterans of Foreign Wars, Bush said that Quayle "did not go to Canada, he did not burn his draft card, and he damn sure didn't burn the American flag." Of course, fleeing to Canada and burning his draft card would have been bizarre behaviors for someone whose wealthy family got him out of Vietnam via the Indiana National Guard. Still, Bush showed admirable restraint by not bragging about other things that Quayle didn't do, such as assassinating Archduke Franz Ferdinand or exploding the Hindenburg.

With only a month to go until his vice presidential debate with the Texas senator Lloyd Bentsen, Michael Dukakis's running mate, Quayle had to change the narrative, and fast. For an appearance at the City Club of Chicago, his staff handed him a gravitas-building script about military affairs, despite the caveat that "he can't read a

---

* In *Standing Firm*, Quayle expresses moral outrage at Spencer trashing him before spending many paragraphs trashing Spencer.

speech." (That blunt assessment came from his wife.) In the words of a campaign aide, Joe Canzeri, "He didn't want anything on paper. His eyes would glaze over." His aversion to reading might have been due to a derisory attention span. "He was like a kid," Canzeri said. "Ask him to turn off a light, and by the time he gets to the switch, he's forgotten what he went for."* As we've discussed, reading is a pretty good indicator of intellectual curiosity, and, unfortunately, there's scant evidence that Quayle read anything besides his golf score. On those rare occasions when his eyes fell upon the printed page, what he gleaned was iffy. He said that Robert K. Massie's classic account of the Romanovs' fall, *Nicholas and Alexandra*, "shows how people that are really very weird can get into sensitive positions and have a tremendous impact on history." (Indeed.) At the City Club of Chicago, Quayle, vastly overestimating his improv skills, ditched his prepared text and decided to wing it. The result was an incident that the *Los Angeles Times* reported under the headline "Quayle Remarks Appear to Bewilder Audience."

Calling himself an "agnostic" about trusting the Soviet Union, he said, "I put myself down as an agnostic because I'm hopeful," causing his audience to become less than agnostic about whether he knew the meaning of the word "agnostic." Hitting his stride, he quoted from an indispensable reference book on weapons policy, the novel *Red Storm Rising* by Tom Clancy. Just when the City Club of Chicago thought he couldn't get any more erudite, Quayle took a deep dive into the subject of the North Atlantic Treaty Organization. Arguing that "the strategy of NATO is not an offensive strategy," he demonstrated that Tom Clancy wasn't the only foreign policy expert

---

*As Quayle makes clear in *Standing Firm*, he didn't like Canzeri any more than he liked Spencer.

he heeded: he also listened to the legendary Indiana basketball coach Bobby Knight. "He says there is nothing that a good defense cannot beat a better offense," he said, garbling whatever wisdom Knight was trying to impart. Belatedly realizing that what he'd just said made zero sense, he added, "In other words, a good offense wins." Then, as if to prove his mind was capable of holding two opposing thoughts simultaneously, he asserted that NATO's strategy is "not defense," just moments after saying it was.*

How could Stu Spencer, the man who kept Reagan on script and Ford under wraps, let Quayle fly off the rails? Spencer claimed it was all part of his plan: he wanted Quayle to flop as a form of obedience training, like letting a rambunctious spaniel shock itself on an invisible fence. As he explained to his fellow Quayle-minder Canzeri, "I want him to step on his dick, and then we'll own him again." After the VP debate, however, during which the candidate would step on his dick roughly once a minute, Spencer would give up on owning Quayle and settle for disowning him.

By the night of October 5, when he took the debate stage at the Civic Auditorium in Omaha, Quayle was a nervous wreck: a shadow of his former self, which made him a shadow of a cipher. Capitalizing on fears that his vacuity could pose an existential threat to the nation, Democratic operatives mocked him that night merely by wearing buttons reading "President Quayle." What transpired over the following ninety minutes was an epochal event in the Ridicule stage

---

*Quayle confuses matters further, if that's possible, in *Standing Firm*, by attributing an entirely opposite insight to Knight: "Indiana's great basketball coach, Bobby Knight, used to say that the best offense can never beat a really good defense." Alas, Knight didn't say that, either. He said, "Good basketball always starts with good defense." Elsewhere in the book, Quayle redeems himself somewhat by making a wholly accurate statement about defense as it pertained to his 1988 campaign: "I was reduced to a defensive crouch."

of ignorance, a catastrophe on the order of the eruption of Mount Vesuvius or the movie *Cats*. The first question from moderator Judy Woodruff set the grisly tone for the night. Raising the issue of his qualifications—or, more precisely, his disqualifications—Woodruff brought up criticism from an unwelcome source: Quayle's fellow Republicans. Bob Dole, the Senate Minority Leader, had said that "a better-qualified person could have been chosen"; most likely, the better-qualified person Bob Dole had in mind was Bob Dole. More scathingly, former secretary of state Alexander Haig called Quayle's selection "the dumbest call George Bush could have made." It was particularly damning that Haig, who alarmed the nation with his Strangelovian "I'm in control here" outburst from the White House podium after Ronald Reagan was shot in 1981, was freaking out at the prospect of Quayle someday being in control.

Quayle, in a peculiar gambit intended to silence his doubters, decided to demonstrate his qualifications by barking a random series of technical terms related to national defense. (It was unclear whether they came from a briefing book or *The Hunt for Red October*.) "In national security and arms control," he said, "you have to understand the relationship between a ballistic missile, a warhead, what throw weight, what megatonnage is. You better understand about telemetry and encryption." True enough, but, in addition to saying those terms aloud, it would have helped if he'd shown that he knew what they meant. As it was, Quayle seemed to be flaunting his ability to recite polysyllabic words; you half expected him to blurt out "cantilever" or "pomegranate."

When ABC's Brit Hume asked him the decidedly non-gotcha question about what he'd do if tragic circumstances thrust him into the presidency, his response was so tortured that his inquisitors kept giving him mulligans, wishfully thinking he might do better if he took another swing. Instead of being grateful for the do-overs,

Quayle grew peevish, accusing the journalists of asking him the same question four times. Tom Brokaw corrected him, saying that the actual number was three; on top of all his other deficits, it now appeared that Quayle couldn't count.

Just as remarkable as the answers Quayle gave were the endless pauses he took on the road to giving them. Never had a politician produced such lengthy blank stares in response to questions he should have anticipated.* These hiatuses, often occurring midsentence, threatened to eclipse the eighteen minutes of silence that gave Richard Nixon's secretary, Rose Mary Woods, fifteen minutes of fame. When Quayle began an answer, a viewer couldn't be blamed for going to the kitchen, frying up an omelet, and returning to the TV without fear of missing anything.

The most famous moment of the debate, of course, belonged to Bentsen, who deployed the mother of all debate zingers. His withering takedown, alas, was made possible by Quayle himself, who foolishly stepped into a bear trap of his own creation. Despite the debate-night assessment by ABC's Peter Jennings that Bentsen's legendary burn was "perhaps the most spontaneous moment of the evening," it was anything but.

On the campaign trail, Quayle had repeatedly compared his experience in government favorably to that of John F. Kennedy; a ballsy move, to be sure, but not terribly surprising for a man who had also convinced himself that he was Robert Redford. The Dukakis campaign harvested clips of Quayle riffing on this grandiose theme and handed them to a young Ohio congressman, Dennis Eckart, who was

---

*With one possible exception: in 1979, Senator Edward M. Kennedy was struck dumb when CBS's Roger Mudd asked, "Why do you want to be president?" in an interview whose sole purpose was to promote his desire to be president.

to be Quayle's stand-in for a series of mock debates with Bentsen.* During one practice session, when Eckart-as-Quayle suggested that he and Kennedy were of equal stature, Bentsen was aghast. Susan Estrich, Dukakis's campaign manager, remembered the incredulous Texan asking, "Does he really do that?" At that point, the zinger-formulating equivalent of the Manhattan Project was underway. The only question was whether Bentsen would have an opportunity to drop the bomb.

Fifty-eight minutes into the debate, Quayle, who'd been reliably inarticulate all night, seemed to draw on unexpected reserves of coherence to give Bentsen the perfect setup: "I have as much experience in the Congress as Jack Kennedy did when he sought the presidency." The Bush team must've been shitting bricks: they'd specifically warned Quayle against hoisting himself up to JFK's pedestal. Bentsen, who up to this point had comported himself like a sly old cat, seemingly content to toy with Quayle as if he were a yarn mouse, was spring-loaded and ready to pounce. As Estrich recalled, "I turned to the key supporters gathered in the holding room and said, 'Here it comes.' And it did."

You probably know what Bentsen said next, but, because it never gets old, voilà: "Senator, I served with Jack Kennedy. I knew Jack Kennedy. Jack Kennedy was a friend of mine. Senator, you're no Jack Kennedy." According to the helpful transcript provided by the Commission on Presidential Debates, Bentsen's remarks provoked "prolonged shouts and applause." As Roger Ailes recalled, "Once that happened . . . I said good night." Bentsen knew he'd delivered a coup de grâce. "I saw his Adam's apple going up and down," the Texan said later.

---

*In 2016, Eckhart still preserved a holy relic from those sparring matches: the page from a yellow legal pad on which the Ohioan had scribbled, "Quayle thinks he's JFK!"

From that point on, Quayle resembled Jack Kennedy only if you could picture JFK first learning the outcome of the Bay of Pigs invasion. In the debate's waning minutes, Quayle had no choice but to go for a Hail Mary, employing the patented Reagan technique of uncorking a totally unverifiable anecdote. He claimed that his ninety-seven-year-old grandmother once told him, "You can do anything you want to if you just set your mind to it, and go to work." It was a stretch to see how this corny chestnut, which leaned on the words "mind" and "work," applied to Dan Quayle. To borrow terminology from the polysyllabic Quayle lexicon, it went over like a balloon of massive megatonnage.

Across the political spectrum, the reviews were brutal. In a column titled "Roboflop," the *New Republic*'s Hendrik Hertzberg referred to Quayle's "pee-pants performance." The conservative columnist George Will observed that, as VP, "Quayle will not be trusted to handle even the more serious foreign funerals." On a morning-after call-in show on C-SPAN, a Cleveland woman suggested, in all seriousness, that Quayle be drug-tested. She didn't indicate which pharmaceuticals she suspected him of using, but they couldn't possibly have been in the performance-enhancing family.

The most devastating notices, however, came from Bushworld. An anonymous staffer compared Quayle to "a wounded fawn" and said the campaign would need to "potty-train" him. The campaign chairman, James Baker, managed to put a positive spin on the debate while eviscerating Quayle: "When you think about what might have happened, we have to be pretty happy."* Woodward and Broder reported that, when Baker and Stu Spencer convened to discuss Roboflop's future, "the decision was made to 'go out and bury him,' by

---

* Only one person in the Bush campaign seemed to have thought Quayle won the debate: Quayle. "I was convinced we came out on top," he said.

scheduling Quayle only for events likely to generate minimal national news coverage." For the remainder of the campaign, he was packed off to the political equivalent of boarding school.

Despite Quayle's abysmal performance, the Republican ticket was headed for victory—in part because the Democrats, ignoring the Curse of Adlai Stevenson, had given the egghead strategy another shot. During the race for the nomination, the Democratic presidential field had featured no fewer than *five* eggheads. Eugene McCarthy was back, in a quixotic attempt to rekindle the magic of '68. From Adlai's home state of Illinois came Senator Paul Simon, who cemented his Poindexter cred by voluntarily wearing a bow tie. Also running was the former Colorado senator Gary Hart, a cerebral Yale Law School graduate and the author of such beach reads as *America Can Win: The Case for Military Reform*, who was the front-runner until he was photographed in a less-than-cerebral pose on a Bimini-bound yacht called *Monkey Business*.* Hart's fascination with technology led some in the media to call him an "Atari Democrat," an honor shared by another contender, Senator Al Gore of Tennessee. And, rounding out this historic roster of geeks and dweebs, the eventual nominee: the Massachusetts governor, Michael Dukakis.

People seeking more information about the Democrats' standard-

---

* Hart's reputation as a military expert suffered somewhat during a Democratic presidential primary debate in 1984. The moderator asked what the candidates would do if a Czech airline entered American airspace and headed straight for NORAD. "If the people that they looked in and saw had uniforms on, I'd shoot the aircraft down," Hart said. "If they were civilians, I'd just let it keep going." Hart's answer provided fodder for another debater who was better versed in air travel: the Ohio senator and ex-astronaut John Glenn. "Let me say first, I think there's such a lack of fundamental understanding by saying we're going to go up and peek in the window of this thing and see if they have military uniforms on," Glenn said as the audience erupted in laughter.

bearer most frequently google the phrase "Michael Dukakis tank." The regrettable photo op they find, in which a goofily helmeted Dukakis goes for a ride in a sixty-eight-ton Abrams Main Battle Tank, was intended to silence the Bush campaign's accusation that he was weak on defense. Instead, Dukakis drew widespread comparisons to the world's most famous beagle, Snoopy.

A televised debate with Bush would soon make Dukakis nostalgic for his joyride in the Abrams. The CNN anchor Bernard Shaw began the evening with this nuanced policy question about the governor's wife: "Governor, if Kitty Dukakis were raped and murdered, would you favor an irrevocable death penalty for the killer?" In what proved to be a fatal mistake, Dukakis gave an intellectually coherent response. "No, I don't, Bernard, and I think you know that I've opposed the death penalty during all of my life," he said. "I don't see any evidence that it's a deterrent, and I think there are better and more effective ways to deal with violent crime." This answer showed Dukakis could remain cool under pressure, a commendable quality in a president. The media, however, preferred that an aspirant for that job go batshit crazy, and roasted Dukakis for not doing so. In their view, his failure to rend his garments, howl with rage, and vow revenge on his wife's hypothetical assailant disqualified him from holding office anywhere but Massachusetts.

After the debate, Kitty Dukakis said what her husband probably should have: "It was an outrageous question." The three female journalists on the debate panel—Ann Compton, Margaret Warner, and Andrea Mitchell—had all tried to convince Shaw not to use Mrs. Dukakis's name for the purposes of his attention-seeking stunt. Dismissive of the women, Shaw said, "I disagree with each of you and I'm not changing anything." Though some blame Shaw's question for ending Dukakis's political career, the career it should have ended was Shaw's.

Dukakis's debate "gaffe," however, wasn't the only TV phenomenon boosting the Bush campaign. Republicans blanketed the airwaves with the face of a man who'd be crucial to their success: William Horton. A convicted Massachusetts murderer, Horton went on a violent crime spree made possible by a weekend prison furlough program that Dukakis supported. Lee Atwater, Bush's campaign manager and an expert at weaponizing bigotry, changed the first name of Horton, who was Black, to "Willie" for racist attack ads that left nothing to the imagination. "By the time we're finished," Atwater said, "they're going to wonder whether Willie Horton is Dukakis's running mate." Not content to leave them wondering, Republicans sent out a fundraising letter emblazoned with photos of Dukakis and Horton and the highly rhetorical question "Is this your pro-family team for 1988?" For Atwater's outstanding achievement in the field of racist campaigning, the Republican National Committee named him chairman.

Atwater, of course, was only picking up where Ronald Reagan left off. In a startlingly candid 1981 interview, he traced the evolution of racist dog whistles in political campaigns: "You start out in 1954 by saying, 'N—, n—, n—.' By 1968 you can't say 'n—'—that hurts you. Backfires. So you say stuff like forced busing, states' rights, and all that stuff." During the 1988 campaign, Atwater worked with Bush's son George W. Bush, and they grew close. When the Horton ads catapulted his dad to victory, W. must have been impressed. He'd find bigotry useful in future campaigns of his own.

Meanwhile, if the Quayle ordeal taught Bush Senior anything about the perils of choosing an unqualified nominee for an important position, he didn't show it. If anything, winning big despite the albatross of Quayle might have emboldened him: in 1991, he tapped a man with only one year of judicial experience to serve on the United States Supreme Court. Thirty years later, the nation is still paying the price for his selection of Clarence Thomas.

One of the loudest voices supporting Thomas was a rising young neocon named Bill Kristol, whose record of embracing unfit candidates might be without peer in American political history. In 1988, he managed the campaign of his former Harvard roommate Alan Keyes, who was running for the U.S. Senate in Maryland. Keyes, a political neophyte who'd lived in the state only three years, seemed bent on appealing to voters who felt Ronald Reagan had been too cuddly toward the poor. When a homeless woman asked the reasonable question of what he'd do for her as senator, Keyes snapped, "Nothing. There's nothing I can do for you. The question is, what are you going to do for yourself?" Maryland's voters, evidently deciding there was nothing Keyes could do for them, chose his Democratic opponent, Paul Sarbanes, by a twenty-four-point margin. Having gained invaluable experience working for a monumental loser, Kristol was now suited for a new job: chief of staff to Dan Quayle.

In this post, Kristol soon earned the oxymoronic sobriquet "Quayle's Brain." The grand strategies emanating from said brain were brainless. Kristol hoped Quayle's position on Bush's "Space Council" would transform his image from floundering airhead to visionary futurist. Instead, it gave him an opportunity to sound like Carl Sagan's stupid brother: "Space is almost infinite. As a matter of fact, we think it is infinite." As debate raged over whether the space inside Quayle's head was infinite, Kristol had another genius idea: allowing the vice president to pick a fight with a popular sitcom character.

Quayle started the feud on May 19, 1992, in a speech to California's Commonwealth Club about the recent Los Angeles riots. Flaunting his skills as a master detective, Quayle said, "When I have been asked during these last weeks who caused the riots and the killing in L.A., my answer has been direct and simple: Who is to blame for the riots? The rioters are to blame. Who is to blame for the killings? The killers are to blame." But, just when his audience was about to exclaim, "Case closed!" Quayle introduced a twist worthy of Agatha Christie: the *real* culprit wasn't the rioters or the killers, but a fictional newswoman portrayed on CBS by Candice Bergen. Arguing that the rise of single-parent households had somehow caused Los Angeles to burn, Quayle scolded, "It doesn't help matters when prime-time TV has Murphy Brown, a character who supposedly epitomizes today's intelligent, highly paid professional woman, mocking the importance of fathers by bearing a child alone and calling it just another lifestyle choice." He underscored this point the following day, declaring, "Illegitimacy is something we should talk about in terms of not having it."

In the end, this ill-advised tussle proved only that, in addition to losing a debate to Lloyd Bentsen, Quayle was capable of losing one to a person who didn't exist. The producers of *Murphy Brown* mined the controversy for ratings, while Quayle became the most unpopular vice president in modern history, notching 63 percent disapproval.* Embarrassingly, it emerged that Quayle had never watched *Murphy Brown*. The fiasco should have sent Bill Kristol into hiding, but his role in the Age of Ignorance wasn't over. When another egregiously unqualified candidate burst onto the scene two decades later, Bill Kristol rose again, as we'll see.

Describing his approach to his job, Quayle said, "One word sums up probably the responsibility of any vice president, and that one word is 'to be prepared.'" Though he went to the trouble of plagiarizing the Boy Scouts' motto, circumstances never required Quayle to assume the presidency; one word that sums up probably the American

---

* Quayle held the record for vice presidential unpopularity until July 2007, when he gave way to the formidable Dick Cheney.

people's feeling about that was "to be relieved." He reassured the nation that "[w]e are ready for any unforeseen event that may or may not occur," but Quayle's tenure as Bush's wingman proved blessedly uneventful. His archnemesis turned out to be not Candice Bergen but syntax. The *New York Times* published this harrowing account of his attempt, after a speech in Phoenix, to answer an audience member's question about the White House's proposal for medical malpractice reform:

> Mr. Quayle, an earnest look on his face, began to fidget. "I, I can't tell you exactly what we do on that pain and suffering in the—" the Vice President said, his voice trailing off as he looked offstage toward Kevin E. Moley, the deputy secretary of the Department of Health and Human Services, who has been coaching him. "Kevin, what do we do on the pain and suffering on our malpractice proposal?"
>
> After listening briefly to Mr. Moley, Mr. Quayle continued. "So, it doesn't address it specifically," he said. "The state—the states could in fact—what we basically do is—try to do—is get the states to come up with medical malpractice legislation. We have, I think it's five criteria in our suggested recommendations. But once they meet the five criteria, then they get a favorable distribution from us if they meet—basically forcing the states to adopt this medical malpractice legislation, and that's the way that you do it."

Quayle once observed, "Verbosity leads to unclear, inarticulate things"; on the international stage, he produced an impressive stream of them. Four months into his vice presidency, he said, "I believe we are on an irreversible trend toward more freedom and democracy— but that could change." Speaking in El Salvador, he let that nation's government know that "[w]e expect them to work toward the elimination of human rights." On a return visit, he posed with a Soviet anti-tank rocket, holding it backward so the muzzle pointed toward him. But these embarrassments can't compete with the most memorable episode of his vice presidency: the incident that has made "Dan Quayle potato" the most popular Google search involving his name.

On June 15, 1992, Quayle visited Munoz Rivera Elementary School, in Trenton, New Jersey. What began as a harmless pro-education event for a man who'd once observed, "Quite frankly, teachers are the only profession that teach our children" became the most nightmarish spelling bee in history. After a student named William Figueroa correctly spelled "potato" on the chalkboard, Quayle advised him, "Add a little bit to the end there. . . . [Y]ou're right phonetically, but . . ." Once he'd hectored young William into disfiguring his answer by adding an *e*, Quayle beamed and the assembled kids, understandably assuming that the person who might be called upon to lead the free world was better informed than their peer, applauded.

Quayle was roasted nonstop for his blunder, including by Figueroa, who called the vice president an "idiot." The twelve-year-old tried to walk back that insult while appearing on David Letterman's late-night talk show, but his recantation made matters worse: "I know he's not an idiot, but he needs to study more. Do you have to go to college to be vice president?" Quayle had used his Murphy Brown speech to pontificate about "personal responsibility," but he took none for his spelling error. Instead, he blamed it on an index card provided by a member of the only profession that teach our children.* The whole nasty incident must have reinforced his long-standing hatred of school, not to mention words written on paper.

---

* Bill Kristol, the Forrest Gump of political disasters, was present at the spelling bee. He asked an advance man, "Has anyone checked the cards?" Satisfied with the affirmative response, Kristol didn't bother to check the cards.

But the question of whether Quayle, had he not been misled by that infernal index card, might have correctly spelled the name of a common root vegetable is beside the point. The episode is significant for two other reasons.

First, it illustrates the astonishing reality that, as recently as 1992, misspelling a word could damage a politician's career. Today, revisiting an era in American politics when spelling mattered is, sadly, like traveling to Colonial Williamsburg. In today's politics, if spelling is relevant at all, it's just another lightning rod for tribal grievances. In 2020, an online clip of Quayle's spelling mishap inspired this comment by someone using the handle "lib hypocrites": "The travesty was that Quayle wasn't wrong. Either way is acceptable. Just more railroading by the leftist media." Adding more fuel to this raging partisan debate, "potato" is the only correct spelling recognized by the *Merriam-Webster* dictionary, a notorious antifa publication.

Second, the spelling bee catastrophe underscores a more serious political deficit of Quayle's than his lack of knowledge: his utter lack of the talent necessary to conceal his lack of knowledge. When Quayle didn't know something, we knew he didn't know. He freaked out, he panicked, he got snippy. He kept riffing, nonsensically, believing he was circling the facts when he was only circling the drain.

In addition to dreaming that he was JFK, Quayle might also have imagined himself as the hero of his favorite movie: Ferris Bueller, the smart-ass who could talk his way out of anything. The character in that film Quayle most resembled was Principal Rooney, an overconfident, easily enraged dolt whom Ferris outwits again and again. Ferris's watchword—"Life moves pretty fast. If you don't stop and look around once in a while, you could miss it"—reflects an insouciance that Quayle might have had as a golf star in high school, or as a Deke at DePauw, but never during the 1988 campaign or his vice presidency. By then, everything moved too fast for him.

There have been forty-nine vice presidents of the United States, and they can be sorted into three categories: the famous, like John Adams, who got his own HBO miniseries; the infamous, like Spiro Agnew, who did for "nolo contendere" what Warren G. Harding did for "normalcy"; and the forgotten, like George Clinton, who, despite serving under both Thomas Jefferson and James Madison, never achieved the fame of his namesake, George E. Clinton, the founder of Parliament-Funkadelic.* In the years since the electorate ousted George H. W. Bush and his veep, Quayle has tried to avoid winding up in that last category. Striving to be more than a historical footnote, he's been an avid supporter of the Quayle Vice Presidential Learning Center, an educational institution dedicated to teaching students about all the U.S. vice presidents, but one in particular.

Although the museum, located in Quayle's hometown of Huntington, Indiana, is funded by a shadowy nonprofit called the Dan Quayle Commemorative Foundation, there's no mystery shrouding the identity of the shrine's principal donor of artifacts. Quaylologists will swoon at the 425 boxes of the former veep's papers; if they include memoranda intended for Quayle's consumption, they're undoubtedly in mint condition. There's the toy truck he played with as a child before trading it for golf clubs; also on display are his golf clubs. Possibly the biggest draw among these curios—the *Mona Lisa* of the Quayle Center—is his raggedy law school diploma,

---

*The more famous George Clinton heralded another Clinton's ascension to the presidency in 1993 by recording a memorable song, "Paint the White House Black."

which the Quayle family dog, Barnaby, considered a chew toy, not realizing how many grandfatherly greenbacks it cost.

To fulfill its educational mission, the museum offers something called "Quayle Quiz," which it describes as "an in-depth examination of the life and career of Vice President, Dan Quayle." (The extraneous comma is an unintentional tribute to Quayle's grammar.) To further the museum's mission of educating youngsters about "Vice President, Dan Quayle," I will now offer a little-noted postscript to his vice presidency.

In 1999, hoping, perhaps, that voters had decided a president might never be called upon to spell "potato," Quayle entered the race for the 2000 Republican presidential nomination. (During his wilderness years, he'd made one attempt to own his spelling mishap, appearing in a 1994 Super Bowl ad for—what else?—Wavy Lay's potato chips, acting opposite a teenage Elijah Wood. One of them would go on to bigger things.) There's a YouTube video of him announcing his candidacy, and it's oddly moving: receiving a thunderous ovation from his hometown crowd, Quayle exclaims, "I accept your nomination!" The joke doesn't land, possibly because, since Dan Quayle's saying it, the audience isn't sure whether he's being funny or just inaccurate. But his bid had the support of at least one future Republican luminary: a pollster named Kellyanne Fitzgerald, who would later become famous under her married name for inventing something called "alternative facts." Asked by a *New York Times* reporter why she'd chosen to work for Quayle instead of another Republican hopeful, she said, "I don't deal with nonserious men in my personal or professional life."

Unfortunately, Quayle's chances of winning the nomination turned out to be very nonserious. On August 14, 1999, he finished eighth in Iowa's influential Ames Straw Poll. In a further humiliation, the seventh-place finisher was Bill Kristol's electorally challenged college roommate, Alan Keyes. This experience was sufficiently traumatic to convince Quayle to quit the race. "There's a time to stay and there's a time to fold," he said, sounding like a Kenny Rogers who couldn't rhyme. Quayle, whom George Bush had chosen in 1988 to be George Bush 2.0, had been demolished by the winner of the straw poll, George Bush 3.0—who happened to be named George Bush.

2

THE SECOND STAGE: ACCEPTANCE

As Dan Quayle melted into the bulging population of presidential also-rans, Calvin Trillin wrote this valediction in *The Nation*:

Farewell, once more, J. Danforth Quayle.
Although we know it's sad to fail,
Remember, you were once obscure—
Considered lightweight, immature.
A Bush then snatched you from the pack.
Another Bush now puts you back.

Before Quayle saunters offstage, though, we must give him his due: he was the crash test dummy who enabled George W. Bush to take the wheel. Without his groundbreaking work in the field of bar-lowering, would we ever have experienced the Iraq War, the shredding of civil liberties under the Patriot Act, and the catastrophically inept response to Hurricane Katrina?

Although Bush won 31 percent in the Ames Straw Poll and Quayle garnered a measly 4, the two candidates had more in common than

Iowans might have realized. Don't believe me? Take this quiz, which I call "Bush or Quayle?"

1. Who was admitted to college as a third-generation legacy?
ANSWER: Both. As you may remember, both Quayle's father and grandfather went to DePauw; Bush's father and grandfather attended Yale. As for membership in the academically challenged DKE frat, Quayle was a third-generation Deke, while Bush had only his father to grease his admission. Quayle, however, never got into an even more exclusive fraternity to which both W. and H. W. belonged: U.S. presidents who invaded Iraq.

2. Whose family had links to right-wing extremists?
ANSWER: Both. Dan Quayle's father worshipped Robert W. Welch Jr., the crazypants founder of the John Birch Society. But Bush's grandfather Prescott Bush outdid Jim Quayle by working for an investment bank that helped build the Third Reich. In 2003, newly declassified documents in the U.S. National Archives revealed that this bank, Brown Brothers Harriman, enabled German businessman Fritz Thyssen to funnel cash to Hitler in the 1930s. This revelation makes W.'s denunciation of the Axis of Evil seem positively Oedipal, since his grandpa worked so hard to build the original evil Axis.

3. Who used family connections to avoid going to Vietnam?
ANSWER: Both. The two fortunate sons found military posts far from the Mekong Delta: Quayle in the Indiana National Guard and Bush in the Texas Air National Guard. We thank them for their service.

4. Who was accused of plagiarism?
ANSWER: Both. Quayle was accused of plagiarizing in college, though no damning evidence ever emerged. Bush, on the other

hand, lifted entire passages from numerous other sources when he wrote—or rather, collated—his 2010 memoir, *Decision Points*.

5. Who had an adviser known as his "brain"?
ANSWER: Again, both. Bill Kristol, of course, had the dubious honor of being called "Quayle's Brain," and Karl Rove, the charming man we'll meet in this chapter, was known as "Bush's Brain." Rule of thumb: when a politician's brain resides somewhere other than in the politician, uh-oh.

6. Who was a C student in college?
ANSWER: Have you detected a pattern? Yes, just as Quayle's C average was a drag on the Deke house's GPA, Bush's Yale transcript was a monument to mediocrity. But, before you turn this data point into a decision point, remember: a college transcript is an unreliable predicter of presidential performance. Though an average student, Bush went on to become one of the worst presidents in U.S. history.

Bush's feeble grades at Yale didn't hurt his popularity at the frat. Thanks to his tireless backslapping and an approach to partying that could be summarized as No Beer Left Behind, the Dekes elected him president. He was so beloved that, during his first White House bid, his pals pumped the DKE alumni network for campaign contributions. One former classmate on the receiving end of such a pitch couldn't hide his disbelief. "Look," he said, "president of the fraternity was *one* thing. . . ."

Out of the mouths of bros. The same qualities that made Bush a bodacious president of DKE—overconfidence and recklessness—made him a cataclysmic commander in chief. Crowning himself the Decider, he made hasty choices, as if the most important goal were ending a meeting early so he could go for a jog. If Reagan sometimes channeled Winston Churchill, even tailoring faux Churchillian quotations to his own purposes, George W. Bush's apparent role model was more recent: Maverick, the character Tom Cruise played in *Top Gun.* Bush's need for speed informed everything he did: he biked fast, ran fast, and even ate fast, inhaling a hot dog in seconds. Though this velocity might have earned him the gold in a running/biking/wiener-eating triathlon, it made his presidency a fiasco. An intellectually curious man might take weeks absorbing information to make a decision that W., with no information whatsoever, could dash off before lunch. "I'm not afraid to make decisions," Bush boasted. "Matter of fact, I like this aspect of the presidency." Unlike Quayle, who flailed desperately when he didn't know something, Bush mocked knowledge as an affectation of the elites and made ignorance proof of his authenticity. His swaggering pride in how little he knew—and he knew very, very little—made George W. Bush the father of the second stage of ignorance: Acceptance.

For Bush, born just a few blocks from the Yale campus, but raised in West Texas, the rowdy Deke house was an escape from what he saw as the oppressive seriousness of his fellow Yalies, who seemed to spend all their time doing heinously unfun stuff like going to class and learning. "I wasn't exactly an Ivy League scholar," he told the *Texas Monthly* in 1994. "I had fun at Yale," he later said. "I got a lot of great friends out of Yale. And I didn't pay attention." The academic atmosphere in New Haven inspired in Bush a level of scorn that made Reagan's crack about universities "subsidizing intellectual curiosity" seem tolerant. "What angered me was the way such people at Yale felt so intellectually superior and so righteous," Bush informed the *Texas Monthly.* "They thought they had all the answers."

As anyone who graded his college exams could attest, W. didn't have all the answers. "[H]e's not at home in the more intellectual, very intellectual . . . more intellectual and more cerebral," his cousin Elsie Walker somewhat repetitiously noted. The anti-knowledge bias that Bush displayed at Yale had only hardened by the time he became president. As his former speechwriter David Frum wrote, "Conspicuous intelligence seemed actively unwelcome in the Bush White House."

With all the free time that not paying attention opened up for him, W. had plenty of room on his college schedule for pranks. While his classmates protested the Vietnam War, Bush stuck it to the Man by stealing a Christmas wreath from a local hotel to repurpose as decor for the Deke house. (His enthusiasm for such hijinks might explain his administration's surprisingly relaxed boys-will-be-boys reaction to the looting of Baghdad in 2003.) Another example of DKE tomfoolery—the jolly practice of applying a hot branding iron to the backs of pledges—resulted in Bush's first appearance, in 1967, in the *New York Times*: "A former president of Delta said that the branding is done with a hot coathanger. But the former president, George Bush, a Yale senior, said that the resulting wound is 'only a cigarette burn.'" This nonchalant pro-torture stance surely would have earned praise from a fellow Yalie, Dick Cheney, who'd unfortunately flunked out a few years earlier.

"I would agree that he's not contemplative or reflective," a Yale classmate/master of understatement said about Dubya, in 2000. "He's not a guy who would go off by himself thinking of something. He's more likely to be hiding in a tree to jump down on somebody." While Bush found his Yale classmates snobby and humorless, you couldn't blame them for failing to see the hilarity in a smirking W. plummeting toward them from his arboreal perch.

Pursuing his passion for flight, Bush joined the Texas Air National

Guard when his draft deferment expired. Omitting any reference to family connections that might have smoothed his admission to the Guard's cushy "Champagne Unit," packed with sons of the rich and powerful, Bush told the *Houston Chronicle*, "They could sense I would be one of the great pilots of all time." In 2002, reflecting on his record of valor, he said, "I've been to war. I've raised twins. If I had a choice, I'd rather go to war." By 2003, having invaded two countries in two years, Bush's preference for going to war would be unquestionable. As for the ordeal of raising his own daughters, that must have seemed more harrowing than his Champagne Unit stint, when he saw action mostly in war-torn Houston. To alleviate the stress of this tour of duty, W. threw himself into boozy poolside antics at the Melrose Place–like apartment complex where he lived, Chateau Dijon. As funny as that name is, it's even funnier if you imagine Dubya trying to pronounce it. His drinking career seemingly flowered during this period. At a society fete, he approached an elegant older woman who was a member of his parents' circle and asked, "So, what's sex like after fifty, anyway?"

In 1973, having distinguished himself in the military mainly by skipping his mandatory physical, Bush decided that law school would be the perfect place to put his talent for not paying attention to its best use. The admissions office of the University of Texas School of Law disagreed. Responding to a supplicant who'd advocated for Bush's acceptance, the dean of the law school, W. Page Keeton, wrote, "I am sure young Mr. Bush has all the many amiable qualities you describe, and so will find a place at one of the many fine institutions around the country. But not at the University of Texas." Having failed in his attempt to learn anything about torts, Bush would later dedicate himself, as governor of Texas, to tort reform.

Dubya didn't let rejection by UT Law School get him down. Instead, he aimed a little lower and applied to Harvard Business

School. Admission accomplished. An HBS instructor, Rudy Winston, remembered his initial impression of the future president: "The first day I came in the class, [Bush] and several other students were sailing paper airplanes around the class and they looked at me kind of funny, but they ended up stopping." Bush's origami sorties, however, wouldn't become an ongoing nuisance for his peers; like Dan Quayle, W. only attended class when the mood struck. Unsurprisingly, in the words of one classmate, "He's sort of a guy who got an MBA but it didn't take." A female classmate of Bush's was more pointed: "When I first heard he was running for the presidency I laughed until I couldn't see through the tears in my eyes. I just thought 'The nation is going to hell in a hand-basket. If he can be president maybe I can be the Queen of England.' "

Other events during this phase of W.'s life seemed to prove the old adage that, while you can take the bro out of the Deke House, it's significantly harder to extract the Deke House from the bro, even if the bro in question is pushing thirty. One night in 1973, after some strenuous carousing with his youngest brother, Marvin, Bush announced his return to his parents' DC home by smashing his car into trash cans. A fuming George H. W. Bush summoned his inebriated adult son to his den. At that point, shit got real, as W. uttered the immortal words, "You want to go mano a mano right here?" Cooler heads, or at least the cooler head of H. W., prevailed. Had fisticuffs ensued, the two Bushes would have made presidential history, since there's no record of John Quincy Adams going mano a mano with John.

In 1976, the year Dan Quayle used his overpowering sex appeal to get elected to the House, W. also got involved with government, racking up a DUI while visiting his family's compound in Kennebunkport, Maine. (Interestingly, Bush's worst calamities always seemed to happen in places his father got to first: DC, Kennebunkport, Iraq.)

One year later, W. was adrift, a thirty-one-year-old dude with an MBA and a DUI. Hampered by a slim résumé and meager skills, he did what any young man with few prospects would do: he ran for Congress.

Though W.'s impulsive bid in Texas's Nineteenth Congressional District surprised his family, his father, possibly hoping that serving in the House would keep W. out of vehicular mischief, provided him with a campaign adviser: Karl Rove. In their book about Rove, *Bush's Brain*, James Moore and Wayne Slater described Bush and his Brain's special bond: "[E]ach harbored a deep suspicion of the gratuitous intellectualism of the Ivy League." Soon Rove would be raising money from Republican notables plucked from Bush Senior's Rolodex, including one who would someday play a key role in an equally impetuous but more catastrophic adventure of W.'s: Donald Rumsfeld.

A no-budget four-minute film produced for Bush's first campaign shows a young W. driving down the dusty roads of West Texas, looking for unsuspecting voters to accost; the Oldsmobile Cutlass he drives, like everyone he meets, is white. Given his history, Bush might have felt it important to show that, when necessary, he could drive safely. A narrator intones, "George Bush. Businessman. Independent oil and gas producer. And now a candidate for Congress." Of the four items on that list, only number one and number four—his name and candidacy—were, strictly speaking, true. Bush's "business" at this point, Arbusto Energy, existed only on paper, and his claim to being an independent oil and gas producer was accurate only in the sense that he was independent of having produced either one.

After W. is shown hitting fly balls for Little Leaguers, the scene shifts to voter testimonials that lack the spontaneity customarily found in hostage videos. "George Bush has a sharp mind; he's done his homework well," says one woman, parting company with the UT admissions office. Bush touts his attendance at Midland,

Texas, public schools for his elementary and junior high years, wisely avoiding any mention of having graduated from high school two thousand miles away, at Phillips Academy, in Andover, Massachusetts. His savvy omission of this elitist red flag makes a subsequent statement by the narrator all the more head-scratching: "He later attended Yale, then Harvard Business School."

Why Bush thought name-checking these two institutions was a good idea for a congressional candidate in West Texas defies explanation, but his Ivy League degrees provided irresistible fodder for his Democratic opponent, the folksy good old boy Kent Hance, who treated them as if they were prior convictions. No one, however, did a better job of portraying Bush as a wine-sippin', brie-tastin' city slicker than Bush himself. In an appearance at a farm near the town of Dimmitt, Bush gushed, "Today is the first time I've been on a real farm." He also released an ad showing him jogging, an activity as alien to West Texas in 1978 as clog dancing. Seizing on Bush's goof, Hance cracked, "The only time folks around here go running is when somebody's chasing 'em."

In a radio ad for Hance, an announcer drawled, "In 1961, when Kent Hance graduated from Dimmitt High School in the Nineteenth Congressional District, his opponent George W. Bush was attending Andover Academy, in Massachusetts. In 1965, when Kent Hance graduated from Texas Tech, his opponent was at Yale University. And while Kent Hance graduated from University of Texas Law School, his opponent—get this, folks—was attending Harvard. We don't need someone from the Northeast telling us what our problems are." You have to give Hance credit for not issuing flyers with a doctored photo of Bush wearing a top hat and monocle.

Ultimately, Bush's familiar nemesis, alcohol, proved his undoing in the race, though in an unexpected way. After his campaign held a "Bush Bash" campaign event offering free beer to collegians, Hance uttered a variation on his favorite burn: "Maybe it's a cool thing to do at Harvard or Yale." Bush lost the election but learned a valuable political lesson: in future races, he'd do his darnedest to appear as folksy, homespun, and uneducated as possible. Only when he felt his mental capacity was being insulted did he drop his smirking mask of unsophistication. In 1999, when CNN's Larry King asked him about pundits calling him dim, he shot back, "They ignored the fact that I went to Yale and Harvard."

After losing the election, Bush turned his attention to his previously notional oil exploration company, Arbusto Energy. Failing to anticipate the mockery an oil-drilling outfit with the word "bust" in its name might attract, Bush began a search for petroleum that proved roughly as successful as his later quest for WMDs. Through a bewildering series of name changes and mergers—bewildering, that is, to Bush's investors, who lost millions—the original Arbusto was eventually absorbed into a company called Harken Energy, allowing Bush to walk off with a profit. His career as an oilman was notable mainly for allegations of insider trading, suggesting that, had he never run for office, he could easily have worked at Enron. His fishy maneuvers didn't escape the attention of the SEC, which began investigating Harken in 1991—when, in a massive stroke of good fortune, Bush happened to share the first and last name with the president of the United States.* After the SEC shut down its Harken probe in 1993, Dubya decided to give politics another shot. Having lost his only campaign when he ran for Congress, he decided that his next move was obvious: run for governor of the whole damn state.

---

* W.'s brother Neil might have been even luckier: despite his central role in the Silverado Savings and Loan scandal, which cost taxpayers more than a billion dollars, he remained mysteriously unindicted.

"I wouldn't say that patience is one of George's greatest qualities," his wife, Laura, told the *Texas Monthly* in 1994. "He doesn't need to evaluate and reevaluate a decision. He doesn't try to overthink. He likes action." This assessment would prove ominously insightful, as Texas, the United States, and the Persian Gulf would discover.

Amazingly, the wholly unqualified Bush had considered running for governor even earlier, in 1990. His father nixed that idea, fearing that an embarrassing defeat for his son could hurt his own reelection chances in 1992. (H. W. wound up losing anyway.) Before Bush Senior shut Junior down, though, Karl Rove and Dubya roamed Texas, visiting a series of experts in a quixotic attempt to give the vacant fortysomething the appearance of knowledge about state government. One expert they consulted was an Austin lawyer named Harry Whittington, who, in 2006, was repaid for his kindness when Bush's vice president, Dick Cheney, shot him in the face during a quail hunt.*

In 1993, with Bush Senior's political career officially dead, Junior got the all-clear to run for governor. Once again, Rove assumed the task of educating Dubya, this time spending months funneling information into him. These civics lessons were far less successful than those Stu Spencer had arranged during Reagan's first gubernatorial bid. Bush's gift for not paying attention, a source of pride for him at Yale, remained intact. In *Bush's Brain*, a Republican state senator named Bill Ratliff recalled two daylong sessions he spent trying, and failing, to educate the man who would be governor:

---

* After the shooting, Whittington apologized to Cheney for allowing his face to stray into the airspace of the vice president's birdshot. "My family and I are deeply sorry for all that Vice President Cheney and his family have had to go through this past week," said Whittington, who, in addition to injuries to his face, neck, and torso, suffered a heart attack and a collapsed lung.

"He didn't know much," said Ratliff, who was chairman of the Senate Education Committee. "He knew that public schools were hidebound in too many regulations and needed to go to a more market-based approach. He didn't take notes that I remember. It was me very much trying to point out all of this stream of everything I knew about public education and he was trying to absorb it."

At one meeting on welfare and the state's network of social services programs, Bush had trouble distinguishing between Medicaid, the federal government's medical program for the poor, and Medicare.

"Now, I hear these two. They're different. What's the difference between the two?" Bush asked, according to an aide.

After witnessing his candidate bomb his tutorials, Rove repurposed another tactic of Stu Spencer's: the Rose Garden strategy, which had hidden both Ford and Reagan from the media. Molly Ivins, in her book *Shrub: The Short but Happy Political Life of George W. Bush*, reported, "In September 1993 Rove wrote a memo urging the campaign to 'limit GWB's appearance . . . to reduce the attention of the Capitol press corps.' This is the first known instance of Rove's preference for not letting Bush loose in any unstructured situations and for keeping him away from the press." Bush, Ivins noted, "was almost fanatically 'on message'—mostly because he didn't know enough to wing it. Every time he tried, he got into trouble."

In *Bush's Brain*, Moore and Slater recount one such train wreck. Bush prided himself on overseeing the work of his speechwriters, telling them, "When you're developing things, I'm going to tell you what I believe. You guys are the wordsmiths. You can smith it out." But in November 1993, after Bush delivered a speech on education that had been smithed out for him, he had an unfortunate impromptu encounter with a member of the press:

When the reporter asked him a question about the workings of the state's education agency, apparently not in his briefing book, Bush stood for a moment, blinking.

He did not know the answer.

Exactly how would his plan change the school-finance formula?

He didn't know.

How much would it cost?

Again, he demurred.

"Will voters know how much money would be involved before election?"

Bush shifted from foot to foot, his brain swimming.

"Probably not."

During the campaign, political insiders started comparing Bush to a movie character well known to those familiar with the tragic tale of Dan Quayle: the empty vessel played by Robert Redford in *The Candidate*.

Given how often Bush revealed his ignorance, you could be forgiven for wondering how the hell he got elected governor in 1994. The narrative advanced by Bush partisans was that he dazzled Texans in a televised debate with the incumbent Democrat, Ann Richards. (The race was something of a grudge match for Bush, since the salty Richards had landed that "silver foot" zinger about W.'s dad at the 1988 DNC.) The truth is a little more complicated.

First, Richards might have contributed more to her defeat than Bush did, since she waged what all agree was an atrocious campaign. Negative press coverage compounded her mistakes. Speaking to a huge crowd of teachers two months before the election, she said, "You know how it is. You are working your tail off and doing a good job and then some jerk comes along and tells you it's not good enough." This remark was taken out of context to accuse Richards of calling W. a jerk—not a ladylike thing to do in Texas, apparently.

Second, Bush's debate performance was a case of surpassing low expectations. Mary Beth Rogers, Richards's campaign chair, remembered, "I realized that the press was in awe of Bush because he didn't make a major mistake. . . . So people thought, 'This guy's not so bad. There's nothing scary about him.'" (Low expectations would also benefit Bush in his 2000 debates with Al Gore, another time people would erroneously conclude he wasn't scary.)

And third, Bush got the final boost he needed from a well-orchestrated whispering campaign accusing Richards of packing her gubernatorial staff with lesbians. Although the Bush team denied any involvement in this effort, which targeted the Bible-thumping precincts of East Texas, the ensuing anti-gay panic mirrored the bigotry stoked by his dad's Willie Horton strategy six years earlier. Bush called Karl Rove "the Lee Atwater of Texas politics," intending that as the highest praise. Indeed, a later Bush-Rove campaign gem would have made Atwater proud: their use of push-polling in the 2000 South Carolina primary to spread the lie that Senator John McCain had fathered an illegitimate Black child. Like Yale and DKE, the Bush family tradition of appearing genteel while weaponizing bigotry was part of W.'s inheritance.

If you thought that, by becoming governor of Texas, W. would at long last accrue the knowledge and gravitas befitting a man of his years—he was, on the day of his inauguration, forty-eight—you'd be mistaken. As Robert Draper notes in *Dead Certain: The Presidency of George W. Bush*, "[A]t an event for Republican governors in Williamsburg, Virginia, shortly after his election, he came off to some as a good-time Charlie rather than a man of gubernatorial stature. The leadership in the state capital picked up on the cocksure mien as well. And a Texas reporter was startled to hear the newly elected governor tell him, 'Blacks didn't come out for me like the Hispanics did. So they're not gonna see much help from me.' " At a news conference about a heat wave that had already resulted in eighty deaths and rampaging forest fires, Bush gave a sneak preview of his devil-may-care response to Hurricane Katrina. Dubya called a Forestry Service official to the podium by yelling, "Tree Man, get up here!" As the official spoke, Bush stuck out his tongue and puffed out his cheeks, imitating a blowfish.

Assessing Bush as governor, Molly Ivins wrote, "From the record, it appears that he doesn't know much, doesn't do much, and doesn't care much about governing. . . . [H]e seems to have a rather short attention span and often seems impatient to move on to the next topic or project." Confirming Ivins's take, Bush acknowledged, "I don't like long meetings." He also disliked long books. When asked, in 1999, to name something he wasn't good at, he replied, "Sitting down and reading a 500-page book on public policy or philosophy or something."* Although he avoided reading, he stressed its importance to America's students. A month after becoming president, he asserted, "You teach a child to read, and he or her will be able to pass a literacy test."

After Texas spent $1.8 million investigating a Texas A&M bonfire that killed twelve people, Governor Bush read neither the 261-page report nor the thirty-six-page summary. "I highlighted half a page," said his chief of staff, Clay Johnson. "He read that." To Johnson, who'd been Dubya's college roommate and fellow Deke, Bush's work

---

* Bush said during a Republican primary debate in December 1999 that his favorite political philosopher was Jesus, who considerately never wrote a five-hundred-page book. The Sermon on the Mount comes in at a zippy 2,500 words, which Bush could polish off in three or four sittings.

ethic couldn't have been a shocker. Johnson said a typical workweek for his boss amounted to "two hard half days." Considering that Bush clocked in for only about eight hours a week, one wonders how the Decider managed to decide the fate of the 152 men and women whose executions he approved (a record for gubernatorial serial killing surpassed only by his successor, the fellow pro-lifer Rick Perry, who offed 278). No biggie: living up to his wife's assessment of him as a man who abhorred deliberation, he halved the time allotted for considering a death row case, when possible, from thirty minutes to fifteen. That left plenty of time for a jog.

Defending his controversial decision to execute Gary Graham, a convicted murderer whom many believed was innocent, Bush said, "This case has had full analyzation and has been looked at a lot. I understand the emotionality of death row penalty cases." He somewhat undermined the credibility of his analyzation, however, when he declared, "I do not believe we've put a guilty . . . I mean, innocent person to death in the state of Texas."

Willie Nelson once said, "I'm from Texas, and one of the reasons I like Texas is because there's no one in control." This aphorism might help explain W.'s popularity as governor; to borrow another phrase from Willie, Bush never tried to convince Texans they were always on his mind. By 1998, the state's voters seemed so pleased with the many things Dubya didn't know or do that they elected him to a second term. His signature accomplishment as governor was turning the bountiful budget surplus inherited from Ann Richards into a massive deficit, by recklessly cutting taxes. Now a rising star in the Republican Party, he wondered: Could he do to the USA what he'd done to Texas?

As a Southern governor running for president, Dubya hoped to replicate the success of the outgoing White House occupant: Bill

Clinton. The Arkansas governor's presidential bid in 1992 had threatened, at first, to become yet another casualty of the Curse of Adlai Stevenson, with some questioning whether Clinton, an alumnus of Georgetown, Oxford, and Yale Law School, was too wonky to win. "Wonks are not new to public life, but they rarely make it to the White House," wrote the *Baltimore Sun*'s Jon Morgan. "Former presidential candidate Adlai Stevenson was a wonk. So [is] Michael Dukakis. . . . Voters tend to be suspicious of overtly intellectual leaders, especially if they come across as snobbish." In 1988, Dan Quayle had tried to convince people not to be terrified by how dumb he was. In 1992, Clinton had to convince people not to be terrified by how smart he was. To pull this off, he transformed himself into someone who would never in a million years be confused with a wonk: Elvis.

You might think that doing cheesy Elvis impersonations was beneath the dignity of a former Rhodes Scholar and aspiring commander in chief, but that's the strategy that Bill Clinton chose. He made himself so synonymous with the King that, during a New York campaign stop, two talk show hosts asked him to perform his rendition of "Don't Be Cruel." (He wound up croaking out the chorus for Charlie Rose.) His campaign underscored the Elvis theme by playing the song "Graceland" at his rallies.

As summer approached, Elvis, in the form of Bill Clinton, remained alive. On June 3, lagging in the polls behind both Dubya's dad and the independent candidate Ross Perot, Clinton appeared on *The Arsenio Hall Show* wearing shades and blowing something that sounded vaguely like "Heartbreak Hotel" on a sax. The stunt helped reassure voters that, despite his academic attainments, Clinton could be dumb when necessary. (As president, he continued to demonstrate that capability, even when it was the opposite of necessary.)

Basking in the afterglow of the *Arsenio* stunt, Clinton amped up his tributes to the King. The cultural critic Greil Marcus detailed

Presley's increasingly surreal role in the Clinton campaign: "In July 'Elvis Aron Presley' was listed in the party literature as the 'Entertainment Coordinator' of the Democratic Convention. [Vice presidential nominee] Al Gore told the convention it had always been his dream to come 'to Madison Square Garden and be the warm-up act for Elvis.'"* All of Clinton's Elvismania appeared to provoke George H. W. Bush, who started sounding like a cranky 1950s dad telling his kids to turn down that noisy rock and roll. It was typical of Bush Senior's implacable squareness that he decided to weigh in on the wrong side of a culture war that had been settled decades earlier. He wisecracked that, if Clinton were elected, "America will be checking into the 'Heartbreak Hotel.'" Maybe Bush's speechwriters originally wanted him to claim that Clinton was nothing but a hound dog, but thought better of it.

Once elected, Clinton dropped his Elvis act and started imitating another anti-wonk: Ronald Reagan. One of the first trips he took after the election was to Southern California, where he sought an audience with Ron and Nancy. After his presidency wobbled early on, he hired as his chief spokesman Reagan's former communications director, David Gergen, the man who praised Ronnie's fictitious anecdotes as "forms of moral instruction." On the fiftieth anniversary of D-Day, Clinton prepared for his speech at Normandy by borrowing a tape from the Reagan Library to see what Ron had said on the fortieth. Bill treated the Gipper's repository like Blockbuster Video: in preparation for foreign trips, he checked out tapes of Reagan giving speeches in Canada, Japan, Korea, and Indonesia. In an odd

---

*At least they had the restraint not to claim that Elvis, if he were in fact alive, would have voted for the Democrats, though they might have had some justification: the only time the resolutely apolitical King tipped his hand was in 1956, when he expressed his admiration for . . . Adlai Stevenson! "I don't dig the intellectual bit, but I'm telling you, man, he knows the most," Elvis said.

move for a Democratic president who ran against Reagan's VP, Clinton wrote a fond tribute to Ronnie in *Vanity Fair*: "We remember the sunniness of his temperament during eight years in office." (Of course, that sunniness was only possible because Reagan ignored the decidedly unsunny plight of the unemployed, the homeless, the hungry, and those dying of AIDS, among others.) In his 1996 State of the Union address, Bill performed a cover version of one of Reagan's biggest hits. "The era of big government is over," he announced. By the time Clinton's reelection campaign brazenly copied Reagan's Morning in America theme, his relentless Ronniephilia was starting to piss off members of Reagan's party. "Clinton Staff Annoys Republicans by Tapping Successful Reagan Style: '96 Campaign Adapts Its Optimistic Themes," read a headline in the *Baltimore Sun*. One GOP aide groused, "I guess when we see him take out an ax and start clearing the brush behind the White House, we'll see that the transformation is complete."

The rewards Clinton reaped by emulating Reagan weren't lost on Karl Rove. As W. readied his first presidential campaign, Rove urged him to buy a ranchette in Crawford, Texas, to serve as a Reaganesque backdrop for photo ops. Before long, Dubya was yanking on the pull cord of his very own chain saw, fixing to clear some brush.

Although Rove had succeeded in hiding Bush's ignorance about the workings of state government—up to a point—when W. announced his candidacy for president, on June 13, 1999, Bush's Brain faced a far more unnerving task: how to conceal his candidate's near-total obliviousness about countries other than the United States of America. He redeployed the Rose Garden strategy, claiming that Bush would be too busy governatin' to make himself available for public viewings. Theoretically, the two hard half days that Bush put in at the office each week would have left ample time for voters to kick his tires, but Rove would have none of it. On the rare occasions when he did let Bubble Boy out, it became clear that the candidate was a work in progress. When asked on *Meet the Press* if he had a take on Vladimir Putin, he replied, "I really don't. I will if I'm the president." (His eventual take—that he had looked Putin in the eye and got "a sense of his soul"—turned out to be worse than no take.) One week after he announced his candidacy, he confused Slovakia with Slovenia. "Nobody needs to tell me what I believe," he told *Talk* magazine. "But I do need someone to tell me where Kosovo is." He also, it seemed, needed someone to tell him what to call the people who lived there: he called Kosovars "Kosovarians," much as he called East Timorese "East Timorians," and Greeks "Grecians." Attempting a quick injection of gravitas, Rove slated Bush to give a major foreign policy address at the Reagan Library. Thus a man who'd confused Slovakia and Slovenia sought to boost his geopolitical cred by speaking at the shrine to a man who'd confused Brazil and Bolivia.

Even when talking about his native land, W. spewed nonsense impenetrable to the average Americanian. In New Hampshire, he unspooled this incoherent take on how the internet might spark an economic revival in rural areas: "The nature of the new economy is going to create all sorts of interesting opportunities and problems. . . . The interesting opportunities are, capital will move freely when we're a global nation in a global world. We're a nation in a global world. The ability to communicate—and capital to move quickly because of the new economy—is changing the nature of the world." "Has he been taking lessons from Dan Quayle?" the journalist David Corn asked. But just as Bush threatened to follow his fellow Deke into political oblivion, he avoided that dire fate—thanks, improbably, to his own ignorance.

Bush caught his lucky break in a state not known for its beneficence toward Republican presidential candidates: Massachusetts. On November 3, 1999, Karl Rove inexplicably let Bush be interviewed on Boston's WHDH-TV by Andy Hiller, a local political reporter with a reputation for vivisecting his guests. One of Hiller's favorite bits was to humiliate politicians by subjecting them to a lightning round. The following transcript captures the ensuing demolition:

HILLER:	Can you name the president of Chechnya?
BUSH:	No, can you?
HILLER:	Can you name the president of Taiwan?
BUSH:	Yeah, Lee.
HILLER:	Can you name the general who is in charge of Pakistan?
BUSH:	Wait, wait, is this 50 Questions?
HILLER:	No, it's four questions of four leaders in four hot spots.
BUSH:	The new Pakistani general, he's just been elected— not elected, this guy took over office. It appears this guy is going to bring stability to the country, and I think that's good news for the subcontinent.
HILLER:	Can you name him?
BUSH:	General. I can't name the general. General.
HILLER:	And the prime minister of India?
BUSH:	The new prime minister of India is [pause]. No. Can you name the foreign minister of Mexico?
HILLER:	No, sir, but I would say to that, I'm not running for president.

A man who wanted to be the next commander in chief had just bombed a foreign policy quiz. He'd answered only one out of four questions correctly, which, in letter-grade terms, would be an F. As with Gerald Ford's "Soviet domination" gaffe, there could be only one possible upshot. In unison, the media excoriated the disastrous performance . . . of *Andy Hiller*.

"The person who is running for president is seeking to be the leader of the free world, not a *Jeopardy* contestant," said Bush's communications director, Karen Hughes. "I would venture to guess that 99.9 percent of most Americans and probably most candidates could not answer 'Who is the president of Chechnya?'" The nation's pundits, acting as a Greek (or is it Grecian?) chorus, parroted Hughes's sound bite, *Jeopardy* reference and all. On TV shows such as *The NewsHour with Jim Lehrer*, they condemned the pop quiz, attacking the examiner and not the dunce. Astoundingly, Bush's F on the pop quiz had become an A for his campaign. As Jonathan Chait noted in *The New Republic*, "Bush advisers have confided their pleasure at the pop quiz 'fiasco,' saying it makes their man seem like a normal guy." The former Nixon and Reagan aide Pat Buchanan concurred: "[N]ot only does he not know a great deal, he's defiant about it. He likes the idea." Indeed, Bush appeared on ABC and gave his obliviousness a Texas-sized hug. "America understands that a guy doesn't know the name of every single foreign leader," he said. "That's not what Americans are making their choices on about who's going to be the president. . . . People are making their choices based upon judgment, based upon vision, based upon philosophy."

Like the discovery of the double helix or the invention of soap, George W. Bush's pop quiz was pivotal, the moment that marked the end of the Ridicule stage. Acceptance had begun. Politicians and their advisers now realized that they could flaunt ignorance instead of hiding it.

Having defended Bush when he blanked on Chechnya, the media were still coddling him three months later when he displayed his cluelessness about a somewhat less obscure country: Canada. After a rally in Michigan, the Canadian comedian Rick Mercer, posing as a journalist, had this risible exchange with the future leader of the free world:

MERCER: Governor Bush, a question from Canada. A question
            from Canada.
BUSH: What about it?
MERCER: Prime Minister Jean Poutine said that he wouldn't
            endorse any candidate. He says that you look like the
            man who should lead the free world into the twenty-
            first century.
BUSH: I'm honored. Thank you.
MERCER: Yeah, so what do you think about that? How's his
            endorsement?
BUSH: Well, I appreciate his strong statement. He
            understands I believe in free trade. He understands
            I want to make sure our relations with our most
            important neighbor to the north of us, the
            Canadians, is strong. And we'll work closely together.

Bush would never get to "work closely together" with Jean Pou-tine, because the prime minister of "our most important neighbor to the north" was actually named Jean Chrétien, and had been since 1993. "Poutine," on the other hand, is a favorite semi-digestible French-Canadian dish, a mixture of cheese curds and fries smothered in brown gravy.* To the extent that anyone in the American press

---

*The reception that Chrétien's government eventually gave Bush as president might have made him wish he'd been dealing with Jean Poutine instead. After Chrétien's director of communications, Françoise Ducros, was overheard saying of Bush, "What a moron," the prime minister issued a tepid statement calling Dubya "a friend of mine. He's not a moron at all."

noted this incident, they defended Bush. The *Washington Post*'s Al Kamen said, "I guess I'm a little sympathetic. He was a little tired." For the remainder of the race, the media would continue to grade Bush on a pass/fail basis—and would often pass him even when it was clear that he had failed. If only he'd had such easy graders at Yale.

Dubya, once in danger of becoming the next Quayle, had rewritten the rules. Rather than try to answer questions that baffled him, as his fellow Deke had so torturously done, Bush would project calm acceptance of how little he knew. Aided by the largely fawning media, Bush's ignorance became an asset: something voters could relate to, a sign he was "authentic" and "down-to-earth." When W. expressed scorn for Yale classmates who had "all the answers," he was onto something. After all, no one likes a know-it-all. Especially one named Al Gore.

Remember when Al Gore claimed that he invented the internet? No, you don't, because he never did. During a CNN interview on March 9, 1999, he said, "During my service in the United States Congress, I took the initiative in creating the Internet." The quote went little noticed until two days later, when Declan McCullagh wrote a short post about it for *Wired*. Though Gore was touting only his legislative contribution to the web's development, Republican leaders Trent Lott and Dick Armey seized on the *Wired* story and started faxing sarcastic press releases mocking Gore as the internet's self-styled "inventor." On October 17, 2000, McCullagh seemed remorseful about the runaway train he'd sent down the tracks. "If it's true that Al Gore created the Internet, then I created the 'Al Gore created the Internet' story," he wrote. "[I]t's now as much a part of the American political firmament as the incident involving that other vice president, a schoolchild, and a very unfortunate spelling of potato." Hoping to repair some of the damage he'd wreaked, he noted,

"[W]hile Gore certainly didn't create the Internet, he was one of the first politicians to realize that those bearded, bespectacled researchers were busy crafting something that could, just maybe, become pretty important." Coming three weeks before the election, this clarification was a little tardy.

The "Al Gore invented the internet" joke unfairly popularized his image as a grandiose fibber, but also reinforced another damaging perception about the vice president: that he was an elitist wonk whose obsession with science and technology alienated "ordinary people." In a column in the *Christian Science Monitor* in early 2000, under the headline "An Uneasiness with Al Gore?," Godfrey Sperling questioned Gore's electoral appeal, comparing him to—oh, no!— Adlai Stevenson. By October, that comparison was still being made, this time by the conservative columnist George F. Will: "In 1952 and 1956 the Democratic nominee was an early prototype of Gore. Adlai Stevenson . . . like Gore, was susceptible to strange ideas supposedly grounded in science."* The parallels between Gore and Stevenson were so compelling that the *Washington Post*'s Richard Cohen was still writing about them two years *after* the election, asking, "Is Al Gore destined to be the Adlai Stevenson of our age?"

Unlike Bill Clinton, who responded to the March of Ignorance by grabbing his sax and marching along, his vice president seemed unaware that appearing too brainy could hurt him at the ballot box. He spoke freely—and, in retrospect, unwisely—about books he'd read. In a *New Yorker* profile titled—what else?—"After Elvis," Louis Menand asked him to name some of his influences. Gore eagerly complied, name-checking Reinhold Niebuhr, Edmund Husserl, and

---

* One of those strange ideas Will alluded to was climate change, which Gore warned about in his 1992 book, *Earth in the Balance*. Gore's book has aged much better than Will's column.

Maurice Merleau-Ponty, the author of that juicy page-turner *Phe-nomenology of Perception.*

After Bush read (or skimmed) the Gore profile, he was far from intimidated; he was stoked. Bush had no intention of competing with Gore on the field of knowledge; instead, he'd play to win on the field of ignorance. Bush broadcast *his* status as a bibliophile by declaring, "One of the great things about books is sometimes there are some fantastic pictures."

Nowhere is the appeal of Bush's callowness on more egregious display than in Alexandra Pelosi's documentary *Journeys with George*, a video diary of her travels with his press entourage in 2000. The tone of the film is jaunty, but because it exposes the total vacuity of not just Bush but the people supposedly covering him, it winds up being more depressing than the collected works of Werner Herzog. Throughout, Bush demonstrates the skills that made him such an effective president—of DKE—as he impishly beguiles members of the press and, in doing so, renders them useless. They seem giddy to be riding with the prom king. Only once in the film's seventy-nine minutes does Pelosi screw up the courage to ask W. a question about policy (capital punishment, one of his rare areas of expertise), and Bush, miffed at her, offers a clipped nonresponse. Instead of answering her question, he hijacks the film's narrative, peppering Pelosi with puerile questions about her crush on a *Newsweek* reporter named Trent; he predicts that she and "*Newsweek* man" will find happiness together. Alas, this prophecy of a love connection, much like Dick Cheney's later prediction about Iraqis greeting U.S. troops as liberators, doesn't pan out.

As the campaign rolled on, the post-pop-quiz Bush paraded his lack of studiousness even more brazenly. He had already taken this approach for a test drive when he told elementary school students in Bedford, New Hampshire, "Some people are saying I prove that if you get a C average, you can end up being successful in life." This appearance wasn't the only time the Decider decided that elementary schools were the perfect venues to showcase how little he knew. An elementary school student in South Carolina stumped him with a gotcha question even more challenging than Hiller's about the president of Chechnya: What was his favorite book as a child? "I can't remember any specific books," he said. Later, responding to a similar query in a written questionnaire, he summoned an answer: *The Very Hungry Caterpillar*. Though that book might have been his favorite, it was published a year after he graduated from Yale.

By the spring of 2000, Bush's ignorance was blossoming into a virtue, just as his campaign had hoped. The *New York Times* reported how the governor of New Mexico, Gary Johnson, had delivered "a populist tribute to Mr. Bush as the antithesis of an egghead" at a rally in Albuquerque. As part of this bizarre endorsement, Johnson

> recounted a conversation that he and Mr. Bush once had about the speakers at a conference of state leaders. "George turns to me," Johnson recalled, "and says, 'What are they talking about?' I said, 'I don't know.' He said, 'You don't know a thing, do you?' And I said, 'Not one thing.' He said, 'Neither do I.' And we kind of high-fived."
>
> . . . Johnson saluted Mr. Bush as the rare "somebody who will rather admit—or rather talk about—the things they don't know and make that really evident."

Johnson, as would later become clear, was another one of those special people who was good at making the things he didn't know really evident. As the 2016 Libertarian Party nominee for president, he offered this response to a question about the Syrian city of Aleppo, whose refugee crisis was front-page news at the time: "And what is Aleppo?"

For his part, Bush continued to participate in foreign policy pop quizzes, if only to show what a regular guy he was by not knowing any of the answers. The *New York Times* reported, "When a writer for *Glamour* magazine recently uttered the word 'Taliban'—the regime in Afghanistan that follows an extreme and repressive version of Islamic law—during a verbal Rorschach test, Mr. Bush could only shake his head in silence. It was only after the writer gave him a hint ('repression of women in Afghanistan') that Mr. Bush replied, 'Oh. I thought you said some band. The Taliban in Afghanistan! Absolutely. Repressive.'" Historians haven't given *Glamour* the credit it deserves for bringing to Bush's attention a regime against whom, less than two years later, he would start America's longest war.

Around the time of Bush's *Glamour* test, he rebuffed a Saudi journalist's foreign affairs question by admitting his ignorance of all such matters: "I don't think you can expect any president to know all things about all subjects." (Okay, but is knowing *some* things about *some* subjects an option?) Instead, he said he'd "surround himself with excellent folks" and "be able to listen and to be able to delegate." J. C. Watts, a Republican congressman from Oklahoma, took up this theme, suggesting at a campaign rally that a Bush White House would have knowledge aplenty, even if it didn't reside in Bush. "You can buy clever," he explained. With Bush vowing to surround himself with excellent folks and buy clever, people were understandably curious about who those excellent clever folks were going to be. The answer, in part, came in a *New York Times* profile of his top foreign policy adviser, a little-known academic named Condoleezza Rice.

In the profile, Rice touts herself as Bush's tutor and foreign policy "quarterback." Dubya, yet again portraying himself as a likably slow-witted pupil, praises his teacher by saying she "can explain to me foreign policy matters in a way I can understand." Rice might have hoped to reassure the nation that Bush was buying clever, but her words did the opposite: "Ms. Rice herself admits that there are vast swaths of the world that are new to her. 'I've been pressed to understand parts of the world that have not been part of my scope,' she said. 'I'm really a Europeanist.'" Although she brags at one point, "I have a really good memory," she has the darnedest time remembering an important fact about, ahem, the Taliban. After alleging that Iran had given money and technology to the regime in Afghanistan, Rice is reminded by her interviewer "that Iran was a bitter enemy of the Taliban and that the two countries had almost gone to war in late 1998. . . . In a subsequent conversation, she said that of course she knew that Iran and the Taliban were enemies." *Of course. The Taliban in Afghanistan. Absolutely. Repressive.*

In 1999, the first *Star Wars* film in sixteen years, *The Phantom Menace*, debuted. The rabid fans' long wait had the unfortunate consequence of creating impossible expectations, so when the movie arrived, Jar Jar Binks and all, it landed with a galactic thud. One year later, as the presidential debates approached, Al Gore would be doomed by similarly toxic hype. In *The Atlantic*, James Fallows devoted thirteen thousand words (!) to an analysis of Gore's evolution as a debater, including this appraisal: "Al Gore is the most lethal debater in politics, a ruthless combatant who will say whatever it takes to win, and who leaves opponents not just beaten but brutalized. But Gore is no natural-born killer. He studied hard to become the man he is today." That assessment contrasted with the below-sea-level expectations accorded George W. Bush. As Molly Ivins observed, "[A]ll he had to do was clear a matchbox."

At the first debate, in Boston, the media showered Gore with the

kind of rapturous love they'd previously reserved for Jar Jar. Some
of the criticism was valid; his stagy, contemptuous sighing at Bush's
remarks sounded like a nationally televised lung exam. But his performance didn't justify the clobbering he got from some members
of the Fourth Estate, who found a new aspect of Gore to dislike:
his makeup. The vice president was slathered in a thick coat of it to
mask a sunburn, and the resulting orange hue provided pundits with
a ready-made, glib take on the entire evening. They likened Gore
to the Addams Family's butler, Lurch; "Herman Munster doing a
bad Ronald Reagan impression"; and "a big, orange, waxy, wickless
candle." Mike Conklin of the *Chicago Tribune* explored this crucial
campaign issue by interviewing an expert panel of cosmeticians:

> "He was too overdone even by TV standards and that's scary," said
> makeup artist Ingrid Myles, who, before the sun even rises, makes
> everyone look presentable on WGN-Ch. 9's early-morning news
> show. "He looked like he was embalmed," added Andrea Nichols,
> who is Myles' counterpart on WFLD-Ch. 32's morning show.
>
> Neither had a problem with Bush's look Tuesday night, but
> Myles has three suggestions for Gore's makeup person at next week's
> debate: (1) lighter foundation ("You have to be darker for TV, but
> not that dark"); (2) less blush on the cheeks ("he didn't need any");
> and (3) better transition ("his neck was too light for his face").
> Myles said things could have been worse for the veep, though. The
> room temperature was a cool 65 degrees; imagine if it had been hot
> enough to cause his makeup to run!

Imagine! Imagine, also, if too much rouge had disqualified others in American history from becoming president. The White House
would have been off-limits to George Washington, who went a little
crazy with blush before he posed for his iconic portrait. In *Amusing*

Ourselves to Death, Neil Postman observed that, in a political land-scape dominated by television, "[W]e may have reached the point where cosmetics has replaced ideology as the field of expertise over which a politician must have competent control."

Because Bush won the expectations game, not to mention the not-looking-like-a-candle game, he emerged from the first debate with an even bigger smirk than usual. Acknowledging that he'd indeed cleared a matchbox, he said, "Well, a lot of folks don't think I can string a sentence together so when I was able to do so, the expectations were so low that all I had to do was say, 'Hi, I'm George W. Bush.'" W. had gleaned a valuable lesson from his failed 1978 congressional bid, when the folksy Kent Hance painted him as an effete, Ivy League–educated snob. As Hance later observed, Bush learned never to be "out-good-old-boyed again. He's going to be the good old boy next door." And so he was in 2000, becoming Kent Hance 2.0 and letting Gore be George W. Bush circa 1978.

As Election Day approached, Bush became a walking mixtape of inanities. At the second debate, he declared, "We've got to work with Nigeria. It's an important continent." (Possibly overcompensating for that error, as president he would call Africa a nation.) Referring to the Clinton-Lewinsky scandal during an appearance in Illinois, he said, "That's a chapter, the last chapter of the twentieth, twentieth, twenty-first century that most of us would rather forget. The last chapter of the twentieth century. This is the first chapter of the twenty-first century."

At the Al Smith Dinner, a charity fundraiser where politicians traditionally roast themselves and one another, Bush owned his ignorance as much as Reagan had owned his sloth. His foreign policy pop quiz might have been long forgotten, but Bush chose to invoke its memory: "Foreign policy's been a big issue in this campaign and we just had some really good news out of Yugoslavia—I'm especially pleased that Mr. Milošević has stepped down. It's one less polysyl-labic name for me to remember." (Kind of a weird joke about a re-cent genocide, but okay.) In contrast with Quayle, who got snippy whenever the subject of his college career arose, Bush celebrated his reputation as a shitty student: "I see Bill Buckley's here tonight—fellow Yale man. We go way back and we have a lot in common. Bill wrote a book at Yale. I read one." The joke kills. It's hilarious how a guy who might soon be president doesn't read anything!

Once Bush was in the White House, he took promoting his dumb-as-a-plank image to new heights. Having already poked fun at his lack of foreign policy knowledge and his aversion to reading, he moved on to a new target: his incoherence. At the Radio and Television Correspondents' Association Dinner in Washington on March 29, 2001, he read from a published collection of his most-mangled utterances. ("I know the human being and fish can coexist peacefully." "I understand small business growth. I was one." "More and more of our imports come from overseas.") Bush continued in this vein two months later, when, as Yale's commencement speaker, he repurposed the comment he'd made two years earlier at the el-ementary school in New Hampshire: "To those of you who received honors, awards, and distinctions, I say: well done. And to the C stu-dents, I say: you, too can be president of the United States."

As the Acceptance stage rolled on, Bush cemented his status as the anti-Quayle, trumpeting his poor performance in college as much as his fellow Deke had tried to hide his. In 2005, the *Washington Post*'s Mark Leibovich reported on Bush's road show to promote his plan for Social Security reform:

> Bush often appears with an "expert" who supports his Social Se-curity plan—some adviser, professor or smarty-pants whom the president likes to use as a foil to contrast with his own academic

record. "I'm a C-student," Bush said proudly in Louisville last week. "He's the PhD. He's the adviser. I'm the president. What does that tell you?"

Bush has always liked to project a common-folk demeanor, but only occasionally mentioned his slacker past during his first term. Now his repertoire includes frequent references to how he paid little attention in class while in college.

When a panelist in Tampa used the word "multitasking," Bush, with a hint of sarcasm, commended her for using a "nice long word, 'multitasking.' Very good. Inject a little intellectual strength in the conversation."

Quayle had tried to sound smart by saying "telemetry"; now Bush was ridiculing someone for saying "multitasking." How far we'd come.

"You never know what your history is going to be like until long after you're gone," Bush once psychedelically observed. In the years since he left office, Dubya hasn't inspired a hagiography industry like Reagan's. Bush's disasters might be too recent and indelible, making his rehabilitation too challenging. But, to the extent that Bush apologists have tried to elevate his reputation, they've hewed to the same stock narrative: 9/11 was the day Bush "became president of the United States." It's a tidy formulation; if Bush's presidency were a screenplay, 9/11 would be a tempting Act I plot point, the inciting incident that forces the hero to find within himself hidden reserves of maturity and grit. The only problem with this arc is that Bush's judgment was bad before 9/11, and worse after it. (If I had to pinpoint the moment when George W. Bush became president, I'd choose December 12, 2000, the day the Supreme Court elected him.)

When Bush was a presidential candidate, his grasp of the threats facing America suggested that one of the greatest might be him. Believing that "a key to foreign policy is to rely on reliance," he said, "There is madmen in the world, and there are terror." (Since he also asked, famously, "Is our children learning?" one expected that his first official act as president would be to cancel the agreement between subjects and verbs.) His attempt to make sense of the post–Cold War world resulted in this heaping bowl of word porridge: "When I was coming up, it was a dangerous world, and you knew exactly who they were. It was us vs. them, and it was clear who them was. Today, we are not so sure who the they are, but we know they're there."

In the early weeks of his presidency, Bush's performance on the international stage was no more encouraging. An official at the British Foreign Office recalled Dubya's first phone conversation with Prime Minister Tony Blair: "It basically consisted of Bush talking about various places in Scotland where he'd got [drunk] when he was young and asking Tony whether he knew them and Tony not really knowing what to say."

Although Bush's lack of intellectual curiosity proved a source of populist appeal during the campaign, it was less than an ideal attribute in the months leading up to 9/11, when he was warned repeatedly that major terror attacks were both likely and imminent. On April 20, 2001, CIA analysts prepared a report for him titled "Bin Laden Planning Multiple Operations." Having failed to rouse Bush with that one, they issued reports with increasingly grabby headlines—"Bin Laden Attacks May Be Imminent," "Bin Laden Planning High Profile Attacks"—as if bouncing horror movie titles off a hard-to-scare focus group. Eventually, they resorted to a President's Daily Brief with a screaming headline dominated by one-syllable words: "UBL [Usama Bin Laden] Threats Are Real." After the CIA's intelligence analyst Michael Morell delivered this PDB to

Bush on Air Force One, W. dismissively responded, "OK, Michael. You've covered your ass."

In August, Bush went on vacation at his ranchette, where he'd become an expert at clearing brush as performatively as Ronnie. While there, W. engaged in another activity familiar to students of the Reagan presidency: he ignored a detailed report requiring his full attention. He received that report, a PDB infamously titled "Bin Laden Determined to Strike in US," on August 6. The document was not just urgent, it was specific, noting "suspicious activity in this country consistent with preparations for hijackings." Bush went fishing.

Bush's allergy to reading had alarmed Richard Clarke, the chief White House counterterrorism adviser, in the early days of his presidency. "The contrast with having briefed his father and Clinton and Gore was so marked," Clarke recalled. "And to be told, frankly, early in the administration, by Condi Rice and [Deputy National Security Adviser] Steve Hadley, you know, Don't give the president a lot of long memos, he's not a big reader—well, shit. I mean, the president of the United States is not a big reader?" In fairness, Clarke never had to brief Ronald Reagan.

Bush's presidency had been directionless before 9/11, the impatient Dubya oppressed by the tedious details of domestic policy. Being president, it turned out, was like running Texas, only with even longer, more boring meetings. The terror attacks solved that problem. September 11 "defined his presidency, giving him the sense of purpose that he had previously lacked," Paul Burka wrote in the *Texas Monthly*. "[I]t transformed him, it focused him and gave a sense of purpose to his presidency that really had not existed before," agreed the conservative commentator Norman Ornstein. "9/11 seized the American with the sense of purpose that his presidency had hitherto lacked," the British journalist Andrew Rawnsley concurred. As his mother, Barbara Bush, would later say when Hurricane Katrina forced New Orleans residents who were "underprivileged anyway" to relocate to the luxurious confines of Houston's Astrodome, 9/11 was "working very well" for George W. Bush.

Ten days after the attacks, he used a joint session of Congress to debut the reductive rhetoric of the War on Terror.* "Either you are with us or you are with the terrorists," he declared, conveniently ignoring the fact that, during the Soviet occupation of Afghanistan, we'd very much been with the terrorists. Details, details! Bush had found his simplistic binary opposition, *us versus terrorists*, to replace Reagan's *us versus communists*.

You didn't need to read a five-hundred-page book to know that Afghanistan was called the Graveyard of Empires; you just had to be paying attention. Unfortunately, Bush's approach to the Afghan War seemed to be "No exit strategy? No problem." No sooner had he invaded Afghanistan than he went fishing for an even bigger war, against a charter member of the freshly fabricated "Axis of Evil." His speechwriter David Frum had borrowed the term "axis" from a fellow wordsmith who'd smithed it out in the 1930s: Benito Mussolini. In a draft presented to his boss, chief speechwriter Michael Gerson, Frum had called a trio of baddies—Iran, Iraq, and North Korea—the "Axis of Hatred." Gerson swapped out "hatred" for the more biblical "evil." This switch accomplished two goals, invoking the memory of Reagan's nickname for the Soviet Union, the Evil Empire; and blowing a dog whistle to let Bush's evangelical base know that he'd been chosen for this mission by God, not just by Sandra Day O'Connor.

In case any members of the Christian right missed Bush's messianic point, he kept repeating it. "Freedom isn't America's gift to the

---

*Even the name of that so-called war was ludicrous, as it suggested that a nation was, for the first time in the history of armed conflict, declaring war against a human emotion. If we defeated terror, what was next—shyness?

world," he'd say. "It is God's gift to mankind." As simple as this statement sounds, the theology behind it is murky. By "freedom," Bush
meant the "democratic" governments that the U.S. was attempting to install by force in Afghanistan and Iraq, regardless of whether
those countries desired them. Did God want everyone in the world
to have democracy? That word appears nowhere in the Bible, possibly because, as many of us learned in grade school, democracy is a
Greek concept. Which God was Bush talking about—Zeus?

In the run-up to Operation Iraqi Freedom, Bush's arguments for
war with Saddam would continue to echo the tactics of Ronald Reagan, who, when he didn't have facts to support his claims, would
make shit up. During the campaign for the 2002 midterms, Robert
Draper reported in *Dead Certain*, Bush's descriptions of Saddam's vil-
lainy grew like brush that W. had no intention of clearing. Stumping
in Tampa, he said of the Iraqi dictator, "We know that he's had connections with Al Qaeda." Moving to Minnesota, he warned, "This
is a man who has had contacts with Al Qaeda. This is a man who
poses a serious threat in many forms—but catch this form: he's the
kind of guy that would love nothing more than to train terrorists and
provide arms to terrorists so they could attack his worst enemy and
leave no fingerprints." By the time Bush got to Sioux Falls, South
Dakota, Saddam had, against the odds, gotten even eviler: "He can't
stand America. He can't stand some of our closest friends. And not
only that: He is—would like nothing better than to hook up with
one of these shadowy terrorist networks like Al Qaeda, provide some
weapons and training to them, let them come and do his dirty work,
and we wouldn't be able to see his fingerprints on his action." In a
surprising omission, Bush never accused Saddam of trying to buy
vodka with food stamps.

The absence of any credible intelligence that Saddam possessed
weapons of mass destruction didn't trouble Bush's incurious mind as

he marched toward war. It was hard to argue facts with someone who, like the Blues Brothers, believed he was on a mission from God. In 2002, the journalist Ron Suskind got an earful from a White House aide who confirmed that Bush was now operating untethered from knowledge: "The aide said that guys like me were 'in what we call the reality-based community,' which he defined as people who 'believe that solutions emerge from your judicious study of discernible reality.' I nodded and murmured something about enlightenment principles and empiricism. He cut me off. 'That's not the way the world really works anymore,' he continued. 'We're an empire now, and when we act, we create our own reality. And while you're studying that reality—judiciously, as you will—we'll act again, creating other new realities, which you can study too, and that's how things will sort out. We're history's actors . . . and you, all of you, will be left to just study what we do.'" In Bushworld, it was the journalists' job to study the actions of people who did no studying whatsoever.

Though he'd certainly agree with Reagan that "facts are stupid things," Bush thought nuance was even stupider. He told Senator Joe Biden, "Joe, I don't do nuance." CNN's Candy Crowley heard him say, "In Texas, we don't do nuance," explaining his mental limitations as if they were a regional quirk, like chicken-frying your steak. He complained of aides "nuancing him to death," though it's impossible to picture Bush sitting still long enough for that to happen. Dubya couldn't stand nuance even when he wasn't in the room where the nuancing was taking place. In the spring of 2002, as Condoleezza Rice met with a group of senators in the West Wing, Bush popped his head in and blurted, "Fuck Saddam. We're taking him out."

Unfortunately, when contemplating a $2 trillion war, nuance comes in handy. At a White House meeting in early 2003, three Iraqi Americans briefed Bush on the complications the U.S. would inevitably encounter if it pressed forward with its war plans. According to

Peter Galbraith, the former U.S. ambassador to Croatia, as the meeting progressed it gradually dawned on Bush that there were weird-sounding groups of people in Iraq called Sunnis and Shiites. Baffled, he exclaimed, "I thought the Iraqis were Muslims!"

The year the U.S. invaded Iraq, 486 American soldiers were killed, with another 2,416 wounded; 12,152 Iraqi civilians died. The number of weapons of mass destruction found stood stubbornly at zero. Still, Dubya wasn't going to let any of these statistics dampen his prankish sense of humor. The following March, he performed a comedy routine at the Radio and Television Correspondents' Association Dinner, narrating slides of himself clownishly looking for WMDs in the Oval Office. "Those weapons of mass destruction have got to be here somewhere," he said as a slide showed him looking under a piece of furniture. "Nope, no weapons over there," he said, laughing at the hilarity of it all. "Maybe under here." The cringeworthy bit was interminable.

By the end of 2005, 2,181 U.S. soldiers had died in Iraq and 16,365 had been wounded; the number of dead civilians topped 40,000. On NBC, he was asked about Dick Cheney's prediction that Iraqis would welcome American troops as liberators. "I think we are welcomed, but it was not a peaceful welcome," he said. Given all the bad news, Bush had to be inventive to keep the mood light at the White House. On July 20, 2005, he had a high-tech whoopee cushion rigged under Karl Rove's chair in the Cabinet Room and set it off during a senior staff meeting. As Bob Woodward reported in *State of Denial*, "Everyone laughed."

One month later, Bush had to sit through a meeting he found far less entertaining: a briefing on Hurricane Katrina. During that session, held nineteen hours before the storm hit New Orleans, Max

Mayfield of the National Hurricane Center emphasized, "I don't think anyone can tell you with any degree of confidence right now whether the levees will be topped or not, but that's obviously a very, very grave concern." Despite that concern, the Decider, uncharacteristically abstaining from what he considered the most enjoyable part of his job, made no decisions—except to end the meeting as quickly as possible. After receiving a briefing that could be summarized as "Katrina Determined to Strike in Louisiana," he couldn't think of a single question to ask the experts. Four days later, after the storm had ravaged New Orleans and killed more than 1,800 people, he once again showed the gift for not paying attention that he'd nurtured at Yale. "I don't think anybody anticipated the breach of the levees," he declared.

Bush became more engaged, if not more comprehending, when the global financial crisis struck in 2008. Working on an address to the nation about the government's plan to bail out the financial sector, Bush's speechwriters were urged to include the words "a bold decision." As one of those writers, Matt Latimer, recalled, "The president seemed to be thinking of his memoirs. 'This might go in as a big decision,' he mused." There was only one problem: the Decider didn't seem to know, exactly, what he'd decided on. He wanted his speech to explain that the government's proposed purchase of troubled assets would ultimately benefit the taxpayers because, as he kept repeating to his speechwriters, "We're buying low and selling high." One of his aides became alarmed and, pulling the writers aside, told them, "The president is misunderstanding this proposal. . . . He has the wrong idea in his head." When W. received the final draft of the speech, the absence of the phrase "buy low and sell high" perplexed him. At that point, his aides had to inform him that this notion existed only in his mind, and not in the actual plan. According to

Latimer, "When it was explained to him that his concept of the bail-
out proposal wasn't correct, the president was momentarily speech-
less. He threw up his hands in frustration. 'Why did I sign on to this
proposal if I don't understand what it does?' "

In 2000, a poll famously asked voters which presidential candidate
they'd rather have a beer with; Bush, not requiring the Supreme
Court's help in this contest, beat Gore, 40 percent to 37. The survey
was commissioned not by a political party or news outlet but by the
marketing team behind Samuel Adams beer. Nevertheless, seizing on
the beer quiz as an excellent way to elevate the national political conversation, Zogby, an allegedly reputable polling company, asked the
question again in 2004. This time, 57 percent of undecided voters
favored Bush over John Kerry, somehow thinking it wise to inebri-
ate someone already capable of starting a ruinous war while sober.
The beer quiz has been a staple of stupid campaign coverage ever
since, underscoring the condescending assumption that voters want
a president who, in the pollsters' parlance, is just like them.

    I don't want a president who's just like me. I'm pretty sure I'd suck
at the job. I want a president to be better than I am: smarter, braver,
calmer, and more patient. When a country faces war, economic col-
lapse, or contagion, I'm not sure it's Miller Time. Lincoln may have
been our greatest president, but he wouldn't be in my top hundred
potential drinking buddies. He could get kind of dark.

Before the invasion of Iraq, Secretary of State Colin Powell reminded
Bush of the so-called Pottery Barn rule: "You break it, you own
it." Bush violated the Pottery Barn rule and then some, leaving behind the debris of not just Iraq but also the United States of America.
By his final year in office, his brand had mutated from lack of studiousness to utter thickness. At one White House press conference, a

reporter asked him a question that, as a former "independent oil and gas producer," he should have aced:

> REPORTER: What's your advice to the average American who is hurting now, facing the prospect of 4 dollar a gallon gasoline? A lot of people facing—
>
> BUSH: Wait a minute, what's you just say? You're predicting 4 dollar a gallon—
>
> REPORTER: A number of analysts are predicting 4 dollar a gallon this spring when they reformulate—
>
> BUSH: That's interesting, I hadn't heard of that.

As Bush's presidency limped to the exit, some wondered whether electing a candidate who passed the beer quiz but failed all the others was such a good idea, after all. Perhaps to capitalize on the backlash against stupidity, in 2007 Al Gore published a book called *The Assault on Reason*. Some interpreted the timing as a sign that Gore was contemplating another presidential bid. Ultimately, he declined, possibly deciding that spending another year being mocked for inventing the internet wasn't the best use of his time. Democratic egghead fanciers needn't have despaired, however: in Gore's place came a brand new nerd, Barack Obama.

As a presidential candidate, Obama faced serious obstacles. He was a Black man in a country that had elected only white presidents, at least a dozen of whom had, at one time or another, enslaved Black people. He had foreign-sounding first and last names, and a middle name that also belonged to a Middle Eastern tyrant the U.S. military had chased into a spider hole. For voters who weren't prone to racism or xenophobia, there was the question of his inexperience: at the time he announced his candidacy, he had served in the United States Senate only two years. Still, to some commentators, none of these obstacles was as daunting as this: he reminded them of—RUN FOR COVER!—Adlai Stevenson.

On November 3, 2007, the former Reagan speechwriter Peggy Noonan wrote in the *Wall Street Journal* that "Barack Obama, with his elegance and verbal fluency, really did seem like that great and famous political figure from his home state of Illinois—Adlai Stevenson." On November 4, Steve Clemons of the New America Foundation concurred: "As things look now, Barack Obama is running an Adlai Stevenson campaign." Ned Temko, in the *Guardian*, made the comparison seem even more undesirable: "Obama can by now have little doubt that his 'Adlai problem' is no laughing matter." Jeering from the sidelines, Karl Rove contributed the not-entirely-coherent observation that Obama was "a vitamin-deficient Adlai Stevenson." Huh?

One person determined to avoid comparisons between Adlai Stevenson and Barack Obama, however, was Barack Obama. In an interview with the *Reno Gazette-Journal*, he revealed who his *actual* role model was: "I think Ronald Reagan changed the trajectory of America. . . . He put us on a fundamentally different path because the country was ready for it. . . . [H]e tapped into what people were already feeling, which was we want clarity, we want optimism, we want a return to that sense of dynamism and entrepreneurship that had been missing." That's right: the critically acclaimed author and former president of the *Harvard Law Review* was taking inspiration from a man who didn't know that South America contained different countries. It was a testament to the viselike grip of the Age of Ignorance that another of our most informed politicians was paying tribute to one of our least.

Like Bill Clinton, Obama borrowed from Reagan, drenching his campaign in the Gipper's generic sunniness. For instance: "I've found as I say all across this land a longing among our people for hope." Obama in 2008? Nope: Reagan in 1980. Decades after Reagan made hope his brand, both Clinton and Obama produced their own knockoffs. Bill, who had the great good fortune to be born in a town called Hope, Arkansas, starred in a promotional film shown at the 1992 Democratic National Convention called *The Man from Hope*; Barack, born in Honolulu, had to settle for publishing a 2006 book called *The Audacity of Hope*. While Obama followed Reagan's example, he steered clear of Gore's; you never heard Barack savoring his favorite bits from *Phenomenology of Perception*. Instead, he tried to appear like a regular guy, sometimes with hilarious results. During a campaign stop in Pennsylvania, his familiarity with the local brew, Yuengling, was as shaky as Dan Quayle's grasp of NATO. Later, he went bowling, expertly avoiding the pins.

By and large, though, Obama's accommodation to the Acceptance stage was subtler than those ill-conceived stunts. The high-flown eloquence that was criticized for being too Adlai-ish in 2007 was, by 2008, mostly missing from a stump speech that leaned on two one-syllable words, "hope" and "change," as well as a combination of three others: "Yes, we can!" * It's hard to imagine Adlai saying any of this, just as it's impossible to picture him yelling, "Fired up! Ready to go!" Unless, of course, he could do it in Latin.

As successful as Obama's simplified messaging was, some supporters felt he was insulting his audience's intelligence. In an interview with *Playboy* in 2013, the actor Samuel L. Jackson, who'd backed Obama in both his presidential bids, accused him of "promoting mediocrity" by sounding less educated than he was. "[S]top trying to 'relate,'" Jackson said. "Be a leader. Be fucking presidential. Look, I grew up in a society where I could say 'It ain't' or 'What it be' to my

---

*Reinforcing the impression that Obama was infantilizing his audience, this was also the catchphrase of the popular children's show character Bob the Builder.

friends. But when I'm out presenting myself to the world as me, who graduated from college, who had family who cared about me, who has a well-read background, I fucking conjugate." When the star of *Snakes on a Plane* accuses you of dumbing things down, attention must be paid.

For the moment, though, let's set this rhetorical critique aside. True, Obama wasn't immune to the Age of Ignorance, but his role in it was mainly reactive. He did nothing to usher it from its second stage, Acceptance, into its third, most hideous stage, Celebration. Was another politician up to that task? You betcha.

Much has been made of John McCain's reckless selection, during his 2008 presidential run, of the woefully unqualified Sarah Palin as his running mate. In reality, Palin wasn't a wild aberration from the national Republican candidates who preceded her but, rather, a logical result of the trend they embodied. The inanities she spewed were no more absurd than those of George W. Bush, whose warm embrace of his own ignorance softened the ground for her. Palin had much in common with Bush, who had much in common with Quayle. Therefore, according to the transitive property of stupidity, Palin also had a great deal in common with Quayle.

But the descent of the bar in the twenty years between Quayle's candidacy and Palin's made their destinies diverge. Quayle's cluelessness, exposed during the Ridicule stage, consigned him to oblivion. Palin's, unfurling majestically during the Acceptance stage, guaranteed her best-selling books, well-paid speaking gigs, and a reality TV show.

To many, Palin remains a joke, because when they think of her they're thinking of Tina Fey's impersonation. The comedian's mockery dogged Palin: At Target, a shopper trolled her by yelling, "Oh my God! It's Tina Fey! I love Tina Fey!" (Other customers were amused;

Palin left the store in a huff and drove off.) Fey's imitation became so iconic that, to this day, many people believe that Palin said, "I can see Russia from my house," when in fact she never said anything so concise. It was McCain, not Palin, who first made the laughable claim that Alaska's proximity to Russia somehow prepared her to be commander in chief. Though she later concurred, in an interview with ABC's Charlie Gibson, what she told Gibson was technically true: from Alaska's Little Diomede Island, in the middle of the Bering Strait, you can see Vladimir Putin's homeland. But, as we learned from the story about Al Gore inventing the internet, in the Information Age jokes travel faster than information.

If Tina Fey fans thought Palin was ludicrous, however, their view was far from unanimous. Millions watched Fey's *SNL* performances, but many millions more didn't—and a lot of them considered Palin a hero. The bar having been lowered for her by 2008, she returned the favor by lowering it even further, inspiring a clown car of candidates to run for office in 2010 and 2012. That, however, was not her crowning achievement. With her toxic brew of ignorance and grievance, Sarah Palin was the gateway ignoramus who led to Donald Trump.

The McCain campaign staff could have saved themselves much heartache if, during Palin's vetting, they had rung up one of the foremost authorities on Alaska's governor: a young man named Levi Johnston. The boyfriend of Palin's eldest daughter, Bristol, Johnston described himself on Myspace as follows: "I'm a fuckin' redneck who likes to snowboard and ride dirt bikes. But I live to play hockey. I like to go camping and hang out with the boys, do some fishing, shoot some shit and just fuckin' chillin' I guess. . . . Ya fuck with me I'll kick ass." When he learned of Palin's selection, he assumed someone was, indeed, fucking with him: "I thought, Was this woman—who, at home, would literally say things that did not make sense—really running for vice president?" The governor's good news turned out to be bad news for Levi—or, more specifically, for his mullet, which Palin demanded he prune before his appearance at the 2008 Republican National Convention.

We should forgive Levi for being flabbergasted by the elevation of Bristol's incoherent mom, as he was far from alone. On the day of her unveiling, the *New York Times* quizzically observed, "The choice of Ms. Palin was reminiscent of former President George Bush's selection of Dan Quayle, then a barely known senator from Indiana as his running mate in 1988." News of the pick prompted Barack Obama's running mate, Joe Biden, to ask, "Who's Sarah Palin?" But to those who'd been paying attention to the ineluctable rise of Sarah Barracuda (as her high school basketball teammates called her), her selection wasn't so shocking. Despite her carefully cultivated "just your average hockey mom" image, by 2008 Palin had already been a politician for sixteen years, starting with her election to the Wasilla, Alaska, city council at age twenty-eight. After two winning campaigns for mayor and one near-miss bid for lieutenant governor, she won the state's top job in 2006. It was one year after that triumph that Palin's ship came in—literally.

The ship in question was Holland America Line's MS *Oosterdam*, which, given its pivotal role in catapulting Sarah Palin onto the national scene, deserves a special place in maritime history alongside the *Lusitania* and the *Titanic*. As Jane Mayer reported in the *New Yorker*, two major conservative publications, the *Weekly Standard* and the *National Review*, had sponsored a luxury Alaskan cruise, bringing to Juneau such VIPs as George W. Bush's former speechwriter Michael "Axis of Evil" Gerson, the Fox News commentator Fred Barnes, and Dan Quayle's former chief of staff Bill Kristol. Upon meeting Palin, the seafaring Republicans proved far more easily impressed than Levi Johnston. Gerson called her "a mix between Annie Oakley and Joan of Arc," somehow neglecting to compare her to Eleanor of Aquitaine and Marie Curie. Barnes said he was "struck by how smart Palin was, and how unusually confident. Maybe because she had been a beauty queen, and a star athlete, and succeeded at almost everything she had done."

The "beauty queen" part seemed to make a particularly big impression on the male cruise passengers. Barnes called her "exceptionally pretty." Jay Nordlinger, in a post on the *National Review* website, called her "a former beauty-pageant contestant, and a real honey, too. Am I allowed to say that? Probably not, but too bad." No Republican vice presidential prospect had released such crazy-making pheromones since Dan Quayle.

Speaking of Quayle, no passenger on the Alaska cruise was more blown away by Sarah Barracuda than Kristol, who seemed convinced that Palin, like his former boss, had the stuff of vice presidential greatness. The savvy talent spotter who boosted Clarence Thomas and Alan Keyes began tub-thumping for Palin. Mayer reported, "[A]s early as June 29th, two months before McCain chose her, Kristol predicted on 'Fox News Sunday' that 'McCain's going to put Sarah Palin, the governor of Alaska, on the ticket.' He described her as 'fantastic,' saying that she could go one-on-one against Obama in basketball, and possibly siphon off Hillary Clinton's supporters. He pointed out that she was a 'mother of five' and a reformer. 'Go for the gold here with Sarah Palin,' he said. The moderator, Chris Wallace, finally had to ask Kristol, 'Can we please get off Sarah Palin?' "

No, we couldn't. Three weeks later, again on Fox, he called her "my heartthrob." At this point, the lovesick Kristol was practically holding a boom box over his head. "I don't know if I can make it through the next three months without her on the ticket," he said. Fortunately for him, and less so for John McCain, his wish came true. A friend of McCain's, describing Kristol's sober contribution to the deliberative process, said that he "was out there shaking the pom-poms."

The man the McCain campaign enlisted to vet Kristol's heart-throb was a lawyer named A. B. Culvahouse. Vetting a running mate traditionally takes months, but Culvahouse, operating within the hurry-up offense of the campaign, completed his "work" in a matter of days. No one summed up Palin's vetting better than Levi Johnston: "I have been more diligent tracking a moose than anyone seemed to have been in choosing the Republican vice-presidential nominee."

Culvahouse later explained why he thought Palin would help the ticket: She had "a certain aura about her" and "an engaging personality. . . . [I]t was clear she had a personality that fills the room." These were remarkable conclusions about someone whom Culvahouse had spoken to only over the phone. Given how obsessed the Republican shipmates had been with Palin's history as a beauty queen, it's no surprise that the questions Culvahouse lobbed her way were the kind a pageant host would ask a contestant, such as "Why do you want to be vice president?" His questions were such softballs that it fell to Palin to suggest a more probing one: "Here's what you should really ask me is why I went to so many schools."

The tangled tale of Palin's education was indeed worth examining, since it appeared she'd been intent on visiting more colleges than *U.S. News & World Report*. Her academic career brought to mind the lament of John "Bluto" Blutarsky, John Belushi's character in *Animal House*: "Christ. Seven years of college down the drain." She nearly equaled Bluto's record, attending six colleges in six years.* She began at the University of Hawaii at Hilo, in 1982, leaving a few

---

* Like Elizabeth Taylor's two marriages to Richard Burton, Palin's two stints at University of Idaho are being counted twice.

weeks later after finding it too rainy. She moved to Hawaii Pacific University, but lasted there only through the fall of her freshman year. Then it was on to North Idaho College, which seemed, at least for a little while, like a keeper: she stayed for two whole semesters. But the University of Idaho beckoned. There, in an ironic decision for the future scourge of the "lamestream media," she majored in journalism.

We're not done yet! By the fall of 1985, higher education's answer to Carmen Sandiego was back in Alaska, attending Matanuska-Susitna College. Seemingly afflicted by seller's remorse, she hastened back to the University of Idaho in the spring of 1986 and, astoundingly, managed to stay there until 1987, when, much to the relief of the nation's college registrars, she graduated. Given how convoluted this itinerary was, it's odd that Culvahouse didn't consider it worthy of scrutiny. Asked whether the McCain campaign had been in touch, a spokeswoman for the University of Idaho said, "Our office was not contacted by anyone."

Even if Culvahouse had reached out to Palin's manifold alma maters, however, it's unlikely that he would have turned up much: Sarah roamed the nation's universities like a ninja, leaving no trace. Unlike Dan Quayle's professor at DePauw, who vividly remembered the frustration of gazing into his student's vacant blue eyes, no one at Palin's schools seemed to have the foggiest recollection of her. "It's the funniest damn thing," said Jim Fisher, whose journalism class Palin took at the University of Idaho. "No one can recall her." Roy Atwood, who was her academic adviser at Idaho, also drew a blank. The *Los Angeles Times* reported that "interviews with a dozen professors yielded not a single snippet of a memory." An Idaho classmate suggested that Palin had been close to her resident adviser, Jill Loranger Clark, but that account came as a surprise to Clark: "I can honestly tell you I have no idea who she was." Only Kim

"Tilly" Ketchum, a high school classmate who attended North Idaho with Palin, could summon a memorable college anecdote about her. "Someone pulled the fire alarm next to my door," Ketchum said. "We all were told there is an invisible dye that squirts onto your hand when you pull the alarm and you're not going to be able to hide. And Sarah looked at her hands, and said, 'Oh my God, look!' And she went and confessed."

If Palin's failure to stay at one college barely long enough to unpack her toothbrush suggested a certain flightiness, her former aide John Bitney confirmed that assessment: "She has a remarkably short attention span." Colleen Cottle, who served on the Wasilla city council when Palin was mayor, said that she "had no attention span—with Sarah it was always 'What's the flavor of the day?'" Many of her colleagues in Alaska would have echoed this opinion—if only Culvahouse had placed a call to any of them.

Contrary to this scatterbrained image, though, there were times when Palin proved capable of intense and sustained concentration: when she was engaged in a personal vendetta. The best example of this laser focus was the sordid case of her sister's ex-husband, the Alaska state trooper Mike Wooten, whom Palin tormented over a period of several years, using her position in government to do so. Her vindictive campaign culminated in her controversial decision, as governor, to fire Alaska Public Safety Commissioner Walt Monegan after he refused to fire Wooten. The so-called Troopergate scandal sparked a bipartisan probe conducted by the investigator Stephen Branchflower, whose report concluded that, "in attempting to get Trooper Wooten fired," Palin had "abused her power as governor." Coming in at 263 pages, it's unlikely she read it.

Troopergate didn't dampen the McCain campaign's passion for Palin. Even more mystifyingly, neither did her appearance on a 2007 episode of *Charlie Rose*, where her signature verbal style, featuring run-on sentences that sound like a spilled bag of Bananagrams, was on glorious display. When Rose asked if she thought education was a "significant challenge for a governor because it's primarily a state responsibility," she unleashed this torrent: "Well, absolutely, it is. For the state of Alaska, though, our biggest issues are energy issues, so that we can pay for a world-class education system up there. Our energy issues surround the fact that Alaska is very, very wealthy in reserves, oil and gas reserves, but we are not given the ability right now, or I guess the permission, by some, to go ahead and develop those resources and flow that oil and gas into the rest of the United States of America to help secure our United States so that we can quit being so reliant on foreign sources of energy, but a clean safe domestic supply of energy being produced in Alaska. Again we are very rich in the reserves, we just need that ability to tap them and flow into hungry markets our oil and our gas, so development of our resources." Just in case you thought you missed something, Palin responded to a question about education with an answer that had zero to do with education. Instead, she took 146 words to say what could have been said in three: "Drill, baby, drill." (Say what you will about Palin's short attention span, it takes a certain amount of focus, not to mention lung capacity, to give an answer that long.) In fact, Palin responded to nearly every one of Rose's queries with an answer about oil and gas production in Alaska, suggesting a somewhat limited command of issues outside the realm of oil and gas production in Alaska. To his credit, Culvahouse expressed reservations about this unusual performance, but the campaign's honchos overruled him. "We loved her appearance on *Charlie Rose*," they said. McCain's campaign manager, Steve Schmidt, went further: "She's a star!"

Members of McCain's inner circle had convinced themselves that Palin could attract disaffected Democratic women upset by their party's failure to nominate Hillary Clinton—a realignment possible only if those women overlooked the fact that Clinton and Palin had as much in common ideologically as Batman and the Joker. In her book *Notes from the Cracked Ceiling*, Anne E. Kornblut reported that the testosterone-heavy McCain team reached its conclusion about Palin's appeal to women without consulting one key demographic: any actual women.

In his final recommendation to McCain, Culvahouse offered this optimistic assessment of Palin's preparedness to be president: "She will not be ready on January 20, but she has the smarts to get there." When Culvahouse described her as "high risk, high reward," that was all McCain needed to pull the trigger. "You shouldn't have told me that," he replied. "I've been a risk taker all of my life." But as much as the self-styled "maverick" liked to credit the impetuous decision to his gambler's temperament, the choice of Palin also owed much to the not-very-deliberative process of his former political rival George W. Bush. After nearly eight years of W.'s fact-resistant decisions, including the disastrous call to invade a foreign country populated by mysterious people called Sunnis and Shiites, choosing a demonstrably unfit running mate after a shambolic vetting process seemed like no big deal. Even Culvahouse's description of how McCain picked Palin had an eerie echo of Bush: "John was the decider."

So, for that matter, did Palin's expression of otherworldly calm when she was told she'd been chosen: "It's God's plan." Her claim that Providence played a role in her selection, however, drew a skeptical response from Levi Johnston. "Sarah told the world that her being chosen was God's plan," he wrote. "It would be the first time I had ever heard her mention the fella."

With Palin's vetting complete, Culvahouse's involvement in the McCain campaign was over, but his role in the Age of Ignorance was not. Given how roundly his evaluation of Palin was assailed, it would have been safe to assume he'd never again be asked to choose anything more momentous than pizza toppings. That wasn't the case. In 2016, he embarked on a second tour of duty when he was tapped to vet running mates for Republican presidential nominee Donald J. Trump.

To assess the depth and breadth of her ignorance, let's ask a version of a question we've asked before: What does Sarah Palin know?

The McCain campaign didn't explore this question too thoroughly during the vetting process. Only after she was selected did the campaign's manager, Steve Schmidt, spend enough time with her to learn the horrifying truth: in his words, "She doesn't know anything."

Palin believed that the British armed forces were under the command of the Queen. She didn't know the difference between England and the United Kingdom, and had never heard of Margaret Thatcher.* She was also shaky when it came to a former British colony, the United States of America. Answering a question about the phrase "under God" in the Pledge of Allegiance, Palin opined, "If it was good enough for the Founding Fathers, it's good enough for me and I'll fight in defense of our Pledge of Allegiance." We'll never know whether it was good enough for the Founding Fathers because the Pledge of Allegiance wasn't written until 1892; the reference to God was inserted in 1954.

With so little time to prep Palin for her first media inquisition, the interview with ABC's Charlie Gibson, the McCain team clung to the belief (or hope) that she was a "quick study." There's a grand Republican tradition of this brand of delusion. In 1999,

---

* Once Palin figured out who Thatcher was, she declared the Iron Lady one of her heroes. Even so, she didn't seem to know too many details about her: in 2010, she sought a meeting with Thatcher, unaware that she was in the throes of dementia.

Lawrence B. Lindsey, who was giving the budding presidential candidate George W. Bush a desperately needed crash course in economics, claimed, "He has a strong sense of character. And he's a quick study." After Quayle was named the GOP vice presidential nominee, in 1988, Senator Bob Dole, who had earlier questioned his colleague's qualifications, stated, "Dan Quayle, as I've said before, is a very quick study." Going back a couple decades further, Ronald Reagan's longtime associate Michael Deaver recalled the Gipper's preparation for his first gubernatorial run: "I think he had to learn, but he was a quick study." It makes you wonder how Deaver's boss, the White House chief of staff Howard Baker, would have appraised the president. "He was a quick study," Baker said. The lesson here: when someone calls you "a quick study," you don't know shit.

And so Palin's quick-studying commenced. As John Heilemann and Mark Halperin reported in *Game Change*, Palin's tutors treated her like a tabula rasa: "They sat Palin down at a table in the suite, spread out a map of the world, and proceeded to give her a potted history of foreign policy. They started with the Spanish Civil War, then moved on to World War I, World War II, the cold war, and what [lobbyist Randy] Scheunemann liked to call 'the three wars' of today—Iraq, Afghanistan, and the global war on terror." Palin dutifully scrawled all this brand-new information on 5 x 7 cards—not unlike the 5 x 8 cards that Stu Spencer's team had used with Reagan in the mid-1960s. The technology for pouring facts into empty vessels hadn't changed much in the intervening forty years, just an inch.

But, unlike Reagan, whose years of memorizing Hollywood scripts made regurgitating new information a snap, Palin's professional on-camera experience consisted mainly of a stint, in 1988, as a fill-in sports reporter on KTUU-TV, in Anchorage. (Palin: "The Iditarod is of course the biggie, but it's not the only mushing going on.") It soon became questionable whether, as Culvahouse had predicted, she had the smarts to get there. As the journalist Geoffrey Dunn wrote, "[S]he didn't know what countries formed NAFTA, the North American Free Trade Agreement (Canada, the United States, and Mexico). It was said that she didn't know that Africa was a continent and that South Africa was an independent country. She was astonishingly uncertain about municipal, state, and federal distinctions—this after being a mayor and governor. . . . One senior adviser said she couldn't locate Afghanistan on a map." *Game Change* offered an equally grim assessment: "[H]er grasp of rudimentary facts and concepts was minimal. Palin couldn't explain why North and South Korea were separate nations. She didn't know what the Fed did. Asked who attacked America on 9/11, she suggested several times that it was Saddam Hussein. Asked to identify the enemy that her son would be fighting in Iraq, she drew a blank. (Palin's horrified advisers provided her with scripted replies, which she memorized.) Later . . . Palin said to her team, 'I wish I'd paid more attention to this stuff.' "

In Palin's defense, her belief that Saddam Hussein was behind 9/11 indicated that she might indeed have been paying attention— to George W. Bush, who, as we saw, had assiduously spread false-hoods about a nonexistent link between Saddam and Al Qaeda. In an effort to reeducate Palin on this subject, however, Schmidt committed an act of Pollyannaism to rival Gerald Ford's "Whip Inflation Now" campaign: he gave her a copy of Lawrence Wright's 540-page book, *The Looming Tower: Al-Qaeda and the Road to 9/11*. According to Dunn, "[N]o one ever saw her reading from it; she preferred *People* magazine and *Runner's World.*"

That account of Palin's reading preferences chimes with an answer she gave one of Charlie Rose's producers, in 2007, when asked to name her favorite authors: "I love C. S. Lewis—you know, very, very deep—and, um, very intriguing, reading anything from C. S.

Lewis. I love, um, believe it or not, Dr. George Sheehan, from many years ago, he was a *Runner's World* columnist, and I still have some of his columns, Dr. George Sheehan, he's passed away, but, uh, very inspiring, and, um, very motivating, he was an athlete, and I think so much of what you learn in athletics about competition and healthy living that he was really able to encapsulate has stayed with me all these years." You can't help noticing that while Palin called C. S. Lewis very, very deep, her familiarity with Dr. George Sheehan seemed very, very deeper.

In the tradition of Reagan's devotees, Palin's fiercest partisans tried to portray her as a "voracious reader." Nowhere is this campaign more risible than in Kaylene Johnson's *Sarah: How a Hockey Mom Turned the Political Establishment Upside Down,* a book so adoring it could've been written by Bill Kristol. According to Palin's sister Molly, she was a news junkie: "She read the paper from the very top left-hand corner to the bottom right corner to the very last page. . . . She didn't want to miss a word. She didn't just read it—she knew every word she had read and analyzed it." Palin was so well-read, Johnson reports, that her older sister, Heather, sought her help writing book reports: "She was such a bookworm. Whenever I was assigned to read a book, she'd already read it." A photo in Johnson's biography features a bespectacled fourth-grade Sarah and a caption calling her "an avid reader of newspapers and nonfiction books." If we're to believe all this, by the time Palin ran for vice president, she had somehow gotten this raging passion out of her system. As Levi Johnston observed, "I'd never felt that Sarah was all that curious about the world outside Alaska, and I sure never saw her read a book."

Indeed, during her interview with Charlie Gibson, Palin sounded like a student who hadn't done the assigned reading for class. After he asked, "Do you agree with the Bush Doctrine?" there was a Quayle-sized pause before Palin issued a poignant plea for a clue: "In what respect, Charlie?" Unhelpfully, Gibson restated the question without offering her additional information: "What do you interpret it to be?" Palin, demonstrating some familiarity with the word "doctrine," finally replied, "His worldview." Cruelly, Gibson persisted: "No, the Bush Doctrine, enunciated in September 2002, before the Iraq War." At this point, Palin tried to compensate for not knowing the actual answer with a verbal tsunami familiar to anyone who'd caught her on *Charlie Rose*: "I believe that what President Bush has attempted to do is rid this world of Islamic extremism, terrorists who are hell-bent on destroying our nation. There have been blunders along the way, though. There have been mistakes made. And with new leadership, and that's the beauty of American elections, of course, and democracy, is with new leadership comes opportunity to do things better." Palin's ignorance on this point was forgivable; according to Peter D. Feaver, a member of the National Security Council under Bush, there were at least *seven* Bush Doctrines. Under those circumstances, a lot of people might not have known what the Bush Doctrine was— including, probably, Bush.

In what was seen as another gotcha moment from the interview, Gibson asked Palin to defend a statement she'd made at her former place of worship, the Wasilla Assembly of God. In an appearance caught on video, Palin told her audience that American soldiers in Iraq were performing "a task that is from God." Nervously back-tracking with Gibson, she said that she "would never presume to know God's will or to speak God's words." A better answer might have been "What I said was no more crazy-ass than some of the shit our sitting president, George W. Bush, has said." After his second inaugural as governor of Texas, Bush reportedly told the Reverend Richard Land of the Southern Baptist Convention, "I believe God wants me to be president." Not content to run this theory by just one man of the cloth, he revealed to the Reverend James Robison, "I've heard the call. I believe God wants me to run for president." Once the Almighty's wish came true, Bush seemed even more convinced that he was on a task from God. *Time* reported that, after 9/11, Bush "talked of being chosen by the grace of God to lead at that moment." Astoundingly, his dad also believed in the Divine Right of Dubya. "If I'd won that election in 1992, my oldest son would not be president of the United States of America," Bush Senior said. "I think the Lord works in mysterious ways." Mysterious doesn't begin to describe it.

Palin's answers to Gibson's other foreign policy queries, including whether the U.S. had the right to pursue terrorists in Pakistan without its approval, also proved long-winded and bewildering. At one point, Gibson appeared to give up trying to decipher Palinese altogether: "I got lost in a blizzard of words there." In what respect, Charlie? Because so many of Palin's responses avoided being wrong by being incomprehensible, the McCain team felt that she had emerged relatively unscathed.

But the scathing had just begun. Next up was her infamous grilling by CBS's Katie Couric, during which Palin spent most of her time workshopping additional material for Tina Fey. "[I]t's very important when you consider even national security issues with Russia as Putin rears his head and comes into the air space of the United States of America, where—where do they go?" she asked. "It's Alaska. It's just right over the border. It is—from Alaska that we send those out to make sure that an eye is being kept on this very powerful nation, Russia, because they are right there. They are right next to—to our state." Asked to name a newspaper she read, the journalism major responded, "Um, all of them, any of them that have been in front of me over all these years." Asked to provide an example of McCain pushing for financial oversight during his twenty-six years in Congress, she offered, "I'll try to find you some and I'll bring them to ya." But the low point, if you had to choose among many, came when Couric asked whether there were any Supreme Court decisions that she disagreed with besides *Roe v. Wade*:

> PALIN: Well, let's see. There's, of course in the great history of America there have been rulings, there's never going to be absolute consensus by every American. And there are those issues, again, like *Roe v. Wade*, where I believe are best held on a state level and addressed there. So you know, going through the history of America, there would be others but . . .
>
> COURIC: Can you think of any?
>
> PALIN: Well, I would think of . . . any again, that could best be dealt with on a more local level. Maybe I would take issue with. But, you know, as a mayor, and then as a governor and even as a vice president, if I'm so privileged to serve, wouldn't be in a position of changing those things but in supporting the law of the land as it reads today.

It was a dumbfounding moment. All Couric asked was to name one Supreme Court decision. At that point, just say anything: "Ali vs. Frazier."

After revisiting the carnage of the Couric interview, I have to ask: WTF was the McCain campaign thinking? True, the media had been clamoring for access to Palin, but, once it became clear that she'd be subjected to pop quizzes that required her to, you know, *know* things, why didn't they just have her say, in the grand tradition of the 2000 Bush campaign, that she wasn't running for *Jeopardy* champion? Why did Palin's handlers ignore all the hard work that Bush and Quayle had done over the previous two decades to lower the bar?

In his debate with Bentsen, Quayle had shown that there was nothing worse than struggling to answer questions when you didn't know the answers. Bush had triumphed by showing that the only reason to participate in a pop quiz was to devalue the quiz itself—and to declare that knowledge was for suckers who were trying to get a GPA higher than a C. The only quiz Palin ever should have been subjected to was the beer quiz.

No one seemed to understand this better than Palin herself. During her 2006 gubernatorial race, she shared this insight with one of her rivals, Andrew Halcro: "Andrew, I watch you at these debates with no notes, no papers, and yet when asked questions, you spout off facts, figures, and policies, and I'm amazed. But then I look out into the audience and I ask myself, 'Does any of this really matter?'" Halcro later observed that Palin was "a master, not of facts, figures, or insightful policy recommendations, but at the fine art of the non-answer, the glittering generality." She was a direct descendant of Ronald Reagan, who annihilated facts with nonsense like "There you go again." After trying and failing to cram information into Palin for her interviews with Gibson and Couric, the McCain campaign belatedly recognized the error of its ways. As campaign staff prepared her for the VP debate with Joe Biden, they realized that facts were indeed stupid things, and chucked the index cards. Instead, they focused on Palin's strength: glittering generalities. She had no trouble memorizing those.

If all George W. Bush had to do in his debate with Al Gore was "clear a matchbox," the McCain team went into Palin's debate with Biden praying that she'd clear a match. In an audacious gambit, thirteen minutes in, she fired off the following warning shot to the reality-based community: "I may not answer the questions the way that either the moderator or you want to hear, but I'm going to talk straight to the American people and let them know my track record also." History will record that this was one time Sarah Palin told the truth: she kept her word about not answering the questions. Instead, she repurposed her strategy from the *Charlie Rose* interview, pivoting whenever possible—and even when it seemed impossible—to the topic of energy production in Alaska. At other times, she didn't even bother to pivot, and rejected the question outright. Asked about the causes of climate change, she replied, "I don't want to argue about the causes." She was like a prisoner of war, refusing to say anything but her name and serial number. As for glittering generalities, she lifted one of the most famous pronouncements from Reagan's first inaugural address, after feeding it into the Palin-o-matic language mangler: "Patriotic is saying, 'Government, you know, you're not always the solution. In fact, too often you're the problem.'" Forgetting that she'd just said that, or hoping that the audience had forgotten, minutes later she announced that the solution to the financial crisis was more government intervention.

But that was about as wonky as she got. In her interview with Gibson, she'd said that she "didn't blink" when McCain offered her a spot on the ticket; she didn't blink during the debate, either, but she did wink—incessantly. Addressing "Joe Six-Pack" and "hockey moms across the nation," she punctuated so many sentences with a wink that it started to seem less a conspiratorial gesture than an involuntary tic. She tried to score a few points off Biden—or "Senator O'Biden," as she called him, in a verbal slip that the McCain debate-prep team had tried but failed to coach out of her. When Biden said that the solution to the nation's energy needs was not "drill, drill, drill," she fact-checked his comment as if it were a fatal gaffe: "The chant is 'drill, baby, drill,'" she haughtily informed him. She even tried her hand at a "There you go again" moment, at one point telling Senator O'Biden, "Say it ain't so, Joe." It didn't mean anything, but, as Palin had astutely observed to Andrew Halcro, it didn't matter.

When the debate was over, Tina Fey fans were sure that Palin had once again made a fool of herself, and salivated over the mincemeat the comedian would make of her on the next *SNL*. As for the reality-based community, a CNN poll showed Biden besting Palin in the debate, 51 percent to 36. But the people Palin had been aggressively winking at all night told a different story. On Fox News, a post-debate focus group, conducted by the Republican pollster Frank Luntz, gathered at Anheuser-Busch headquarters—an appropriate setting for what turned out to be the latest installment of the beer quiz. Luntz began the segment by indicating that the group was composed of undecided voters who were evenly split about Palin before the debate. Asked whether she won the face-off with Biden, almost all of them raised their hands.

A man with dyed platinum-blond hair spoke first: "I think she just spoke to the people, the American people, and she was direct." A middle-aged woman with a pearl necklace chimed in: "Very energetic, and with a really positive message." An older woman thought Palin "sounded smart and intelligent—knew what she was talking about." Less reckless words of praise came from a man who said, "She was Main Street America. She came across like everybody." In the spirit of the beer quiz, someone indistinguishable from everybody was just the right person to handle the nuclear codes.

The focus group made it painfully clear that there had been rampant grade inflation since Dan Quayle's debate. Expectations for him had been low, yet his performance still inspired a viewer to ask whether he'd been on drugs. But that was during the Ridicule stage; now, in the heart of Acceptance, the focus group was inclined to grade Palin on a curve. Couric's demolition of Sarah Barracuda seemed to create sympathy for her, as Andy Hiller's ambush had done for Dubya. Also helping Palin's cause was the false belief that the Couric interview had somehow been altered to make her look dumb, when anyone could see that a relentless stream of idiocies had gushed uncut from her mouth. "We've seen all week her interviews with—that have been edited—edited interviews with Katie Couric," one woman skeptically said. "We were expecting—I was expecting— her to lose it. It was hers to win or lose, and she won it, I thought." Another woman agreed: "She did very well. She exceeded expectations." Hurrah for not sucking as badly as you were expected to suck!

Luntz asked the voters to comment on the Palin moment that had garnered the most enthusiastic real-time response from the group: when she answered a question about the financial crisis by declaring, "Never again" (without proposing how to keep such a thing from happening never again). One woman said that she liked this rousing but meaningless battle cry "because we all feel very angry about what's going on right now in this country, particularly regarding the economic situation." "I felt it was like a 9/11 moment," a man said. "It was a patriotic thing. We're not going to take this anymore." His comparison of the financial crisis to 9/11 was unintentionally insightful: both disasters might have been averted had George W. Bush been paying attention.

At no point was the grade inflation more glaring than when Luntz asked the question that had been Quayle's kryptonite during his own debate: Was Sarah Palin qualified? There was near-universal assent. One man said, "As a governor, of course she's qualified. She's been down the road." What road? A woman concurred: "She's been there, she's done that, and she's ready to do it again." Been where? Done what? Do what again? Palin wasn't the only person capable of glittering generalities.

Three days later, in the *New York Times*, Bill Kristol was still shaking the pom-poms. Palin had agreed to an interview with him, and the chance to speak to his heartthrob, even over the phone, was enough to make the neocon drool. "It was the first time I'd talked with her since I met her in far more relaxed circumstances in Alaska over a year ago," Kristol wrote, sounding like a besotted middle schooler after a chance encounter with his crush in the cafeteria. Noting that the debate with Biden had scored huge ratings, he posed this question: "[R]eally, shouldn't the public get the benefit of another Biden-Palin debate, or even two? If there's difficulty finding a moderator, I'll be glad to volunteer." Here's another question: Couldn't someone at the *Times* hose this guy down?

As for Palin, her debate performance seemed to infuse her with unwarranted confidence. The day the *Times* published Kristol's love letter, she appeared at a San Francisco fundraiser and praised American soldiers for their work "in our neighboring country of Afghanistan." Later, in an appearance on Fox News, she said that once she and McCain were in power they'd "shore up the strategies that we need over in Iraq and Iran to win these wars," thus expanding the U.S.'s Middle Eastern battlefield into our neighboring country of Iran.

Geography might not have been one of Palin's strengths, but vitriol was. As the campaign entered its final month, Palin launched broadsides against Barack Hussein Obama that stressed his otherness and recalled Dubya's tirades about Saddam Hussein: "Our opponent . . . is someone who sees America, it seems, as being so imperfect, imperfect enough, that he's palling around with terrorists who would target their own country. . . . This is not a man who sees America as you see America and as I see America." As Dubya and Reagan both showed, if you don't have facts to support your case, fear and hate are handy substitutes. Palin's grievance-filled rants riled her running

mate's crowds, which began shouting ugly epithets at the mere mention of Obama's name. As reported in *Game Change*, McCain was
unprepared for what Palin had wrought: "He was startled by the
crazies at his rallies. Who were they?" They'd be back after Obama's
victory, when they'd call themselves the Tea Party.

As Election Day approached, Palin mirrored Bush once again,
though this time less intentionally: she, too, was spectacularly
pranked by a Canadian comedian. While Bush's trickster from "our
most important neighbor to the north" had merely convinced him
that he'd been endorsed by a fictitious Canadian prime minister,
Jean Poutine, Palin's hoaxer was far more ambitious. If the Alaska
governor clung to a dream of being taken seriously on the foreign
stage after her interview with Couric, the dream died three days before the election, when she fielded a call from a person claiming to
be French president Nicolas Sarkozy. The caller was actually Marc-
Antoine Audette, half of a comedy team from Quebec called the
Masked Avengers. The radio duo had spent days setting up the call
through Palin's staff, who astounded the comedians by being just as
oblivious as their boss. "When we started to work on the idea last
Tuesday, we thought it would be mission impossible," Audette told
the *Globe and Mail*. "But after about a dozen calls, we started to
realize it might work, because her staff didn't know the name of the
French president. They asked us to spell it."

Speaking in a crazily exaggerated French accent, Audette picked
up where Bush's prankster left off, tricking Palin into pretend-
ing she recognized the names of imaginary Canadian politicians.
"Some people said in the last days, and I thought that was mean,
that you weren't experienced enough in foreign relations and you
know that's completely false," Audette said. "That's the thing that I
said to my great friend, the prime minister of Canada, Steph Carse."
Palin cheerfully replied, "Well, he's doing fine, too," not realizing

that the actual Canadian prime minister was named Stephen Harper, and that Steph Carse is a Canadian pop singer. Continuing in this vein, Audette offered, "I was wondering, because you are so next to him, one of my good friends, also, the prime minister of Quebec, Mr. Richard Z. Sirois, have you met him recently? Did he come to one of your rallies?" Palin, unaware that Sirois was not the leader of Quebec but a Canadian radio host, said, "I haven't seen him at one of the rallies, but it's been great working with the Canadian officials."

Audette bonded with Palin over their love of hunting: "I just love killing those animals. Mmm, mmm, take away life: that is so fun." Palin laughed in agreement. "Yes, you know, we have a lot in common also," Audette added, "because except from my house I can see Belgium. That's kind of less interesting than you." Amazingly, even after he pointedly reworked Tina Fey's joke, Palin remained unaware that she was being pranked, replying, "Well, see, we're right next door to different countries that we all need to be working with, yes." After five minutes of escalating outlandishness, Audette, who never imagined that Palin would exhibit such sustained cluelessness, ran out of material; he had no alternative but to inform her that she'd been hoodwinked. It's not known whether the taped conversation, which made headlines around the world, changed the mind of the focus group member who said that Palin "sounded smart and intelligent—knew what she was talking about."

Palin's blazing ignorance was such a dominant feature of the 2008 campaign that it tended to obscure a less attention-grabbing reality: her running mate wasn't that well-informed, either. According to *Game Change*, Obama and McCain both conferred with Fed chief Ben Bernanke and Treasury Secretary Henry Paulson about the financial crisis, and those conversations exposed a wide disparity in the thoughtfulness and knowledge of the two candidates:

Obama called Paulson late at night at home and spent two hours discussing the intricate details of regulatory reform. As much as the substantiveness of the discussions struck Paulson, so did their sobriety and maturity. I'll be there publicly for you at any time, Obama told him. I'm going to be president, and I don't want to inherit a financial system that's collapsed.

McCain was in communication with Bernanke and Paulson, too, but to less useful effect. In one exchange with the Fed chairman, McCain compared the causes of the crisis to some recent management troubles at Home Depot. It's kind of like that, isn't it? he asked Bernanke. No, it's not, a flabbergasted Bernanke replied.

Fortunately for Bernanke, that was his last taste of McCain's economic expertise. On November 4, 2008, Obama and Biden clobbered the McCain-Palin ticket. Three years later, McCain's campaign manager, Steve Schmidt, expressed remorse about choosing the VP candidate he'd once called "a star." "I think that she helped usher in an era of know-nothingness and mainstreamed it in the Republican Party to the detriment of the conservative movement," he said. "And I think her nomination trivialized American politics, and had a lot of results that I'm not particularly comfortable with. . . . [I]t was a mistake."

How could a losing candidate who'd been on the national stage for little more than two months have such a profound impact on American politics? In the Information Age, anything is possible—especially with the help of some of the nation's largest media companies.

After Dan Quayle won the vice presidency, in 1988, it was all downhill for him. After Sarah Palin lost the vice presidency, in 2008, the best was yet to come. In a move that could have surprised none of her many college administrators, on July 3, 2009, Palin abruptly announced her resignation as governor, explaining that the best way for her to serve Alaska was not to serve it anymore. The cavalcade of paradoxes that constituted her remarks suggested that, in addition to Dr. George Sheehan of *Runner's World*, one of her favorite authors was Franz Kafka. "Life is too short to compromise time and resources," she said. "It may be tempting and more comfortable to just keep your head down, plod along, and appease those who demand, 'Sit down and shut up,' but that's the worthless, easy path; that's a quitter's way out." Instead of taking the quitter's way out, Palin told Alaska, she would quit.

Her resignation speech sparked wild speculation. Though she said that she didn't want to "go with the flow," because that was something only "dead fish" do, many suspected that her decision had been driven by something other than her desire to differentiate herself from seafood. Was she anticipating a criminal investigation? Did she plan to run for president? As usual, it fell to Levi Johnston to reveal her motives. After the 2008 election, Levi reported, "Sarah was sad for a while. She walked around the house pouting. I had assumed she was going to go back to her job as governor, but a week or two after she got back she started talking about how nice it would be to quit and write a book or do a show and make 'triple the money.' It was, to her, 'not as hard.' She would blatantly say, 'I want to just take this money and quit being governor.'" During the campaign, Palin had broadcast her ignorance. Now it was time to monetize it.

After receiving a $1.25 million advance from HarperCollins, the publishing company owned by Rupert Murdoch, Palin huddled with a ghostwriter, Lynn Vincent, to concoct a memoir called *Going Rogue: An American Life*. We'll never know what each woman contributed, but the book exquisitely captures Palin's knack for getting facts wrong. Each chapter begins with an aphorism, allowing her to continue in the proud Reagan tradition of attributing quotations to famous people who never said them. The biggest howler is the one that kicks off chapter 3: "Our land is everything to us. . . . I will tell you one of the things we remember on our land. We remember that our grandfathers paid for it—with their lives." Though Palin assigns this nugget of wisdom to the famed UCLA basketball coach John Wooden, its actual author was the Native American activist John Wooden Legs. Such bloopers didn't trouble Palin's fans, who propelled *Going Rogue* to number one on the *New York Times* best-seller list.

The success of *Going Rogue* made sequels inevitable. On my bookshelf right now sit the complete literary works of Sarah Palin.* Although it's unclear how many of these books she actually wrote, or read, they were all published. Palin was nothing if not prolific, the Charles Dickens of the Age of Ignorance. In 2010's *America by Heart: Reflections on Family, Faith, and Flag*, Palin decides to flaunt her knowledge of American history. In his review of the book, in the *Philadelphia Inquirer*, Michael D. Schaffer inventoried its avalanche of factual errors. Palin refers to John Adams as a "leading participant" in the Constitutional Convention, in Philadelphia; this could have been true only if Zoom had existed in 1787, since Adams was 3,500 miles away, serving as Minister Plenipotentiary to the Court of St. James's. In a similar vein, she defends her opposition to the separation of church and state by noting that Benjamin Franklin proposed opening each session of that same convention with a prayer; she omits the bothersome fact that his idea wasn't adopted. At one point, though, she does follow historical precedent: she asserts that

---

*If you're interested in acquiring any or all of them, DM me. I'm a highly motivated seller.

"patriotic Americans" aren't being racist by attacking Obama's policies because they are merely advocating "smaller federal government and a return to federalism—otherwise known as states' rights." Here she reproduces the white supremacist dog whistle that Ronald Reagan used in his 1980 speech near Philadelphia, Mississippi. The Philadelphia where Reagan appeared left a deeper impression on Palin than the Philadelphia where John Adams didn't.

After *America by Heart*, Palin's books keep getting shorter, which their author might have seen as a virtue, and which I, as a reader, most certainly do. *Good Tidings and Great Joy: Protecting the Heart of Christmas*, from 2013, is positively tiny: at approximately 5 x 7, it's the same size as the index cards that Palin used to prep for her interview with Couric. A festive Christmas wreath on the cover seems to promise a warm, home-for-the-holidays read, but you can't judge this book by its cover. *Good Tidings and Great Joy* turns out to be a screed against Palin's usual roster of enemies: liberals, the government, and the lamestream media, all of whom are engaged in a satanic conspiracy to wreck Christmas. Jarringly, she closes the book with a chapter of holiday recipes, including "Juanita's Soft, Gooey Oatmeal Raisin White Chocolate-Chip Heaven." Prominently featuring the words "white" and "heaven," it might be the most Sarah Palin cookie recipe ever.

And then there's 2015's *Sweet Freedom: A Devotional*. Having saved American history and Christmas in her two previous books, Palin here turns her attention to the Bible, citing more than two hundred scriptural passages and offering her unique commentary on each. After "Forgive me, for I have sinned [Romans 3:23]," Palin provides this illuminating gloss: "Every single human being has sinned and will sin again. Darn it. I'm right there at the top having to acknowledge mine. Double darn." *Sweet Freedom* appears to be Palin's final book—unless, of course, it turns out that she's been secretly writing a novel, which, given her extraordinary verbal style, could turn out like *Finnegans Wake*.

Books were only a teeny sliver of the burgeoning Palin media empire. In 2010, Roger Ailes, the former Nixon/Reagan/Bush/Quayle adviser and now the chairman and CEO of Fox News Channel, gave her a multiyear deal at $1 million per annum. "It's wonderful to be part of a place that so values fair and balanced news," the renowned news junkie said. It wasn't long, though, before Fox experienced buyer's remorse. One year later, a source close to Ailes told *New York* magazine's Gabriel Sherman, "He thinks Palin is an idiot. He thinks she's stupid."

In 2010, though, she was still bankable—so much that The Learning Channel wanted to go into business with her, despite the obvious risk to a network with the word "learning" in its name. TLC, formerly home to such reality shows as *Jon & Kate Plus 8*, announced that it was picking up *Sarah Palin's Alaska*, which the channel described as a show "about the remarkable Governor Palin." Produced by Mark Burnett, the creator of the money-gushing CBS series *Survivor*, the show's goal, in Palin's words, was to bring "the wonder and majesty of Alaska to all Americans." In the series, however, no one seems more amazed by Alaska, and at times unfamiliar with it, than its former governor. In an episode ironically titled "She's a Great Shot," Palin stalks caribou with her dad and turns out to be the worst Republican hunter since Dick Cheney. It's an odd performance for the vehement Second Amendment defender, who awkwardly handles her weapon as if holding a gun for the first time in her life. That might have been the case. As Levi Johnston informs us, "Sarah kept a gun under her bed, but she had no idea how to load it, much less shoot it. She once pulled it out, shook some bullets out of their box, and asked me to show her what to do." Although the caribou is not one of nature's smaller targets, Palin has trouble hitting it.

Fortunately for her, Burnett has managed to find the one caribou in Alaska as slow on the uptake as she is; she misses four times before the antlered dude realizes that it's time to get the heck out of there. ("Get settled down, Sarah!" her father pleads.) TLC canceled the low-rated series after its initial run. Though something of a setback for Palin, the axing was no big deal for Burnett, who was busy not only with *Survivor* but with another long-running hit reality show: *The Apprentice.*

As America continued its march through the Acceptance stage, some in the media—possibly afraid, as they had been with Reagan, to attack a politician whose popularity they'd underestimated—were eager to give Palin a pass, or even a boost. Back when ignorance was still in its Ridicule stage, no one had been more dogged in his investigation of Dan Quayle than the *Washington Post*'s David S. Broder. Three years after Quayle was sworn in as vice president, Broder and his *Post* colleague Bob Woodward were still trying to get him to release his noisome college transcript. Though the former Deke finally yielded, up to a point—offering them a verbal summary of his grades at DePauw—Quayle, in his signature snippy style, called the reporters' relentless pursuit of his transcript "irrelevant and rather demeaning." Fast-forward to 2010. Confronted with Palin—a far less qualified politician than Quayle (I can't believe I just typed that)—Broder was starting to sound like Bill Kristol shaking his pom-poms. He began his February 11 column by putting the political establishment on notice: "Take Sarah Palin seriously." Calling her "a public figure at the top of her game—a politician who knows who she is and how to sell herself," Broder praised the half-term governor's "pitch-perfect" message. "There are times," Broder wrote, "when the American people are looking for something more: for an Eisenhower, who liberated Europe; an FDR or a Kennedy or a Bush, all unashamed aristocrats;

or an Obama, with eloquence and brains. But in the present mood of the country, Palin is by all odds a threat to the more uptight Republican aspirants such as Mitt Romney and Tim Pawlenty—and potentially, to Obama as well." Considering that he saw her as a viable threat to be president in two years, this should have been a good moment for Broder to start looking for her college grades, as he'd done with Quayle. He didn't. "In the present mood of the country," Broder was much like the voters he presumed to understand: he was looking for less.

One pitch-perfect Palin performance that dazzled Broder was her keynote address to the National Tea Party Convention in Nashville, in 2010. The Tea Party had emerged, the previous year, as a grassroots movement of mainly older white conservatives. It soon drew the attention of the Koch brothers, Rupert Murdoch, and other powerful Republicans, who lavished it with money and publicity in hopes of manipulating its voters. While the billionaires' goals were easy to summarize—the elimination of taxes and regulations on their businesses—the actual Tea Partiers' agenda was more eclectic. They favored small government, but wanted government to play an active role in kicking immigrants out of the country. They wanted fewer handouts for the young, the poor, and people of color, but wanted government to keep its hands off their own Medicare and Social Security. They worshipped the Constitution, but selectively: they revered the Second Amendment, which allowed them to own guns, but weren't so keen on the First, which let Muslims build mosques. Although the media sometimes called the Tea Party a rejection of establishment Republicanism, that wasn't entirely accurate. According to *The Tea Party and the Remaking of Republican Conservatism* by Theda Skocpol and Vanessa Williamson, "In talking to Tea Party activists, you hear echoes of Reagan-era stories of 'welfare queens.'" Dick Armey, the former House Majority Leader who had faxed the fraudulent press release about Al Gore "inventing the internet," was both an establishment Republican and a Tea Party overlord. Ultimately, there was only one governing principle uniting this unwieldy group: the conviction that Barack Hussein Obama was Satan. (Even on this topic, though, there was some disagreement, as Tea Partiers split over whether the president was a communist, a Nazi, or both.) Since she'd already spent months polishing her crowd-pleasing anti-Obama stand-up set, Palin saw the Tea Party as an ideal opportunity to extend her brand.

The ex-governor could be counted on to bring down the house at Tea Party events, even when her speeches were a tangle of contradictions that made her gubernatorial resignation sound Ciceronian. In the Tea Party convention speech that prompted Broder to urge the political establishment to take her seriously, she asked, "How can I make sure that I, that you, that we're in a position of nobody being able to succeed?" At a Tea Party rally in Searchlight, Nevada, she told the crowd, much of it holding signs extolling the Constitution, "Our vision for America is anchored in time-tested truths that the government that governs least governs best, that the Constitution provides the path to a more perfect union—it's the Constitution." Moments later, though, she declared, "In these volatile times when we are a nation at war, now more than ever is when we need a commander in chief, not a constitutional law professor lecturing us from a lectern."

Palin would solidify her position of power in the Tea Party by endorsing as many candidates as she could in the 2010 midterms, using a vetting process as half-assed as the one that landed her on McCain's ticket. In the parlance of the vetting trade, she was pulling a Culvahouse. Like George W. Bush and John McCain before her, Palin was now the Decider, dispensing endorsements with the precision of a lawn sprinkler. Some candidates were so surprised to receive her blessing that they feared they were being pranked, Masked

Avengers–style. Rita Meyer, a Republican gubernatorial candidate in Wyoming, got a call on her cell phone informing her of Palin's endorsement only an hour before Sarah Barracuda announced it on her Facebook page. "[M]y campaign staff was taken completely by surprise by Sarah Palin's endorsement," Meyer said. Leo Hough, an aide to the Iowa gubernatorial candidate Terry Branstad, was flabbergasted after receiving a Palin endorsement by phone. "I was listening very carefully to make sure it was her and to make sure it wasn't a hoax, because there are a lot of hoaxes going around," he said. "I did identify that it was her after a few seconds."

Some 2010 candidates greeted their Palin endorsement with something less than jubilation. Palin gave no warning before a Fox News appearance in which she praised the former wrestling executive Linda McMahon, the GOP's Senate candidate in Connecticut, as a fellow "mama grizzly." McMahon wasn't that into her. "Palin's certainly entitled to make any opinion on any race that she would like," a campaign spokesman said tepidly. "Linda is running her own race, and she'll continue to do that through Election Day." It was striking that a candidate who had spent her career in the company of men pretend-fighting in capes, masks, and tights feared that an association with Palin might undermine her seriousness.

But most Tea Party candidates luxuriated in the mama grizzly's bear hug. Rand Paul, an ophthalmologist running for the U.S. Senate in Kentucky, was one Tea Party aspirant grateful for the Palin nod. "Governor Palin is providing tremendous leadership as the Tea Party movement and constitutional conservatives strive to take our country back," he declared. "Sarah Palin is a giant in American politics. I am proud to receive her support." A sterling exemplar of the Acceptance stage of ignorance, Paul was alarmingly open about how little he knew. Explaining that he didn't understand the mining industry well enough to regulate it, he warned voters, "[D]on't give me the power in Washington to be making rules." (Deal!) During the Q&A portion of a meeting of the Christian Home Educators of Kentucky—not exactly hostile ground for the likes of Paul—he was asked how old the Earth was. "I forgot to say I was only taking easy questions," he said. "I'm gonna pass on the age of the Earth. I think I'm just gonna have to pass on that one." Armed with this profound understanding of science, Paul would later appoint himself Grand Inquisitor whenever Dr. Anthony Fauci, the world's most esteemed virologist, testified before the Senate.

Another Tea Party candidate with intriguing scientific views was Ron Johnson, a failed class-ring salesman who was running for the U.S. Senate in Wisconsin. In an interview with the *Milwaukee Journal Sentinel* on August 16, 2010, Johnson, who had previously called claims that climate change was man-made "lunacy" and their adherents "crazy," advanced his own unique theory about the phenomenon. First, he offered some historical perspective, asserting that the Earth was pretty warm during the Middle Ages, when "it's not like there were tons of cars on the road"; for that reason, he declared, "I absolutely do not believe in the science of man-caused climate change. It's not proven by any stretch of the imagination." Then, demonstrating a stretch of imagination all his own, he offered, "It's far more likely that it's just sunspot activity or just something in the geologic eons of time." Like Rand Paul, Johnson has now been in the Senate for more than ten years, which to many people seem like the geologic eons of time.*

One GOP candidate who didn't get Palin's endorsement fared

---

*Johnson flaunted his scientific chops again in 2021 when he advised Wisconsin's citizens, "Standard gargle, mouthwash, has been proven to kill the coronavirus." The makers of Listerine disagreed, posting this statement online in bold: **LISTERINE® Antiseptic is not intended to prevent or treat COVID-19 and should be used only as directed on the product label."**

less well at the ballot box, but had only himself to blame. During a campaign event in June, Ken Buck, running for U.S. Senate in Colorado, wearied of answering questions posed by birthers, the not-insignificant Tea Party faction that believed Barack Obama was born in Kenya. Afterward, the exasperated Buck was caught on tape saying, "Will you tell those dumbasses at the Tea Party to stop asking questions about birth certificates while I'm on camera?" We'll never know how many votes this reckless moment of sanity cost him, but Buck lost in November.

Electoral losses that Palin had no choice but to take personally belonged to two candidates she'd anointed as fellow mama grizzlies, Sharron Angle and Christine O'Donnell. Angle's bid for the U.S. Senate, in Nevada, got off to an auspicious start when her chief rival in the GOP primary turned out to be Sue Lowden. The hapless Lowden did Angle a huge favor by offering this outside-the-box health-care proposal: "[B]efore we all started having health care, in the olden days our grandparents, they would bring a chicken to the doctor, they would say I'll paint your house." After her poultry-based medical plan came in for more than its share of derision, she doubled down, producing a letter from a doctor who asserted, "I have bartered with patients—for alfalfa hay, a bathtub, yard work and horse shoeing in exchange for my care." On the day of the primary, Republican voters showed that they weren't in desperate need of alfalfa hay, horseshoeing, or Sue Lowden, and voted for Angle instead.

But Angle, it turned out, had some unusual notions of her own. Concurring with Ron Johnson about climate change, she said that she didn't "buy into the whole . . . man-caused global warming, man-caused climate change mantra of the left. I believe that there's not sound science to back that up." She did, however, believe that there was sound science linking abortion to breast cancer. She didn't believe that the Constitution guaranteed the separation of church and state, conveniently ignoring that the First Amendment does just that. She was, however, a big fan of another part of the document: she mused that, if conservatives didn't prevail in the midterms, their supporters might need to seek what she called "Second Amendment remedies." * She supported eliminating the IRS and auditing the Fed, which put her at odds with Palin, who didn't know what the Fed did. She claimed that Dearborn, Michigan, was being ruled by Sharia law. Finally, she supported the privatization of Social Security, praising similar efforts by Chile's Augusto Pinochet. "Sometimes dictators have good ideas," she noted. Nevada's voters, apparently less pro-Pinochet than Angle, reelected the Democratic incumbent, Senator Harry Reid.

The mama grizzly known as Christine O'Donnell was Palin's pick for the U.S. Senate seat in Delaware formerly held by Palin's debate rival, "Say It Ain't So, Joe" O'Biden. The founder of an organization called Savior's Alliance for Lifting the Truth (SALT), O'Donnell outdid every other evangelical Christian running for office in her opposition to sex. Not only was she opposed to people having sex before marriage, and to people having sex with people of the same gender, she also objected to people having sex with themselves. At first glance, O'Donnell's staunch anti-masturbation views seemed at odds with the Tea Party's opposition to big government intruding on people's lives, not to mention the Declaration of Independence's enshrinement of the pursuit of happiness, but such contradictions didn't shake her certainty. She was certain about a lot. A staunch creationist, she threw down this memorable challenge to Charles Darwin: "You know what, evolution is a myth. . . . Why aren't monkeys

---

* With this remark, she was a trailblazer of sorts, since in 2016 Donald J. Trump suggested that, if Hillary Clinton were elected, that outcome could be fixed by "Second Amendment people."

still evolving into humans?" (Perhaps they are, but at a very slow pace, because they're spending too much time masturbating.) But monkeys weren't the mammals keeping O'Donnell awake at night. In an appearance on Fox News, she warned, "American scientific companies are crossbreeding humans and animals and coming up with mice with fully functioning human brains." Delaware voters might have wondered whether science could help O'Donnell grow a similar feature.

To be fair, O'Donnell wasn't the only politician bent on thwarting a gene-spliced race of half-man, half-mouse monstrosities. In his 2006 State of the Union address, George W. Bush called for banning "the most egregious abuses of medical research," including "creating human-animal hybrids." (Showing admirable restraint, he didn't say, "Either you're with us, or you're with the centaurs.") Senator Sam Brownback, a Republican from Kansas, answered Bush's call, sponsoring the Human-Animal Hybrid Prohibition Act of 2007. "What was once only science fiction is now becoming a reality, and we need to ensure that experimentation and subsequent ramifications do not outpace ethical discussion and societal decisions," Brownback said. "History does not look kindly on those who violate the dignity of the human person." (Fair enough, but Brownback's ringing defense of the "human person" raised the weird possibility that there might also be a non-human one. A dolphin person?) The controversy continued to rage in 2015, when the Georgia state representative Tom Kirby's website drew a hard line: "The mixing of Human Embryos with Jellyfish cells to create a glow in the dark human, we say not in Georgia."

As improbable as it might seem, O'Donnell's anti-masturbation, anti-supermice comments weren't the biggest drag on her campaign: that distinction went to the discovery that she was a witch—or, at the very least, a former one. A clip from a 1999 appearance on the

TV show *Politically Incorrect* emerged in which she'd volunteered, "I dabbled in witchcraft," before adding, in a witchy version of Bill Clinton's infamous "I didn't inhale" comment, "I never joined a coven." Offering more tantalizing details, she went on. "One of my first dates with a witch was on a satanic altar, and I didn't know it. I mean, there's a little blood there and stuff like that. . . . We went to a movie and then had a little midnight picnic on a satanic altar." Suddenly, a few youthful necromantic indiscretions were jeopardizing all the hard work she'd done to court evangelicals with her perfectly reasonable comments about the non-evolution of monkeys and the sin of spanking them. Instead of asking, "Who among us hasn't had a picnic on a satanic altar?" O'Donnell compounded the damage: she filmed a political ad that became an instant classic, in which she somehow declared with a straight face, "I'm not a witch." O'Donnell, who went on to lose by 16 percent, might have done better if she'd stopped pandering to Christians altogether and tried to increase voter turnout among Delaware's Wiccans.

Palin's zest for endorsing candidates she knew little or nothing about would also haunt her in the 2012 election cycle, in a comedy of errors that played out in three acts. I will do my best to re-create it for you.

Act I: Palin endorsed Richard Mourdock for the U.S. Senate seat in Indiana. So far, so good: Mourdock bested the incumbent Republican senator, Richard Lugar, in the party's primary.

Act II: In Missouri's Senate primary, Palin opted not to endorse Todd Akin, who went on to become the Republican nominee. Then, in an interview with a St. Louis television station, Akin, a longtime antiabortion activist, was asked whether women who become pregnant in cases of rape should be permitted to terminate such pregnancies. In a response that would add a new term to the political lexicon, Akin replied, "First of all, from what I understand from doctors, that's really rare. If it's a legitimate rape, the female body has ways to try to shut that whole thing down." Akin's "legitimate rape" comment, complete with its baffling attribution of sentience to the uterus, sparked widespread outrage—including from Palin, who urged him to quit the race. "This is not going in his favor, so you have to step aside from self, from yourself, your desire to get in there and serve and do what you believe is right, and you have to, in a sense, take one for the team," she said. "You have to step aside. Hand the mantle to someone else." Akin ignored the Alaskan interloper's advice to "step aside from self" and stayed in.

And, finally, Act III: Back in Indiana, Palin's handpicked candidate, Mourdock, appeared at a televised debate. Answering a question about abortion, Mourdock demonstrated not only his opposition to that procedure but also his apparent failure to learn anything from the Akin shit show: "I know there are some who disagree, and I respect their point of view, but I believe that life begins at conception. The only exception I have to have an abortion is in that case of the life of the mother. I just struggled with it myself for a long time, but I came to realize: life is that gift from God that I think, even if life begins in that horrible situation of rape, that it is something that God intended to happen." Faced with the daunting challenge of saying something more offensive than "legitimate rape," Mourdock seized the hold-my-beer moment. Palin, who'd exhorted Akin to "take one for the team," found herself in a pickle when it came to Mourdock's comments and, extraordinarily for her, remained silent. On Election Day, her endorsement of Mourdock was for naught: voters in Indiana, much like their counterparts in Missouri, decided that the Senate was better off without a pro-rape caucus.

Palin wasn't the only Tea Party champion whose endorsements

sometimes backfired. Senator Jim DeMint of South Carolina backed Sharron Angle and Christine O'Donnell; also like Palin, he had an original take on what might be called "matters of historical record." After leaving the Senate, in 2013, to become president of the conservative think tank the Heritage Foundation, he gave a radio interview in which he offered this fascinating account of how slavery ended in the U.S.: "Well, the reason that the slaves were eventually freed was the Constitution; it was like the conscience of the American people. . . . But a lot of the move to free the slaves came from the people; it did not come from the federal government. It came from a growing movement among the people, particularly people of faith, that this was wrong." DeMint's claim that the federal government played no role in freeing the slaves betrays, at the very least, a lack of familiarity with Ken Burns's oeuvre. The Heritage Foundation wound up ousting DeMint in 2017, apparently deciding that a think tank should be run by someone more experienced at thinking.

Though Palin would assemble a mixed record as a political endorser, in 2010 she scored a stunning victory in another role: word creator. Park51, a proposed Islamic community center in lower Manhattan, inspired an onslaught of outrage from right-wing critics, who, seizing on its proximity to the site of the 9/11 attacks, branded it the "Ground Zero Mosque." Palin, demonstrating her usual fear of missing out on any controversy that could help draw attention to herself, tweeted, "Ground Zero Mosque supporters: doesn't it stab you in the heart, as it does ours throughout the heartland? Peaceful Muslims, pls refudiate." Had America still been in the Ridicule stage, "refudiate" could have been her "potatoe"; instead, as befit an icon of Acceptance, Palin praised herself for inventing a new word, tweeting, "English is a living language. Shakespeare liked to coin new words too. Got to celebrate it!" The *New Oxford American Dictionary* seemed to share Palin's exultation when it named "refudiate" 2010's Word of the Year. The dictionary folks took some of the luster off her trophy, however, by stating, "Although Palin is likely to be forever branded with the coinage of 'refudiate,' she is by no means the first person to speak or write it—just as Warren G. Harding was not the first to use the word normalcy when he ran his 1920 presidential campaign under the slogan 'A return to normalcy.'" After likening herself to Shakespeare, Palin would have to settle for *Oxford*'s less grandiose but far more accurate comparison to one of the nation's most incompetent presidents.

As the 2012 presidential election cycle neared, speculation abounded that Palin might, after four years of Barack Obama, offer the nation a Return to Abnormalcy. Perhaps to signal that she was a new-and-improved Sarah Palin, vastly better informed than the one Katie Couric had eviscerated, she used a 2011 visit to a Revolutionary War site in Boston to retell the story of Paul Revere's Midnight Ride: "He warned the British that they weren't going be taking away our arms, by ringing those bells, and making sure as he's riding his horse through town to send those warning shots and bells that we were going to be secure and we were going to be free, and we were going to be armed." Millions of schoolchildren who had learned that Revere's mission was to warn the colonists that the British were, in fact, coming, were saddened to learn that Henry Wadsworth Longfellow had lied to them. Revere's actual mission, per Palin, was to warn the British to keep their hands off the colonists' guns, which made him an eighteenth-century antecedent of NRA activists like Charlton Heston. Another detail of Palin's account—the part about Revere "ringing those bells"—was of unknown origin.

Palin might have been inspired to flex her history muscles by the performance, a few months earlier, of her fellow mama grizzly, the Minnesota congresswoman Michele Bachmann. Eyeing a presidential run of her own, Bachmann had parachuted into the site of the first-in-the-nation primary, New Hampshire, where she proceeded to assign the Granite State a previously unknown role in the Revolutionary War: "You're the state where the shot was heard around the world at Lexington and Concord." The response to this praise was subdued, possibly because her audience, unlike the Minnesota congresswoman, knew that the towns she was referring to were located next door, in Massachusetts.

Bachmann could take comfort in knowing that this was far from the most ridiculous historical error she'd made recently. Weeks earlier, in Iowa, she stated that the Founding Fathers "worked tirelessly until slavery was no more in the United States." Since slavery wasn't "no more" until after the Emancipation Proclamation, apparently those guys didn't work tirelessly enough. Complicating their efforts, conceivably, was the fact that three of them, Washington, Jefferson, and Madison, were enslavers themselves. Bachmann later defended her statement, claiming that she'd been referring only to the abolitionism of the Founding Father John Quincy Adams. Eight years old when the Declaration of Independence was signed, Adams was at best a Founding Kid. In light of these utterances, it's perplexing that the conservative commentator Meghan McCain was moved to call Bachmann "the thinking man's Sarah Palin." Asked to explain her reasoning, McCain responded, "She's more smarter." *

Though Bachmann was clearly out of her depth when discussing historical figures in New England, she fared no better on her

---

* While ungrammatical, this comment suggests that the McCain family's assessment of Palin's brain power had declined somewhat since 2008, when Meghan's dad deemed her fit to be president.

home turf. Promoting her candidacy on Fox News, she boasted that she shared a birthplace, Waterloo, Iowa, with the legendary celluloid cowboy John Wayne. Embarrassingly, eagle-eyed fact-checkers realized that Bachmann had confused the birthplace of John Wayne with the onetime home of John Wayne Gacy, the serial killer who became known as the Killer Clown. On the plus side, she gave Gacy no credit whatsoever for signing the Declaration of Independence.

Bachmann's persistent confusion about names, dates, and places sometimes made you wonder if she'd accidentally downloaded a malicious version of Google. If elected president, she vowed, the U.S. would not have an embassy in Iran—not hard to accomplish, since it hadn't had one since Jimmy Carter's presidency. Speaking of Carter, she invoked his name while linking Obama to the 2009 swine flu epidemic: "I find it interesting that it was back in the 1970s that the swine flu broke out then under another Democrat president, Jimmy Carter. And I'm not blaming this on President Obama; I just think it's an interesting coincidence." It would have been an interesting coincidence, except that the epidemic she was referring to happened under a Republican, Gerald Ford. She warned of "the rise of the Soviet Union" in 2011, two decades after it fell. Blasting Obama once more, she said that he "put us in Libya. He is now putting us in Africa," seemingly unaware that, by putting us in Libya, he had already put us in Africa.

One of her more tangled retellings of history occurred on April 27, 2009, when she suggested that FDR caused the Great Depression by signing into law a tariff she called "Hoot Smalley." Actually, the tariff she had in mind was signed into law by FDR's predecessor, Herbert Hoover, and was called Smoot-Hawley. We should give Bachmann partial credit, I suppose, for not referring to the Great Depression as the Date Regression.

Even her attempts at bland pleasantries ran into a buzz saw of factuality. At a rally in Spartanburg, South Carolina, on August 16, 2011, she began by saying, "Before we get started, let's all say happy birthday to Elvis Presley today," prompting a helpful member of her audience to shout, "He died today!" It was, in fact, the anniversary of the King's death. When it came to Elvis knowledge, she was no Bill Clinton.

As the 2012 Republican presidential field took shape, Bachmann would face serious competition—not just for the nomination but for the title of Most Ludicrous. Briefly, the front-runner for both crowns was Rick Perry, the governor of Texas. During his 2010 reelection campaign, the Tea Party favorite had nabbed the endorsement of Palin, who gushed that he "sticks to his guns—and you know how I feel about guns!" (That you don't know how to fire them?) Though he had surpassed the record for most executions by a governor—set by his predecessor, Dubya—the only Texan Perry seemed bent on exterminating during the presidential race was himself. Debating in Michigan, he attempted to flaunt his Tea Party bona fides by listing the government agencies he would eliminate as president: "It's three agencies of government when I get there that are gone: Commerce, Education, and the, um . . . what's the third one there? Let's see," he said, pointing to his temple as if to dislodge his elusive third victim. At the podium to his left, another candidate, Ron Paul, tried to be helpful, but no doubt made things worse for the addled Perry by holding up five fingers and blurting, "You need five." After multiple failed attempts, the governor tried one last time to remember the final answer to his self-inflicted pop quiz: "The third agency of government I would, I would do away with, the Education, the uh, Commerce . . . and let's see . . . I can't. The third one, I can't. Sorry. Oops." Later that night, Perry would extinguish the suspense that had surely been killing the audience by revealing that the third doomed agency was the Department of Energy. Although he never got a chance to eliminate that department as president, he did the next best thing, serving as energy secretary under Donald J. Trump.*

Another prominent passenger in the 2012 clown car was the former U.S. senator Rick Santorum, of Pennsylvania, whose penchant for wearing sweater-vests somehow managed not to be his most mockable attribute. So extreme were Santorum's evangelical views that it sometimes seemed as though he were running not for president but for a slot in the Holy Trinity. In an interview with a Christian blog, he said, "One of the things I will talk about that no president has talked about before is I think the dangers of contraception in this country, the whole sexual libertine idea. Many in the Christian faith have said, 'Well, that's okay. Contraception's okay.' It's *not* okay because it's a license to do things in the sexual realm that is counter to how things are supposed to be." It didn't occur to Santorum that the reason no president had talked about this before was that whoever did would sound insane.

Santorum's opposition to sex grew even more strident if gay people were doing it. Pretty much everything about gay people outraged him, especially their appalling desire to get married. Speaking to a puny audience at a campaign event in an Iowa supermarket, he said, "I can call this napkin a paper towel. But it is a napkin. Why? Because it is what it is. Right? You can call it whatever you want, but it doesn't change the character of what it is. . . . So people come out and say marriage is something else—marriage is the marriage of five people; it can be five, ten, twenty. Marriage can be between fathers and daughters. Marriage can be between any two people, any four people, any ten people, it can be any kind of relationship and we can

---

*Astonishingly, the Michigan debate was not Perry's worst TV performance. After an interview with a reporter in 2005, he sarcastically signed off, "Adios, mofo," under the misimpression that the camera had stopped rolling.

call it marriage. But it doesn't make it marriage." His comparison between gay marriage and a napkin was actually far less offensive than this 2003 statement: "In every society, the definition of marriage has not ever to my knowledge included homosexuality. That's not to pick on homosexuality. It's not, you know, man on child, man on dog, or whatever the case may be. It is one thing." Though these comments weren't terribly persuasive, they did reveal Santorum as a man with a vivid fantasy life.

While Santorum never accused Obama of palling around with terrorists, he did level an equally serious charge against the sitting president: that he was plotting to send more Americans to college. "Oh, I understand why he wants you to go to college," he warned a Michigan audience. "He wants to remake you in his image." (Obama wants you to be educated like him—what a dick!) Santorum had already introduced this anti-getting-smarter theme four years earlier, when he said, "If you were Satan, who would you attack in this day and age? . . . The place where he was, in my mind, the most successful and first—first successful was in academia." Considering that colleges were such a cauldron of evil, it's astonishing that his Tea Party colleague Sarah Palin attended so many of them.

In this sea of ignoramuses, the eventual nominee, the former Massachusetts governor Mitt Romney, decided it would be a bright idea to act dim. At the 2012 Conservative Political Action Conference (CPAC), where he declared himself "severely conservative," he also pretended, in an equally unconvincing gambit, to be a poorly read rube. "There are college students at this conference who are reading Burke and Hayek," he said. "When I was your age, you could have told me they were infielders for the Detroit Tigers." In reality, Romney had graduated with the highest GPA in his class at Brigham Young University's College of Humanities, and went on to earn a combined JD-MBA at Harvard. And so we must salute Romney as an unsung innovator in the Age of Ignorance. His valiant attempt to shape-shift from valedictorian to numbskull would be aped by a horde of cynical Ivy League–educated Republicans a few years later, in the thick of the Celebration stage. His other key innovation— trying to bond with a group of African Americans by singing "Who Let the Dogs Out," complete with barking—has not yet caught on.

No review of the 2012 crop of bar-lowering dunces would be complete without the most ostentatious embodiment of the Acceptance stage of ignorance: Herman Cain, the former president of the other NRA (the National Restaurant Association). Cain's chief qualification for the presidency was his tenure as CEO of Godfather's Pizza, which, according to 2012 rankings by the trade publication *Pizza Today*, was the nation's number eleven pizza chain, edging out its archrival, Hungry Howie's Pizza & Subs. While this might not sound like the résumé of a future commander in chief, it was enough to catapult Cain to the top of the GOP field. (His ascent was later reversed by revelations of his prolific career in sexual harassment. Had he only waited until 2016 to run for president, of course, this would have been no big deal.)

Unlike George W. Bush, who struggled to name his favorite book, Cain had no such difficulty: it was *This Is Herman Cain! My Journey to the White House* by Herman Cain. Many suspected Cain's candidacy was just an elaborate scheme to pump up sales of said book, a theory that only gained traction after it emerged that he'd spent $36,511 in campaign funds on copies. As for books written by others, he didn't appear to have consumed too many. In an interview with the Christian Broadcasting Network (CBN), Cain demonstrated that he'd internalized the lessons of Bush's legendary pop quiz. When the CBN host, David Brody, asked, "Are you ready for the 'gotcha' questions that are coming from the media and others on foreign policy? Who's the president of Uzbekistan?" the former

Godfather's godfather replied, "I'm ready for the 'gotcha' questions, and they're already starting to come. And when they ask me who is the president of Ubeki-beki-beki-beki-stan-stan I'm going to say, you know, I don't know. Do you know? And then I'm going to say, How's that going to create one job?"

Given the state of the 2012 GOP field, the addition of Sarah Palin would have provided much needed gravitas. Indeed, there were Republicans who hoped that she would abandon her various money-spinning schemes and join the fray. One such supporter even made a pseudo-documentary, in 2011, to boost her prospects. In its inverted logic, the film's title couldn't have been more Palinesque: promoting a politician who, in her only run for national office, had been defeated, the movie was called *The Undefeated.* Seemingly the work of a high school filmmaker with limited funds and even more limited talent, it relies on Palin's first-person narration, lifted from the *Going Rogue* audiobook, as well as a hilariously literal use of cheesy stock footage. If someone talks about people burning through money, the filmmaker seems to have no choice but to mash up a shot of matches being lit and a shot of stacks of money. Ultimately, *The Undefeated* was defeated at the box office: while it cost a reported million dollars to produce—all that stock footage was apparently more expensive than it looked—in its initial release it took in a measly $116,381, significantly less than the Republican National Committee paid in 2008 for the VP nominee's wardrobe. More important, the film's underwhelming box office performance failed to persuade Palin to throw her fur-lined hat in the ring.

Sadly, the auteur behind *The Undefeated* joined the long list of people Sarah Barracuda had quit on, including a boatload of college faculties and the entire population of Alaska. He would have to wait until 2016 to find his perfect presidential candidate. The name of this filmmaker was Steve Bannon.

3

THE THIRD STAGE: CELEBRATION

We have reached the final leg of our journey. Before we continue, let's review the first two stages of ignorance. In the first stage, Ridicule, dumb politicians had to pretend to be smart. In the second stage, Acceptance, dumb politicians felt free to seem dumb.

Today, in the third stage, Celebration, smart politicians must pretend to be dumb. For the undisputed icon of this stage, however, no pretense is necessary.

Before we tackle the dire subject of Donald J. Trump's political career, we must pay homage to all the ignoramuses we've explored so far. Had they not danced the limbo under an ever-descending bar, Trump's presidency would have been unthinkable. Thanks to them, it was inevitable.

In his ignorance, though, Trump has lapped all his clueless forebears. Sarah Palin might have had a hate-hate relationship with American history, but only Trump could refer to 9/11 as "7-Eleven." Despite such evidence, there's still some debate about whether Trump is dumb or smart. On one side are people with firsthand knowledge of Trump. On the other is Trump.

"I'm intelligent," he told *Fortune* in 2000. "Some people would say I'm very, very, very intelligent." Trump credited his Ivy League education with helping him achieve his triple-very intelligence. "I went to the Wharton School of Finance," he said in 2004. "I got very good marks. I was a good student. It's the best business school in the world, as far as I'm concerned." As Peter Dreier observed in the *Los Angeles Times*, Trump grew more emphatic in 2011, upgrading himself from a good student to a really good student, and upgrading Wharton's status as well: "Let me tell you, I'm a really smart guy. I was a really good student at the best school in the country." Fearing we'd forgotten where he went to school and what that indicated about his intelligence, he was back to remind us in 2015. "I went to the Wharton School of Finance," he said. "I'm, like, a really smart person." By then, Wharton had become not only the best school in the country, but "probably the hardest school to get into."* He had also developed a theory for why people hadn't given him credit for his prodigious brainpower: "Look, if I were a liberal Democrat, people would say I'm the super genius of all time. The super genius of all time."

His belief in his own super-genius status inspired this tweet, in 2013: "Sorry losers and haters, but my IQ is one of the highest—and you all know it! Please don't feel so stupid or insecure, it's not your fault." Four years later, he was frustrated that people still hadn't realized how smart he was, despite someone's frequent reminders: "You know, people don't understand. I went to an Ivy League college. I was a nice student. I did very well. I'm a very intelligent person." He

---

*Given the gargantuan proportions of Trump's mendacity, this is a small point, but Trump didn't attend Wharton's highly selective and revered graduate school of business. He attended Wharton's undergraduate business program, which is far easier to get into and not as prestigious. Shockingly, he hasn't gone to great lengths to clarify this distinction.

might have persuaded his doubters about his academic achievements if he'd instructed the schools he attended to release his nice transcripts, but he did the opposite. According to the sworn testimony of his former lawyer Michael Cohen, "[He] directed me to threaten his high school, his colleges and the College Board to never release his grades or SAT scores." Maybe he feared that, confronted with his sky-high GPA and scores, we losers and haters would feel stupid and insecure.

Being as smart as Donald J. Trump turns out to be a lonely business. When he ran for president in 2016, he discovered that there was only one expert he could count on to give him foreign policy advice: Donald J. Trump. "I'm speaking with myself, number one, because I have a very good brain and I've said a lot of things," he said on MSNBC's *Morning Joe*, accurately crediting himself with saying a lot of things. "I know what I'm doing, and I listen to a lot of people, I talk to a lot of people, and at the appropriate time I'll tell you who the people are. But my primary consultant is myself, and I have a good instinct for this stuff." And what did his primary consultant tell him? That it would be a mistake to listen to the military's advice about the terrorist group ISIS—because, as he noted, "I know more about ISIS than the generals do." Little did most Americans realize that Trump had been a foreign policy expert for decades. In 1984, he told the *Washington Post* that Ronald Reagan should let him take over arms negotiations with the Soviets: "It would take an hour-and-a-half to learn everything there is to learn about missiles. . . . I think I know most of it anyway." Reagan declined this generous offer, preferring the advice of an astrologer.

By his own account, Trump was an expert in an astounding number of fields. "I know more about courts than any human being on Earth," he said in 2015; not wishing to be typecast as a judicial wonk, he added, six months later, "I know more about renewables than any human being on Earth." It would be extraordinary, to say the least, for an expert in both courts and renewables to know a lot about the tax code, but, according to Trump, "I think nobody knows more about taxes than I do, maybe in the history of the world." As for technology, look out, Elon Musk: "Technology—nobody knows more about technology than me." As for Senator Cory Booker, look out, Senator Cory Booker: "I know more about Cory than he knows about himself." Of Trump's many claims to expertise, though, one might well be true: "Nobody knows debt better than me."

Now that we've reviewed Trump's vigorous, if somewhat repetitious, case for how much he knows, let's explore the opposing view, from people who observed the super-genius workings of his Wharton-educated brain up close. His former national security adviser John Bolton called him "stunningly uninformed." I'm starting with Bolton's comment because, of all the assessments made by members of Trump's inner circle about his mind, it was by far the most flattering. His adviser Sam Nunberg called him an "idiot"; his treasury secretary, Steve Mnuchin, and two of his chiefs of staff, Reince Priebus and John Kelly, reportedly did as well. Somewhat more precisely, H. R. McMaster, the national security adviser who preceded Bolton, allegedly said that Trump had the intelligence of a "kindergartner." More generously, his defense secretary James Mattis purportedly said that he had the comprehension of "a fifth- or sixth-grader." Declining to assign him to a specific grade, his first secretary of state, Rex Tillerson, called him "a fucking moron."

All this is starting to sound a little mean. Isn't there anyone who has something *nice* to say about Trump's intelligence? How about Rupert Murdoch? Surely . . . Oh. Actually, Murdoch called him a "fucking idiot."

So: on the subject of Trump's knowledge, there appears to be a stark difference of opinion between Trump and people who aren't

Trump. To resolve this debate, let's ask a version of my favorite question: What does Donald Trump know?

Let's start with his language skills. According to the Flesch-Kincaid grade-level test, commissioned by the U.S. Navy in 1975 to determine the readability of training manuals, Trump speaks at a fourth-grade level—lower than the fifteen most recent presidents. Contradicting Trump's famous self-assessment on the 2016 campaign trail—"I know words. I have the best words"—he doesn't use many different ones. According to the website Factba.se, which ran a statistical analysis of Trump's utterances, he has only 2,605 unique words in his vocabulary, which, again, is the lowest among recent White House occupants. (By comparison, Barack Obama ranked first with 3,869, a feat that's especially impressive if, as Trump so often claimed, he wasn't even born here.)

Though it's questionable whether Trump has the best words, he definitely has the shortest: with an average length of 1.33 syllables, his words are tinier than those of all the most recent commanders in chief—an astonishing accomplishment when you consider that this list includes George W. Bush. "By every metric and methodology tested, Donald Trump's vocabulary and grammatical structure is significantly more simple, and less diverse, than any President since Herbert Hoover," stated Bill Frischling, the CEO and founder of Factba.se. "The gap between Trump and the next closest president . . . is larger than any other gap using Flesch-Kincaid. Statistically speaking, there is a significant gap."

Let's move on to spelling. Trump's misspellings in office were so abundant that it's daunting to quantify them; fortunately, the masochists at Factba.se did just that. They determined that, as of November 2019, he misspelled a word every five days on Twitter (back when he was still allowed on Twitter). Given his less-than-robust understanding of foreign countries, it was no surprise that he referred to

Prince Charles as the "Prince of Whales"; considering that he was the leader of the Republicans, however, it was weird that he called them "Rupublicans," though that would be a superb name for members of a party founded by RuPaul. He boasted about serving the Clemson football team "hamberders." He called Senator Marco Rubio a "leightweight chocker." In the tradition of Ronald Reagan, who failed to recognize his own son, he misspelled his wife's name, Melania, as "Melanie." The list goes on: *shoebiz, honer, hearby, smocking*, and his most Freudian misspelling of all, *unpresidented*. His favorite words—the monosyllabic kind—offered no safer harbor, as his misspellings of *role, heal, wait, waste*, and *tap* demonstrated. Even more puzzling, he misspelled two words he should've mastered because of their recurring role in his grievances: he typed "lose" and "unfair" as "loose" and "infair." To give you a sense of how much our politicians' literacy has declined, Trump's transcription of Dan Quayle's most famous quotation would read "What a waist it is to loose one's mind."

Now let's explore his unorthodox approach to capitalizing letters. His use of ALL CAPS in his tweets is defensible, I suppose, in the way it would be defensible in a manifesto recovered from a survivalist's mountainside shack. But his habit of randomly capitalizing the first letter of words—"Crime," "Rigged," "Fake," "News"—follows no discernible pattern, unless Trump has been paying homage to the capitalization practices of the eighteenth century. That scenario is unlikely, because, as we'll soon see, that was a historical period he found Very Confusing. As for Trump's use of punctuation, that subject is too broad to be addressed in a book of this length and should be reserved for a doctoral dissertation.*

Reading is a good way to improve your punctuation, not to mention your capitalization and spelling; it's also, as we've seen, an

---

* For starters, he believes an apostrophe is called a hyphen.

indicator of your intellectual curiosity. Trump's reading appears to be as frequent as his attendance at church and the gym. When the Fox News host Megyn Kelly asked him, in 2016, to name the last book he'd read, he replied, "I read passages, I read areas, I read chapters— I don't have the time." Tony Schwartz, the ghostwriter of his image-forging 1987 best seller, *Trump: The Art of the Deal*, told the *New Yorker's* Jane Mayer, "I seriously doubt that Trump has ever read a book straight through in his adult life." As Mayer reported, "Schwartz believes that Trump's short attention span has left him with 'a stunning level of superficial knowledge and plain ignorance.'. . . During the eighteen months that he observed Trump, Schwartz said, he never saw a book on Trump's desk, or elsewhere in his office, or in his apartment." There is, however, one book reportedly in his possession, according to his ex-wife Ivana: he kept a collection of Hitler's speeches, titled *My New Order*, at his bedside. His own oratory suggests that he might have dipped into that one from time to time.

Trump's aversion to reading the work of non–Third Reich authors posed a challenge to those at the White House charged with keeping him semi-informed. According to an email attributed to his chief economic adviser, Gary Cohn, "It's worse than you can imagine. . . . Trump won't read anything—not one-page memos, not the brief policy papers; nothing. He gets up halfway through meetings with world leaders because he is bored."* To brief a man with such a severe case of book hesitancy, his aides resorted to a throwback from the Reagan era, putting on shows featuring graphs, maps, photos, and other word-free visual aids. After noticing that Trump was more likely to read material that mentioned his name, National Security Council staffers tried to trick him into finishing memos by

---

* In 2019, it was reported that Cohn was writing a memoir covering his tenure under Trump, which, one hopes, will be called *It's Worse Than You Can Imagine.*

crowbarring "Trump" into as many paragraphs as possible. "I like bullets or I like as little as possible," Trump told Axios. "I don't need, you know, 200-page reports on something that can be handled on a page." Given that George W. Bush recoiled at the idea of reading a five-hundred-page book, if you do the math, Trump is 60 percent less tolerant of reading than Dubya.

While we're on the subject of math, what does Trump know about that? Since he's spent half a century in the business world, you might expect him to be good with numbers; since he had to file for bankruptcy six times, maybe not. This gaping hole revealed itself in worrisome fashion during an appearance in 2006 with his daughter, Ivanka, and son Don Jr., on Howard Stern's radio show. After asking the younger Don whether he had attended Wharton, Stern issued this follow-up: "What's seventeen times six?" Stumped by this brainteaser, Don Jr. guessed 96 and 94, both incorrect. With Ivanka offering her brother no lifeline, it fell to Dad to save the day. He confidently answered "Eleven-twelve," meaning 1,112. He was off by a mere 1,010. The correct answer is 102.

Trump's math skills seemed to deteriorate from there. After boasting, in 2020, "I know South Korea better than anybody," he declared that Seoul had a population of 38 million, overshooting the correct answer by 28 million. His biggest math mistake, though, was one he made in his first budget, in 2017. That goof, which wasn't exactly a rounding error, totaled $2 trillion. To put this number in perspective, for $2 trillion George W. Bush could have launched a second entirely pointless war in Iraq.

Moving from math to science, Trump shares the skeptical views of his fellow climatologists Ron Johnson and Sharron Angle about something he called, on Twitter, "global waming." Offering a novel theory, he claimed that climate change was "created by and for the Chinese in order to make US manufacturing non-competitive." Instead of worrying about that hoax, however, he urged his followers to focus on a more pressing danger: killer lightbulbs. "Remember, new 'environment friendly' lightbulbs can cause cancer," he tweeted in 2012. "Be careful—the idiots who came up with this stuff don't care." According to Trump, there's nothing more lethal than lightbulbs—with the possible exception of wind farms. "Not only are wind farms disgusting looking, but even worse they are bad for people's health," he tweeted, again in 2012. "The fumes coming up to make these massive windmills is more than anything that we're talking about with natural gas," he later claimed. I'd ask him to produce some numbers to back that up, but, as we've seen, when Trump wanders into the land of numbers, it never ends well. The news about wind turbines was no better in 2019, when Trump hinted darkly, "[T]hey say the noise causes cancer." (Wait, that's lightbulbs' job!) You'd think giving us cancer would satisfy wind power's appetite for destruction, but no. During the same 2020 presidential debate where Trump talked about the "fumes" associated with wind farms, he alleged that the turbines "kills [*sic*] all the birds." The U.S. Fish and Wildlife Service disagreed, stating that the number one threat to birds is cats.

Trump's ignorance about science was on magnificent display at the White House Coronavirus Task Force briefing of April 23, 2020. (Note to any alien scientists in the future who might be reading this book while sifting through the rubble of our civilization: I must stress that this actually happened.) Bill Bryan, the head of the Department of Homeland Security's science and technology division, had just made the seemingly innocuous remark that "the virus dies the quickest in the presence of direct sunlight." This was Trump's cue to offer some intriguing scientific hypotheses. "So supposing we hit the body with a tremendous—whether it's ultraviolet or just very powerful light—and I think you said that hasn't been checked, but you're going to test it," he said, apparently referring to an earlier conversation with Bryan that the official must have found traumatic. "And then I said, supposing you brought the light inside the body, which you can do either through the skin or in some other way, and I think you said you're going to test that, too." Clearly, all this talk of "testing" Trump's deranged idea had been Bryan's desperate gambit to humor him, but it appeared to have had the opposite effect, inspiring him to shoot for a Nobel in medicine. "I see the disinfectant that knocks it out in a minute, one minute," he continued. "And is there a way we can do something like that by injection inside, or almost a cleaning? As you see, it gets in the lungs, it does a tremendous number on the lungs, so it would be interesting to check that."

Checking what would happen if you injected disinfectant into the body, though interesting, would most likely be the job of a coroner. Trump's miracle cure for COVID impelled Reckitt Benckiser, the manufacturer of Lysol, to issue this urgent statement: "As a global leader in health and hygiene products, we must be clear that under no circumstance should our disinfectant products be administered into the human body (through injection, ingestion or any other route)." Despite this warning, some Americans followed Dr. Trump's medical advice. According to the *Wichita Eagle*, in the aftermath of Trump's comments, "the Kansas Poison Control Center reported a more than 40 percent increase in cleaning chemical cases." Fortunately, there were no reported incidents of people trying to swallow flashlights.

Trump might have thought his ingenious medical theories would improve how history remembered his handling of the worst pandemic since 1918—or, as he insisted on calling it, the worst pandemic since 1917. "The closest thing is in 1917, they say, the great pandemic," he said. "It certainly was a terrible thing where they lost anywhere from 50 to 100 million people, probably ended the Second World War." Probably not: the pandemic was over by 1920, and the Second World War didn't begin until 1939.

When it comes to history, Trump's most common errors involve (1) when events happened, and (2) what happened. On only his twelfth day as president, during a breakfast to kick off Black History Month, Trump gave Americans a sense that they hadn't elected Robert Caro. Like Ronald Reagan, he had named only one Black person to his cabinet, Ben Carson, and gave him the same job that Reagan gave his solitary Black cabinet member, secretary of housing and urban development. With Carson at his side, he said, "Frederick Douglass is an example of somebody who's done an amazing job and is being recognized more and more, I notice." Given what an amazing job Fred is doing these days, it seemed a glaring omission that Trump hadn't invited him to the breakfast.

Three months later, when Trump spoke about the president he claimed was his favorite, Andrew Jackson, he revealed confusion about when Jackson was alive. "He was really angry that—he saw what was happening with regard to the Civil War," Trump said of Old Hickory, who, for sixteen years before the Civil War began, had been Dead Hickory. Trump's most surreal mash-up of historical periods, however, occurred during a Fourth of July speech in 2019, when he offered this time-bending narrative of the Revolutionary War: "Our army manned the air, it rammed the ramparts, it took over the airports, it did everything it had to do, and at Fort McHenry, under the rockets' red glare, it had nothing but victory." People were so distracted by the image of eighteenth-century airports—did they have Sbarro back then, too?—that most overlooked the fact that the battle of Fort McHenry occurred during the War of 1812.

Like Ronald Reagan, Trump sometimes placed himself at the center of events in which he'd played no role, or which never happened at all. He claimed repeatedly that he'd been named Michigan's Man of the Year; no such award exists. On more than 150 occasions he took credit for signing a health-care law called Veterans Choice. Such a law does exist, but it was signed, in 2014, by Barack Obama.

Just as Trump supported moving the American embassy in Israel from Tel Aviv to Jerusalem, he seemed to agree with Michele Bachmann that the birthplace of the American Revolution should be relocated from Concord, Massachusetts, to Concord, New Hampshire. "You know how famous Concord is? Concord—that's the same Concord that we read about all the time, right? Concord," he informed members of a Granite State audience—who, having been told by yet another politician that their home was the site of the shot heard 'round the world, might have been starting to believe it. Trump's ignorance of geography, however, makes Bachmann look like Google Maps. "After I had won, everybody was calling me from all over the world," he said in 2017. "I never knew we had so many countries." That's not all he didn't know. He didn't know the difference between England and Great Britain. He didn't know that the Republic of Ireland wasn't part of the UK. As for non-geographical facts about the country whose airports we seized in the 1700s, he didn't know that Britain possessed nuclear weapons, nor did his White House know how to spell the first name of Prime Minister Theresa May. Trump staffers misspelled it "Teresa" three times before someone must have checked Wikipedia.

Trump thought Colorado bordered Mexico. He thought Finland was a part of Russia, and that Belgium is a city. He pronounced Namibia "Nambia" and called Thailand "Thighland," as if it were a strip club. He thought Nepal and Bhutan were parts of India, and called them "Nipple" and "Button." His confusion about India ran a bit deeper; before a 2017 White House visit by Prime Minister Narendra Modi, Trump asked a staffer whether the Indian leader's wife would be joining him on the trip. After being told that Modi and his wife were estranged, Trump responded, "Ah, I think I can set him up with somebody." (Maybe "Teresa"?) He was less friendly during a 2018 meeting with the leaders of Latvia, Estonia, and Lithuania, whom he accused of starting the wars in the Balkans during the 1990s; it eventually dawned on the perplexed trio that he'd confused the Balkans with the Baltics. This mix-up suggested that Trump hadn't engaged in long geopolitical discussions with his Balkan wife, "Melanie."

Having reviewed Trump's ignorance about spelling, reading, math, science, history, and geography, we should wrap up this investigation by considering his grasp of religion. As we saw, George W. Bush set the bar low on this subject by failing to realize that Sunnis and Shiites are Muslims. Trump outdid him. In a 2017 meeting with two Presbyterian pastors, he seemed confused about whether Presbyterians were Christians. Incidentally, he was raised Presbyterian.

Now that we've answered the question "What does Donald Trump know?," let's ask another question, one that Sarah Palin raised so insightfully: "Does any of this really matter?" To millions of his supporters, the answer is no. To them, Trump is successful, smart, and well-informed. In his 1977 interview with David Frost, Richard M. Nixon made his notorious declaration about the legality of a president's actions: "When the president does it, that means that it is not illegal." Trump's followers apply a similar rule to his behavior: When Trump does it, that means that it is not idiotic. Regardless of what he says or does, Trump is right, and the media, always doing a "hit job" on him, are wrong.

Trump's appeal comes into clearer focus if you think of him as a personality from professional wrestling—which, of course, he is. Trump's 2007 face-off with Vince McMahon, the CEO of World Wrestling Entertainment, at *WrestleMania 23* was as essential to his political rise as Abraham Lincoln's 1858 throwdown with Stephen

Douglas. In his book *Empire of Illusion: The End of Literacy and the Triumph of Spectacle*, Chris Hedges analyzes this arena in which Trump thrived. "The success of professional wrestling, like most of the entertainment that envelops our culture, lies not in fooling us that these stories are real," he writes. "Rather, it succeeds because we ask to be fooled. We happily pay for the chance to suspend reality. The wrestlers, like all celebrities, become our vicarious selves. They do what we cannot."

When Trump was elected, many bemoaned our celebrity-obsessed culture, but our obsession with fame, like our anti-intellectualism, is nothing new. Americans have always liked electing famous people, from George Washington to Ulysses S. Grant to Dwight D. Eisenhower. Those celebrities, however, became famous through substantial achievements: winning our independence from Britain, preserving the Union, and saving the world from fascism. Trump became a celebrity in spite of an almost uninterrupted string of failures: six bankruptcies, a laughable football team, a fraudulent university, and a board game no one wanted to play. Once a wrestler steps into the ring, the audience asks to be fooled. But how did someone as blundering as Donald Trump ever get into the ring? His fame has been with us for so long that it's become one of life's certainties, like death and hiding taxes. But how did a guy who's so bad at so much become so famous?

The clinical psychologists Robert Brooks and Sam Goldstein give us a useful framework for understanding Trump's rise to fame. To encourage patients who are beset by a sense of inadequacy, Brooks and Goldstein encourage them to focus not on their deficits but on their "islands of competence": the isolated talents they possess and can build upon. In a vast ocean of ignorance and failure, Donald Trump does indeed have an island of competence, and it has taken him far: a preternatural talent for drawing attention to himself. He captivates by bragging, bullying, and, like Ronald Reagan, telling stories of questionable veracity. His genius for attention-grabbing has proven adaptable, serving him in his multifarious career as a New York tabloid star, TV juggernaut, and internet troll. But, gifted as Trump is, he couldn't have become famous on his own. His unquenchable thirst for the spotlight found a perfect match in the media's ravenous appetite for stories. Trump's fame exploded after 1980, when the first twenty-four-hour news channel, CNN, debuted. Every time his career threatened to flatline, the media were his most dependable defibrillators. He might call the press "the enemy of the people," but for decades it was Donald Trump's best friend.

Like J. Danforth Quayle and George W. Bush, Donald John Trump was born into a third generation of family wealth. His grandfather Friedrich Trump struck it rich during the Klondike Gold Rush not by mining gold but by "mining the miners," in the words of Trump family historian Gwenda Blair. After thousands of would-be prospectors abandoned their worn-out steeds on a treacherous mountain pass aptly named Dead Horse Gulch, Friedrich saw his big chance to break into the restaurant industry. In a forerunner of Trump Steaks, he repurposed the horseflesh as tasty entrées for famished Gold Rushers, thus launching a portfolio of businesses that soon included a highly regarded Arctic brothel. Inheriting the commercial savvy that enabled Friedrich to sell quarter-pound horseberders, his son Fred created a thriving real estate business in New York, building thousands of apartments and refusing to rent them to Black applicants. "My father taught me everything I know," Donald later said.

As a child, Donald Trump displayed both an all-consuming need for attention and an impressive knack for getting it. If you invited him to a birthday party, he'd show his gratitude by throwing cake. At Kew-Forest, the elementary school he attended in Queens, the faculty members he hurled erasers at were the lucky ones; he punched one second-grade teacher in the eye. "I punched my music teacher because I didn't think he knew anything about music," he recounts in *The Art of the Deal.* "Even early on I had a tendency to stand up and make my opinions known in a very forceful way." Not surprisingly, his father decided to dispatch this irrepressible rapscallion to military school. At the New York Military Academy, Donald continued to study the art of bullying. He tormented one of the most diminutive students there, his four-foot-eleven, 120-pound roommate; he even tried to push the cadet out a second-story window. Reflecting on his youthful antics, Trump observed, "When I look at myself in the first grade and I look at myself now, I'm basically the same."

An indifferent student, he got his real education at home. Fred taught him that life was a zero-sum game, with only "killers" and "losers." He provided his son with a chauffeured car to do his paper route, telling him, "You're a king." Thus, he instilled in Donald a deep and abiding respect for democratic norms.

Upon graduation from NYMA, Trump attended college at Fordham, in the Bronx; two years later, he transferred to the undergraduate business program at the University of Pennsylvania. Like Dan Quayle's improbably successful application to the Indiana University School of Law, Trump's admission to Penn was generously lubricated by his family. As his niece Mary Trump reveals in her book *Too Much and Never Enough: How My Family Created the World's Most Dangerous Man,* his older sister, Maryanne, had been doing his homework for him while he was at Fordham, and his brother, Freddy, reached out to a friend in the Penn admissions office. Even with those advantages, "Donald worried that his grade point average, which put him far from the top of his class, would scuttle his efforts to get accepted. To hedge his bets he enlisted Joe Shapiro, a smart kid with a reputation for being a good test taker, to take his SATs for him." It took a village.

Determined to remain on the right side of the killer/loser divide, Donald repaid his brother's help with the Penn admissions office by supplanting him as heir apparent to their father's real estate business. (Freddy, sent off like a failed contestant on *The Apprentice*, would die of alcoholism at forty-two.) Donald's career as his father's junior partner got off to an inauspicious but telling start. In 1973, the U.S. Department of Justice sued Trump Management for discriminating against prospective Black tenants, naming both Trumps as codefendants. "Major Landlord Accused of Antiblack Bias in City," read the headline heralding Donald J. Trump's first appearance on page one of the *New York Times*. Countersuing, the Trumps unleashed their lawyer, Roy Cohn, the disgraced (and, eventually, disbarred) former aide to Senator Joseph McCarthy. Cohn also served as Ronald Reagan's political fixer, and his legal argument was Reaganesque in its disingenuous denial of racism: he advanced the Trumps' claim that they were discriminating not against Blacks but against undesirable "welfare recipients." It's hard to see how said recipients could have hurt the value of the Trump properties if, as Reagan was fond of alleging, they drove Cadillacs and lived like royalty. A judge dismissed the Trumps' countersuit.

Three years later, the *Times* rewarded the young Trump with a glowing and not-very-fact-checked profile. "He is tall, lean and blond, with dazzling white teeth, and he looks ever so much like Robert Redford," wrote Judy Klemesrud, setting the tone for the searing investigative journalism to follow. Klemesrud's credulous account yields too many howlers to mention, but here's an especially wonderful one: "Mr. Trump, who says he is publicity shy, allowed a reporter to accompany him on what he described as a typical work day." (What rare access, Judy!) Amazed that he is to receive an award from a Jewish group, the publicity-shy Trump notes, "I'm not even Jewish, I'm Swedish." (He's neither.) The article also states that he was "a student at the Wharton School of Finance at the University of Pennsylvania, from which he graduated first in his class in 1968." A 1984 *Times* article belatedly corrected this whopper: "Although the school refused comment, the commencement program from 1968 does not list him as graduating with honors of any kind."

My point in reviewing Trump's lie about his Wharton superstardom isn't to quibble about his college performance, since, again, a politician's GPA doesn't tell us much. My point is that, as early as 1976, Trump's island of competence was already a force to be reckoned with: he easily turned a reporter from America's paper of record into a co-creator of his own myth.

Nine years later, he met his most valuable collaborator in that project: Schwartz, the ghostwriter behind *The Art of the Deal*. It's impossible to overstate the importance of this book in establishing the mythical image of Donald Trump as well-informed, successful, and whip-smart. Not only did the best seller bring Trump the fame he craved, it provided the template for *The Apprentice*, which led to Trump's election as president. *The Art of the Deal* must be considered the founding document of the Celebration stage of ignorance.

Schwartz did far more than ghostwrite *The Art of the Deal*: he came up with the book's entire premise and title. (Trump did pose for the soft-focus cover photo.)* As Schwartz tried to gather material by interviewing his subject, Trump's microscopic attention span astounded him. Trump, Schwartz later recalled, was "like a kindergartner who can't sit still in a classroom." Jane Mayer reported in

---

* In the 2020 docuseries *Empires of New York*, Schwartz summarized his and Trump's contributions to *The Art of the Deal*: "I wrote the book, and, miraculously, he read the book."

her 2016 profile of Schwartz that the ghostwriter "regards Trump's inability to concentrate as alarming in a Presidential candidate. 'If he had to be briefed on a crisis in the Situation Room, it's impossible to imagine him paying attention over a long period of time.' " As for the flattering portrayal of Trump in *The Art of the Deal*, Schwartz said, "I created a character far more winning than Trump actually is." After spending a day watching Trump in action, the writer would tell his wife, "He's a living black hole!" According to Mayer, "Schwartz's aim in 'The Art of the Deal' was to present Trump as the hero of every chapter, but, after looking into some of his supposedly brilliant deals, Schwartz concluded that there were cases in which there was no way to make Trump look good. So he sidestepped unflattering incidents and details. 'I didn't consider it my job to investigate,' he says."

One of the more peculiar passages in *The Art of the Deal* disparages an institution that Trump would later invoke as proof of his high intelligence: Wharton. "Perhaps the most important thing I learned at Wharton was not to be overly impressed by academic credentials," Trump/Schwartz writes. "It didn't take me long to realize that there was nothing particularly awesome or exceptional about my classmates, and that I could compete just fine. The other important thing I got from Wharton was a Wharton degree. In my opinion, that degree doesn't prove much, but a lot of people I do business with take it very seriously." These sentiments seem oddly dismissive from someone who insists he graduated first in his class.

For anyone interested in a book that translates *The Art of the Deal* into reality, in 2020 Barbara Res, a construction supervisor who rose to the rank of executive vice president of the Trump Organization, published *Tower of Lies: What My Eighteen Years of Working with Donald Trump Reveals About Him*. Res describes "his lack of concentration, his penchant for diverting big decisions to other people, his collecting of ass-kissers, his mood swings, his ignorance—even in areas of his 'genius,' like construction and finance and real estate." She defines "the Trump way" as "a mix of the nefarious and the ignorant." As for his skills as a self-styled master builder, Res states, "Trump didn't know much about construction (he once said only a masochist could enjoy it) and even less about renovation."

A particularly embarrassing story involves Trump's refusal to do his homework, a tendency that would later make him impervious to his cabinet's desperate attempts to brief him. In the early 1990s, Trump was hoping to demolish the Ambassador Hotel in Los Angeles to make way for an office tower, but he faced opposition from local activists, as well as the LA Unified School District (LAUSD). As the dispute headed to court, Res begged her boss to prepare for his deposition, but Trump, demonstrating his long-standing aversion to learning, participated in only one half-hearted prep session. When it came time to be deposed, Trump was hilariously inept. "I sat next to Donald as the LAUSD lawyer questioned him across the table," Res remembers. "When he asked Trump a question about our lead condemnation lawyer, whose last name was Bitting, Trump replied angrily, 'There was no bidding. We never even got to do a design.' His statement hung in the air; Trump clearly did not have a clue and wasn't even following the questions. He didn't know Bitting was the name of our lawyer, although we'd told him many times, including the previous day."

To drum up publicity for *The Art of the Deal*, Trump employed a promotional strategy later revived by the author of *This Is Herman Cain!*: he pretended to run for president. Trump's friend Roger Stone, who had worked for Nixon and Reagan, scheduled a speech for Trump in Portsmouth, New Hampshire. On October 22, 1987, Trump helicoptered into Portsmouth and drew a capacity crowd at a restaurant called Yoken's. The *New York Times*, which had teased the trip in September with a story titled "Trump Gives a Vague Hint of Candidacy," was on hand to offer its latest breathless account of the developer's exploits, under the headline "New Hampshire Speech Earns Praise for Trump."

Just as the right-wing tentpoles of "The Speech," Reagan's 1964 address, would recur in his oratory for decades, the grievance-filled rant that Trump delivered at Yoken's would be recognizable to anyone who saw him announce his candidacy at Trump Tower in 2015. Trump blamed the country's problems on Japan, Saudi Arabia, and Kuwait, much as he would later assail Japan, Mexico, and China. And he workshopped an early version of his plan to build a great wall and get Mexico to pay for it: he told his Portsmouth audience that he would get those three cheapskate nations to pay off the entire U.S. budget deficit of $200 billion. In 1987, as in 2015, the means by which he would compel foreign governments to cough up billions remained mysterious, but both proposals were crowd-pleasers.

One month later, Trump appeared on Phil Donahue's TV talk show and continued attacking his very own Axis of Evil. "We have countries out there that are our so-called allies, and I use the word 'so-called' because they're a disaster for this country, Japan, Saudi Arabia, Kuwait," he said. Trump's bellicose performance earned him gushing praise from a former commander in chief. "I did not see the program, but Mrs. Nixon told me you were great," read the type-written letter. "As you can imagine, she is an expert on politics and she predicts that whenever you decide to run for office, you will be a winner!"

Receiving fan mail from the only U.S. president to have resigned in disgrace seemed to inflame Trump's political ambitions. After George H. W. Bush wrapped up the 1988 GOP nomination, Trump reached out to Roger Stone's business partner, Lee Atwater, who, as you might remember from the account of his classy Willie Horton strategy, was managing the Bush campaign. The cover boy of *The Art of the Deal* wanted Atwater to know that he'd be available for consideration as Bush's running mate. Bush seemed to find the art of this particular deal wanting; he described Trump's suggestion as "strange and unbelievable."

In Trump's defense, he checked many of the same boxes as the strange and unbelievable person Bush chose as his VP, Dan Quayle. The two men were roughly the same age, from the same generation of family wealth, and allegedly indistinguishable from the same blond movie star. In yet another eerie parallel, they both used family connections to get into college and out of Vietnam. Given these similarities, it's worth imagining the counterfactual history that would have unfolded had Bush chosen Trump over Quayle. In those more innocent days, bad spelling still had the power to end a political career. So many lives would've been saved.

Showing no hard feelings about being snubbed as Bush's VP, Trump popped up at the 1988 Republican National Convention. Once again, his island of competence was in full effect: famous for a book he hadn't written (but had purchased in bulk to cement its best-seller status), he attracted the adoration of the national media. "He's young, he has Robert Redford good looks, he's conservative, and he's rich," CNN's Mary Alice Williams raved before he sat for an interview with Larry King. On the subject of Quayle, who had already bombed his first press conference and was headed for worse, Trump said, "He's a very impressive guy." Asked if he would have agreed to serve as Bush's VP, Trump, responding with typical factuality, said, "I probably would not have done it. I really love what I am doing."

So, what was he doing? During the late 1980s, he started using a new, if pricey, strategy to draw attention to himself: taking out full-page ads in major newspapers to sound off on issues he knew nothing about. On September 2, 1987, in what amounted to a trailer for his upcoming New Hampshire appearance, he paid $98,401 to place ads in the *New York Times*, the *Washington Post,* and the *Boston Globe* calling for "Japan, Saudi Arabia, and others" to pay the U.S. for its defense of the Persian Gulf, which he called "an area of only marginal significance to the United States for its oil supplies." That fact-free assessment was classic Trump: one year earlier, the Associated Press reported that U.S. oil imports had hit a six-year high.

Also intriguing was Trump's suggestion that, once America somehow convinced these bandit nations to fork over billions, we'd use the money to help "our farmers, our sick, our homeless." His sudden concern about the homeless must have surprised the residents of one of his properties in Manhattan, Trump Parc East on Central Park South. A few years earlier, in an effort to oust tenants from their rent-controlled apartments, Trump had made what he considered the ultimate threat: he would move homeless people into vacant units, thus using the homeless to make other people homeless. (He issued this threat via his favorite medium of this era—another newspaper ad.) Weirdly, as president, Trump appeared to exhibit total amnesia about the existence of homelessness during the 1980s. In a 2019 interview with Tucker Carlson of Fox News, he called homelessness "a phenomenon that started two years ago." Seemingly forgetting his 1987 ad, he told Carlson, "We never had this in our lives before in our country."

Trump's most notorious work in the full-page-ad art form appeared in 1989, after five Black and Latino teenagers were charged with beating and sexually assaulting a white female jogger in Central Park. Not waiting for the niceties of due process, he took out ads in four New York newspapers calling for the reinstatement of the state's death penalty. "I want to hate these muggers and murderers," the ad read. "They should be forced to suffer and, when they kill, they should be executed for their crimes." Unlike *The Art of the Deal*, this ad sounded like it was written by Trump, though it's fair to say that it was also indebted to the oeuvre of Lee Atwater. In the end, Trump didn't succeed in bringing back capital punishment, but his call for vengeance likely influenced the conviction of the Central Park Five, who served sentences ranging from six to thirteen years before they were exonerated by DNA evidence. Even after the five sued New York City for malicious prosecution and received a $41 million settlement, Trump refused to apologize for demanding their deaths. Instead, he wheeled out his favorite all-purpose prevarication: "You have people on both sides of that."

As the success of *The Art of the Deal* swelled Trump's ego, he plunged headfirst and eyes closed into industries he knew nothing about. While his catastrophic tenure as a casino proprietor has become legendary, less has been made of his brief but also disastrous career as a racehorse owner. Maybe his grandfather's expertise in making meals of dead horses had convinced him that he knew something about live ones. For whatever reason, in 1988 Trump agreed to pay half a million dollars for a colt named Alibi, whose royal lineage marked him as a potential Triple Crown winner. In one of the more bizarre examples of Trump's compulsion to put his name on things, he renamed the horse "DJ Trump."* Unfortunately, the colt's record was no more winning than his namesake's. Trump (the man) demanded that Trump (the horse) race immediately, against the advice

---

*This meant that, if you include Donald Trump Jr., for a brief time in 1988 there were three mammals with the same name.

of its trainer. After a bug swept through the horse's stable in Florida, Trump, in an early display of his penchant for downplaying viruses, demanded that DJ keep training. The unfortunate colt became infected, lost circulation in his forelegs, and would never race. Meanwhile, his owner, having ruined the animal, tried to back out of paying for him.

In addition to his racehorsing fiasco, Trump bought a football team—the woeful New Jersey Generals of the United States Football League, an entity only slightly longer-lived than Anthony Scaramucci's White House tenure. Trump then went for a sporting trifecta by jumping into professional boxing. Having wormed his way into the inner circle of Mike Tyson, the undisputed heavyweight champion of the world, he flew to Tokyo in February 1990 to watch his friend take on Buster Douglas, a lightly regarded palooka and 42–1 underdog. In one of the biggest upsets in sports history, Douglas dethroned the champ, KO'ing Tyson in the tenth round. For Trump, it was a brutal demonstration of his father's zero-sum worldview: Douglas was now a killer and Tyson a loser. "[I]t's over for him," Trump said. "He'll never come back from this." He was eager to congratulate Douglas after the fight, but didn't want to get anywhere near his friend, the now former champion. "I'm not going to Tyson's dressing room," he said. "I can't go near him. It might rub off. The same thing could happen to me."

And then it did. Having insanely overspent on casinos, an airline, and a yacht, the debt-laden mogul was forced by his bankers to agree to humiliating new terms. Just four months after he feared he might catch a serious case of losing from Tyson, the cover of *Newsweek* featured a photo of a downcast Donald with the headline "Trump: The Fall." (In an unintentional comment on the sorry state of his empire, he shared the cover with a story about "The Suicide Doctor," Jack

Kevorkian, who made headlines by euthanizing the terminally ill.) Trump spent the rest of the 1990s practicing the art of increasingly tiny deals. As the owner of New York's Plaza Hotel, he wouldn't let the director of *Home Alone 2: Lost in New York* film there unless he gave Trump a cameo. The result of this hard-nosed negotiation was a single blink-and-you'll-miss-it line of dialogue: when the film's star, Macaulay Culkin, asks, "Where's the lobby?" Trump replies, "Down the hall and to the left." (Even this fleeting glimpse of Trump proved too much for the Canadian Broadcasting Corporation, which excised his scene from a broadcast in 2014.) Alas, Trump's star turn failed to improve the Plaza's fortunes. The same month that *Home Alone 2* was released, the storied hotel joined Trump's Atlantic City casinos in bankruptcy. Trump's failure in the casino industry might have been brought on, in part, by his ineptitude at arithmetic, as evidenced by this Quaylian comment: "If there is one word to describe Atlantic City, it's Big Business." Worse, as Trump transitioned to his new role as national laughingstock, his status as the country's preeminent populist blowhard was challenged by another formidable attention hog: H. Ross Perot.

The Texas-born founder of Electronic Data Systems, Perot was in some ways the character Trump was impersonating: a self-made billionaire and the chief executive of a large, thriving business. Additionally, his outsidery, anti-trade message, delivered in an East Texas twang during his independent run for the presidency in 1992, prefigured Trump's outsidery, anti-trade message in 2016. When asked about his lack of experience in government, Perot cracked, "I don't have any experience in running up a $4 trillion debt. I don't have any experience in gridlock government, where nobody takes responsibility for anything and everybody blames everybody else." He called the national debt "the crazy aunt we keep down in the basement."

after Buchanan won the Reform Party nomination, his share of the general election vote was a barely detectable 0.42 percent.* "I may have played some role in derailing them as a party," Stone modestly conceded.

But Trump, like Stone, also got what he wanted out of the Reform Party caper: he was indeed on television a lot. A *60 Minutes* segment filmed in 1999 makes spellbinding viewing. As Trump teases Dan Rather for a full twelve minutes about whether he'll run for the Reform Party nomination, you're struck by how similar the clown-candidate Trump of 1999 sounds to the election-winning Trump of 2016. Like Ronald Reagan, he had already polished his act to a high sheen and saw no reason to learn any new bits. When asked about John McCain, he spouts a take that would become infamous sixteen years later: "Does being captured make you a hero? I don't know; I'm not sure." He also gives George W. Bush the insult-comic treatment he'd later lavish on his little brother Jeb. Asked about Dubya, Trump says that he is "very, very saddened by the fact that he certainly doesn't seem like Albert Einstein."

A few years after they both fled the smoldering ruins of the Reform Party, Jesse Ventura and Donald Trump met again. Ventura, having body-slammed Minnesota's $3 billion budget surplus into a $4.5 billion deficit in a mere four years, decided not to seek reelection. Instead, he settled into the role of elder statesman in a field that he actually knew something about: pro wrestling. One night after his induction into the World Wrestling Entertainment Hall of Fame, in 2004, he made a surprise appearance at *WrestleMania XX*. "Let me

---

* Buchanan withdrew to the private sector, where he contented himself by writing a book about how mean Britain had been to wage World War II against those nice Nazis.

say this: what would *WrestleMania* be without Jesse 'The Body' coming out and doing an interview with somebody?" he asked twenty
thousand fans packing Madison Square Garden. "Who is it? It's the
star of the number-one-rated TV show on NBC, *The Apprentice*."
The crowd booed. After Ventura introduced Trump by name, it
booed again.

By giving Trump this greeting, the *WrestleMania* crowd might
have been following the pro-wrestling tradition of booing the villain, or "heel," before a match. Since the premiere, two months earlier, of *The Apprentice*, in which Trump relished the ritual abuse of
his obsequious contestants, he'd become the highest-profile heel in
the country. But his 2004 appearance with Ventura was the last time
WrestleMania fans would boo the heel. By 2007, when he returned
for *WrestleMania 23*, the heel had become a hero, loved and admired
by millions. For orchestrating that miraculous transformation, credit
goes to the creator of *The Apprentice*, Mark Burnett.

The Apprentice was an exquisite work of video chicanery, repack-
aging an inept scion as the preeminent business genius of our time.
"Most of us knew he was a fake," the show's editor, Jonathan Braun,
told *The New Yorker*'s Patrick Radden Keefe, in a 2019 profile of
Burnett. "He had just gone through I don't know how many bankruptcies. But we made him out to be the most important person in
the world. It was like making the court jester the king."

Trump's latest and greatest media defibrillator, Burnett exploited
his star's island of competence. Instead of paying hundreds of thousands of dollars to draw attention to himself with full-page ads,
Trump now received millions from NBC to achieve the same goal.
"I don't think any of us could have known what this would become,"
one of the show's producers told Keefe. "But Donald would not be
President had it not been for that show."

Trump began the first episode with a big lie: "My name's Donald

Trump, and I'm the largest real estate developer in New York." The producers knew that this wasn't true. "We walked through [Trump's] offices and saw chipped furniture," one said. "We saw a crumbling empire at every turn. Our job was to make it seem otherwise." The methods that Stu Spencer had used in the 1960s to make Ronald Reagan ready for prime time were prehistoric compared to the wizardry of Burnett's team, which shot three hundred hours of footage for every hour that aired.

Though he appears nowhere in the show's credits, Reagan deserves special recognition for fostering the ethos it celebrates. *The Apprentice* is a reboot of the fraudulent Trump persona made famous in *The Art of the Deal*, but it also evokes the era of that book's publication, the vicious "greed is good" heyday of New York in the 1980s. "This island is the real jungle," tough-talking Trump says of Manhattan as he rides around in a limo during the show's opening, like Gordon Gekko with a smaller phone. "If you're not careful, it can chew you up and spit you out." Cut to a homeless person sprawled across a bench, the enduring legacy of Reaganomics. With its celebration of life as a Hobbesian, zero-sum game, each season ending with the elevation of one killer over a throng of losers, *The Apprentice* is a show that Fred Trump would have loved.

It's also a show whose success Reagan, as a TV host, would have coveted. The Gipper headlined *General Electric Theater* for eight seasons, but Trump nearly doubled that feat by hosting *The Apprentice* for fifteen. Otherwise, the two shows had much in common. Both series reinvented their stars, who were at career lows, by imbuing them with unearned credibility. Just as the GE show cemented Reagan's image as a reassuring custodian of 1950s values, *The Apprentice* convinced millions that Donald J. Trump was just the right badass to bring back the 1980s and kick the world's losers to the curb. During his presidency, Trump frustrated critics by proving immune to fact-checking, but his status as Teflon Don made sense: *The Apprentice* presented everything he said as unequivocally insightful. Enthroned in his high-back chair, he was the Obi-Wan Kenobi of capitalism. As Keefe reported in *The New Yorker*, Kwame Jackson, a Harvard MBA who was a contestant on the first season, "was struck, when the show aired, by the extent to which Americans fell for the ruse. 'Main Street America saw all those glittery things, the helicopter and the gold-plated sinks, and saw the most successful person in the universe.'" The flimflam succeeded, in part, because of Burnett's genius, but also because Trump—like Ronald Reagan, professional wrestlers, and other charlatans and con men—made people want to be fooled.

By 2011, Trump was on a roll. At the Conservative Political Action Conference (CPAC), in Washington, DC, he raised his political profile by casting doubt on Barack Obama's place of birth. "Our current president came out of nowhere. Came out of nowhere," he declared. "In fact, I'll go a step further: The people that went to school with him, they never saw him, they don't know who he is. It's crazy."

If, as Trump asserted, schoolmates' failure to remember you proves you're a foreigner, this raises troubling questions about his own birthplace. Few Wharton classmates could recall him. "I knew everyone in my class except Donald Trump," Kenneth Kadish told the *Daily Pennsylvanian*, the student-run newspaper of the University of Pennsylvania. "Wharton was a pretty small community back then . . . you knew everyone. Well, except him. . . . It wasn't that [Trump] was just not prominent, it was like he was non-existent." Linda Albert Broidrick, another member of the class of '68, asked more than twenty of her classmates if they'd ever encountered Trump in college. "None recalled seeing or meeting him," she said. But the biggest cloud hanging over Trump might be this: his photo doesn't appear in the Class of '68 yearbook. He came out of nowhere!

Appearing on *The Tonight Show* in 2012, Obama offered a deadpan explanation for both men's mysterious origins. Discussing Trump's long-standing enmity toward him, the president said, "This all dates back to when we were growing up together in Kenya. . . . We had constant run-ins on the soccer field. He wasn't very good, and resented it. When we finally moved to America, I thought it would be over."

Though Obama brushed off Trump's birther lies with humor, Sarah Palin praised the fraudulent claims and Trump's professed willingness to pay for an investigation. "I appreciate that the Donald wants to spend his resources in getting to the bottom of something that so interests him and many Americans—you know, more power to him," she said on Fox News. "He's not just throwing stones from the sidelines; he's digging in there, he's paying for researchers to find out why President Obama would have spent $2 million to not show his birth certificate."*

Two months later, in a summit almost as momentous as Reagan's Geneva meeting with Gorbachev, Palin and Trump convened at a New York City pizza parlor. The tête-à-tête was exactly the sort of news-free stunt Trump had long served up to the grateful media, and which Daniel Boorstin described in his 1961 book, *The Image, or What Happened to the American Dream*. "In the last half century a larger and larger proportion of our experience, of what we read and see and hear, has come to consist of pseudo-events," Boorstin wrote. "We expect more of them and we are given more of them.

---

*On MSNBC, Michael Cohen later told Rachel Maddow that Trump had never paid for such an investigation.

They flood our consciousness. Their multiplication has gone on in the United States at a faster rate than elsewhere." Like most pseudo-events involving Trump, the pizza summit drew widespread coverage, though the horde of journalists in attendance was unable to discern its purpose. Perhaps Palin and Trump were joining forces as detectives to extract from a Kenyan village obstetrician the true story of Obama's birth. Or maybe Palin just wanted Trump's advice on how to star in a reality show that didn't suck.

On June 16, 2015, our perverse American experiment led us to the Gates of Hell, also known as the atrium of Trump Tower. The merger of showbiz and politics that Ronald Reagan had helped launch in the 1960s was ready for a twenty-first-century reboot. In the Ridicule stage, the Gipper had shown that performing talent could triumph over knowledge and competence; to prove the point, however, he still went to the trouble of uttering complete sentences. Now, in the Celebration stage, Donald Trump could ditch that quaint practice. He announced his candidacy for president by riffing like a Dadaist poet.

"Wow. Whoa. That is some group of people. Thousands," he said, looking out at his excited audience, much of which his campaign had paid to attend. (He wasn't even president yet, and he was already creating jobs!) The non sequiturs he spewed demonstrated why Mark Burnett had been wise to shoot three hundred hours of footage for every hour of Trump that saw the light of day: "And, I can tell you, some of the candidates, they went in. They didn't know the air conditioner didn't work. They sweated like dogs. They didn't know the room was too big, because they didn't have anybody there. How are they going to beat ISIS? I don't think it's gonna happen." This was the sound of Trump's brain tuning up, like a demented symphony orchestra. Soon enough, though, he was unfurling the rationale for his presidential campaign, updating Reagan's *us versus communists* and Bush's *us versus terrorists* with a binary opposition of his own: *us versus immigrants.* "When Mexico sends its people, they're not sending their best," he said, sounding like the lead singer in a Pat Buchanan tribute band. "They're not sending you. They're not sending you. They're sending people that have lots of problems, and they're bringing those problems with us. They're bringing drugs. They're bringing crime. They're rapists. And some, I assume, are good people." Before long, though, the non sequiturs were back: "Islamic terrorism is eating up large portions of the Middle East. They've become rich. I'm in competition with them." Trump was in competition with Islamic terrorists? Now, *this* was news. Was he launching his own insurgency—Trump Terror? Eventually, he got back on track: "Now, our country needs—our country needs a truly great leader, and we need a truly great leader now. We need a leader that wrote *The Art of the Deal*." Yes, our country needs Tony Schwartz!

"I'll bring back our jobs from China, from Mexico, from Japan, from so many places," he told the crowd. (He didn't mention Poland. That was wise, because the demolition work that made Trump Tower possible was performed by undocumented workers from that country.) Jobs and trade, though, gave way to the more dire threat of immigrants, who were coming from so many places that Trump couldn't be entirely sure where. "They're sending us not the right people. It's coming from more than Mexico. It's coming from all over South and Latin America, and it's coming probably—probably—from the Middle East. But we don't know. Because we have no protection and we have no competence. We don't know what's happening. And it's got to stop, and it's got to stop fast." The message was clear: we don't know what's happening, but it's got to stop!

As hateful as Trump's rhetoric was, it was part of a grand American tradition. As we saw earlier, anti-immigrant fervor was the engine that drove Millard Fillmore's 1856 presidential campaign as the Know-Nothing nominee. A century and a half before Trump trained his xenophobia on Mexicans, the Know-Nothings had vilified Germans, Irish, and Catholics. They also undermined the validity of elections, suppressed voting, and started riots. Trump's ideology wasn't just toxic—it was derivative.

His borrowing didn't stop there. He lifted Reagan's 1980 campaign slogan, "Let's Make America Great Again," deleting the first word and, in a ballsy move, filing a trademark application for the remaining four. In losing the "Let's," Trump did more than trim the slogan: he turned a relatively benign message into something darker. "Let's Make America Great Again" at least presented the illusion of being a collective invitation, even if it was a disingenuous one, since it didn't extend to anyone outside the all-white cast of Reagan's campaign ads. "Make America Great Again" doesn't even pretend to be an invitation. It's a command.

Trump steamrolled his fellow reality-show contestants in the Republican primary, including the Tea Party gasbag Ted Cruz and Jeb "Please Clap" Bush (whose candidacy failed to capitalize on America's nostalgia for the Iraq War and Hurricane Katrina). Along the way, he garnered endorsements from legends of the first two stages of ignorance: Dan Quayle and Sarah Palin.

Sarah Barracuda was up first, giving Trump her seal of approval before the crucial Iowa caucuses. In her Jabberwocky-like endorsement speech, Palin did what few would have dreamed possible: she made Donald J. Trump seem like a man of few words. "He's got the guts to wear the issues that need to be spoken about and debated on his sleeve, where the rest of some of these establishment candidates, they just wanted to duck and hide," she spouted. "They didn't want to talk about these issues until he brought 'em up. In fact, they've been wearing a, this political correctness kind of like a suicide vest." She contrasted Trump's brave issues-talking-about sleeve with the cowardly apologizing-to-our-enemies sleeve of Barack Obama: "And he, who would negotiate deals, kind of with the skills of a community organizer maybe organizing a neighborhood tea, well, he deciding that, 'No, America would apologize as part of the deal,' as the enemy sends a message to the rest of the world that they capture and we kowtow, and we apologize, and then, we bend over and say, 'Thank you, enemy.'" As Palin nattered on, Trump stood silently to her left, waiting for the whole hot mess to end.

Quayle climbed aboard the crazy train during a May appearance on NBC's *Today* show. Trump's fellow Robert Redford look-alike hadn't been heard from much in recent years. In 2002, he'd popped up on MSNBC to offer his take on the War on Terror by asking, "How many Palestinians were on those airplanes on September 9? None." (No argument there.) Now, decades after he'd struggled to answer the question of whether he was qualified to be president, he struggled to answer the same question about Trump. "On paper, you'd say, 'Well, [Hillary Clinton is] more qualified,'" he began. "But you know what? He's more qualified in the sense that the American people, I think, want an outsider. They want an outsider this time. She is not an outsider, so, if you're looking for an outsider, no, she's not qualified, and he is." The logic of Quayle's answer was Palinesque: If Americans were looking for someone less qualified than Clinton, Trump was more qualified at being unqualified. At any rate, it was nice to see Quayle after so many years: older, but with his speaking style frozen in amber.

One day after Trump's inauguration, the White House initiated a strategy that adviser Steve Bannon called "flooding the zone with shit."* Much like the slogan "Make America Great Again," this idea wasn't new. Trump's former lawyer Roy Cohn deployed it when he produced an imaginary commie-a-day for his boss Senator Joseph McCarthy; Cohn's client Ronald Reagan repurposed it when he spewed a stream of fake quotations, phony anecdotes, and bogus statistics that left fact-checkers breathless; and George W. Bush re-repurposed it when his messianic mendacity plunged the nation into war. The flood of shit began on day two of the new presidency, when the White House press secretary, Sean Spicer, made the easily refutable claim that Trump's inauguration crowd had been larger than Obama's, and was, in fact, the "largest audience to ever witness an inauguration—period—both in person and around the globe." (In a possible homage to Trump's punctuation skills, Spicer said "period" in the middle of a sentence.) Later that week, Kellyanne Conway, formerly Dan Quayle's pollster and now counselor to Trump, appeared on NBC's *Meet the Press* to defend Spicer's statement as an example of what she called "alternative facts."

Under Reagan, facts were "stupid things"; under Bush, facts were the silly obsession of "the reality-based community." Conway was taking the rebranding of facts into a whole new dimension. What did she mean, exactly, by "alternative facts"? Maybe an alternative fact was like an alternative band: something not many people had heard of, but really cool if you knew about it? At any rate, there were many more to come.

Conway herself demonstrated mastery of the alternative-fact genre two weeks after Spicer's maiden foray. Defending Trump's ban on travel from predominantly Muslim countries, she cited the cautionary tale of two Iraqi refugees who masterminded something

---

*In addition to directing the Sarah Palin homage, *The Undefeated*, Bannon had burnished his résumé by running the white-nationalist media outlet Breitbart.

called the "Bowling Green Massacre." Her follow-up statement about the mythical tragedy at Bowling Green at least contained a kernel of truth: "Most people don't know that because it didn't get covered."

If Conway thought she was the master of creating fictitious bloodbaths, though, she would soon be outdone by her boss. At a rally in Florida later that month, Trump bemoaned a terror attack in Sweden that he claimed had occurred the night before: "We've got to keep our country safe. You look at what's happening in Germany, you look at what's happening last night in Sweden. Sweden, who would believe this? Sweden. They took in large numbers. They're having problems like they never thought possible." This lament drew confused reactions from people living in Sweden, where no such attack had occurred. On Twitter, the former Swedish prime minister Carl Bildt asked, "Sweden? Terror attack? What has he been smoking? Questions abound." Some suggested that Trump had been confused by reports of a terror attack in the Pakistani city of Sehwan, which, in fairness, has four letters in common with Sweden. Maybe that was what he'd been smoking—or, as he would say, "smocking."

Though mainstream news outlets highlighted Trump's wild excursions from the truth, such criticism didn't erode his support, for a simple reason: his supporters didn't get their news from mainstream news outlets. Unlike in the Ridicule stage, which ended before the kudzu-like growth of the internet and the advent of social media, in Celebration voters were free to choose only the facts they agreed with. On outlets such as Fox News, Breitbart, right-wing talk radio, and countless Facebook and Twitter accounts, Trump wore an immunity idol around his neck.

Despite his promise at the Republican National Convention to "Make America Safe Again," Trump, two years into his presidency, still hadn't protected the nation from imaginary attackers. Just in time for the 2018 midterm elections, he warned rally crowds about

an ominous "caravan" of miscreants rolling toward the southern border. "Every time you see a Caravan," he tweeted, "or people illegally
coming, or attempting to come, into our Country illegally, think of
and blame the Democrats for not giving us the votes to change our
pathetic Immigration Laws! Remember the Midterms!" The message
was clear: a caravan of marauders was coming to destroy our way of
life, including our right to capitalize any word we want. "In addition to stopping all payments to these countries, which seem to have
almost no control over their population," he threatened, "I must, in
the strongest of terms, ask Mexico to stop this onslaught—and if
unable to do so I will call up the U.S. Military and CLOSE OUR
SOUTHERN BORDER!"

Thanks to Trump's strategic deployment of CAPS LOCK,
military intervention proved unnecessary. One day after the midterms, the dreaded caravan suddenly vanished. Trump and his
media partners at Fox News stopped talking about it. Did this
unexplained evaporation of thousands of the worst evildoers on
the planet trouble his supporters? Not a bit. His strategy of flooding the zone with shit only inspired his disciples in Congress to
try to outflood him.

Some were up to the task, like Representative Marjorie Taylor
Greene, of Georgia, who was elected in 2020. She shared not only
Trump's ignorance but his island of competence. The prolific QAnon
loudmouth began her campaign against verifiable reality as an official of a far-right group with the deceptively benign name Family
America Project. As a leader of FAP, she moderated a Facebook page
promoting, somewhat quaintly, the old-school conspiracy theories
of the John Birch Society. But even Robert W. Welch Jr., that organization's anti-fluoridation founder, might have urged Marge to
get a grip. Among the non-Bircher theories she advanced was that
California wildfires were caused by lasers, fired from outer space, at

the behest of the Jewish banking family the Rothschilds. Her claims had the unintended consequence of stoking the pride of many Jews, including me, who up to that point had felt that our control of the cosmos fell far short of our renowned hammerlock on the media and show business. Her later attempt to establish an Anglo-Saxon caucus in Congress ran aground after such a group was deemed too white supremacist even for today's Republican Party. Its early demise disappointed those of us who'd hoped to witness a pitched medieval battle between the Anglo-Saxon caucus and the inevitable copycat Viking caucus.

Greene's status as the most visibly unhinged member of Congress would face a formidable challenge from a fellow Republican newbie, Colorado's Lauren Boebert. Unlike Greene, whose pre-congressional extremism had been limited to composing hate speech online, Boebert had real-world experience, to the extent that she could be said to reside in the real world. The founding owner of Shooters Grill, a gun-crazy café situated, appropriately enough, in the town of Rifle, Colorado, Boebert said that she started open-carrying a firearm to the restaurant, and encouraging her waitstaff to do the same, after a man was beaten to death in an alley nearby. The assailant, it seems, also perpetrated the Bowling Green Massacre and the terror attack in Sweden, since his existence has never been verified. Once elected to Congress, Boebert tried to turn the House of Representatives into Shooters on the Potomac by bringing a gun, as others might bring their daughters, to work. In a stirring defense of the Second Amendment, Boebert tweeted, "Protecting and defending the Constitution doesn't mean trying to rewrite the parts you don't like," seemingly unaware that the Second Amendment, like every other Amendment, was itself a rewrite of the Constitution. Inspired in part by the gun-toting Coloradan, House Speaker Nancy Pelosi proposed fining members who resisted being screened for firearms. On the plus side,

Boebert made it easy for her constituents to track her attendance in Congress by repeatedly setting off its metal detectors.

"One of the main reasons I'm running is I know a lot about education," Tommy "Tubs" Tuberville said, in 2020, when the former Auburn football coach was running for the U.S. Senate in Alabama. "We've gotten away from teaching world history, American history, state history, civics, government. How did we get here? A lot of these kids don't know." A quick way to improve education would be to identify the schools Tuberville attended and raze them. Tubs thinks that the United States fought World War II "to free Europe of socialism"; impressively, we managed to keep this agenda a secret from one of our key allies, the prominent socialist Joseph Stalin. He thinks the Constitution prohibits one party from controlling all three branches of government, which he defines as "the House, the Senate, and the executive." When it comes to climate change, we can expect many lively scientific debates about its causes between Tuberville and his Republican colleague Ron Johnson, who, as you'll recall, blamed it all on sunspots. "[T]here is one person that changes climate in this country and that is God," Tubs declares.

If there is one person besides God who's capable of changing climate in this country, it might be Representative Louie Gohmert, of Texas. When a deputy chief of the Forest Service testified before Congress, Gohmert inquired, "[I]s there anything that the National Forest Service or [Bureau of Land Management] can do to change the course of the moon's orbit or the Earth's orbit around the sun? Obviously, that would have profound effects on our climate." Obviously! Gohmert should be commended for his creative thinking, but, as any informed citizen can tell you, the only people who can change the orbits of the Earth and the moon are the Rothschilds.

One thing Gohmert doesn't want to change is Alaska's oil pipeline, which, he believes, serves as an aphrodisiac for caribou. "[W]hen they want to go on a date, they invite each other to head over to the pipeline," he said of the horny quadrupeds in 2012. Gohmert is just the latest Republican politician to claim special insight into the sex lives of caribou. Two decades earlier, President George H. W. Bush said of the same pipeline, "The caribou love it. They rub against it and they have babies." Though Rick Santorum spoke in favor of oil pipelines during his presidential campaign in 2011, he omitted any reference to their role in caribou fornication. Most likely, Santorum opposes sex even when caribou are doing it.

Gohmert's brainstorm about altering the orbits of celestial bodies, while tempting and practical, might not mitigate the problem of rising sea levels, according to the Alabama congressman and scientific theorist Mo Brooks. As he explained at a congressional hearing, sea levels are rising not because of climate change but for the most obvious of reasons: *the ocean floor is rising.* "Every time you have that soil or rock, whatever it is, that is deposited into the seas, that forces the sea levels to rise because now you've got less space in those oceans because the bottom is moving up," said Brooks, who, with his election to Congress in 2010, became a prime example of the bottom moving up. Offering an example of the "whatever it is" that is collecting on the ocean floor, he cited the erosion of the White Cliffs of Dover, a rare instance of Brooks using the word "white" in a negative context.

The most ingenious approach to climate change, however, emanated from the mind of Florida's former governor and current senator Rick Scott. Just as Richard Nixon declared, "I'm not a crook," Scott announced, "I'm not a scientist"; unlike Nixon, Scott was rebutting an accusation no one had ever made.* When Scott was governor,

---

* His fellow Florida senator, Marco Rubio, has also denied being a scientist, another entirely unnecessary disclaimer.

his administration employed a revolutionary strategy to eliminate climate change: it reportedly ordered all staffers at the state's Department of Environmental Protection to cease using the terms "climate change" and "global warming." As inspired as this fix was, you could argue that Scott didn't go far enough. Terms he neglected to ban included "catastrophic flooding," "vanishing coastline," and "uninhabitable hellhole."

While we're in Florida, we'd be remiss not to pay tribute to that ultimate specimen of Florida Man, Representative Matt Gaetz. In December 2020, Gaetz demonstrated his fealty to Donald Trump by getting engaged at Mar-a-Lago to a woman named Ginger Luckey, whose last name called to mind how Mar-a-Lago's owner might spell the word "lucky." It was mystifying why Gaetz thought it auspicious to propose at the home of someone with Trump's matrimonial history, but, before long, choosing china would be the least of Matt's problems. After Gaetz came under investigation for child sex trafficking, Republicans grew nostalgic for that solid citizen Roy Moore, their 2017 U.S. Senate candidate from Alabama, who picked up teenagers at the mall but was too much of an old-fashioned gentleman to cross state lines with them.

In their earnest effort to flood the zone with shit, some Trump acolytes in Congress wound up shitting the bed. Exhibit A was Mary Miller, a freshman congresswoman from Illinois, who, in remarks at a pro-Trump rally in Washington on the eve of the Capitol insurrection, made an ill-advised reference to the president's favorite bedside author. "Hitler was right on one thing," she declared. "He said, 'Whoever has the youth has the future.'" Call it a rookie mistake, but someone should have told Miller that, when you start a sentence with "Hitler was right," it's almost impossible to stick the landing. Since all she was trying to say was that children are the future, it's baffling that she didn't quote the far less genocidal Whitney Houston. In fairness, Miller was on the same page as her role model—Trump, that is, not the Führer—who once reportedly told his chief of staff John Kelly, "Hitler did a lot of good things." Her only mistake was saying in public what Trump had said in private. Knowing when and when not to praise Hitler can be tricky.

Though the Celebration stage of ignorance benefited those generously endowed with cluelessness like the Boeberts and the Gohmerts, it posed a challenge to Republicans who had the misfortune of being well-educated and knowledgeable. In a desperate attempt to approximate their leader's appeal, some strenuously pretended to be dumber than they were, imitating Trump like a bunch of sloppy drunks at karaoke.

Luckily for them, the pandemic presented these graduates of some of our nation's finest universities a golden opportunity to simulate idiocy. Gaetz (William & Mary Law School '07) mocked the advice of scientists by showing up on the House floor wearing a cartoonish gas mask; days later, he was forced to quarantine after being exposed to the virus at CPAC. That conservative gathering turned out to be a super-spreader event, also pushing Senator Ted Cruz (Princeton '92, Harvard Law School '95) into seclusion. Although Cruz had already established his anti-science bona fides by casting doubt on both climate change and the theory of evolution, he wasn't content to rest on his stupid laurels. In a reboot of Dan Quayle's brilliant Murphy Brown strategy, he slammed the *Sesame Street* legend Big Bird for spreading sinister pro-vaccination propaganda. Showing that he could also attack a non-avian character, he joined Rand Paul in lambasting Dr. Anthony Fauci. After initially suggesting that the celebrated scientist be fired, the two senators decided that only a criminal prosecution would do. Fauci stubbornly refused to quit, even though his job entailed periodically talking to people like Cruz and Paul.

Possibly fearing that his GOP rivals in Congress were out-duncing him, the Florida governor, Ron DeSantis (Yale '01, Harvard Law School '05), upped the ante. He flatly refused to issue a shelter-in-place order, arguing that imposing a lockdown on Floridians would be "throwing their lives into potential disarray," ignoring the possibility that their lives could also be thrown into disarray by dying. When state senator Oscar Braynon commented, "That is the dumbest shit I have heard in a long time," DeSantis must have done his happy dance. Beneath his faux stupid veneer, though, DeSantis is a big believer in statistics—so much so that he tries to hide them when they make him look bad. As the pandemic raged in his state, the *South Florida Sun Sentinel* reported that he "suppressed unfavorable facts, dispensed dangerous misinformation, dismissed public health professionals, and promoted the views of scientific dissenters." In the summer of 2021, Florida became responsible for a whopping one-fifth of the entire nation's new COVID-19 cases. If, as many predict, DeSantis runs for president, he has already locked up the endorsements of several major variants.

But, when it comes to the title of Most Ginormous Well-Educated Assclown, it's hard to beat Senator Josh Hawley (Stanford University '02, Yale Law School '06). In April 2021, he became the only United States senator to vote against the COVID-19 Hate Crimes Act, a bill tackling the anti–Asian American violence that surged during the pandemic. Sensing a chance to look more imbecilic than all his fellow senators—even Rand Paul!—he grabbed it. Thus, he reinforced the jerkwad status he'd established on January 6, 2021, when a photo of him sending Capitol insurrectionists a supportive fist pump made millions wonder when Pee-wee Herman had joined the alt-right. After that legendary performance, the former U.S. senator John Danforth called his support for Hawley's Senate bid "the worst mistake I ever made in my life." Since Danforth also backed the nomination of Clarence Thomas to the Supreme Court, that's saying something.

When Fred Trump taught his son that the world was divided into killers and losers, he probably didn't guess that this fatherly advice would someday lead to a riot at the U.S. Capitol. After Donald Trump lost the 2020 presidential election, by 7 million votes, the man who refused to go near Mike Tyson for fear that losing might be contagious couldn't accept his own decisive knockout. His ensuing incitement of domestic terrorism was shocking, but perhaps not surprising once you consider the braided histories of the Trump family and the Republican Party. In fact, maybe we should have seen it coming. Because the Age of Ignorance has repeatedly enacted a dark principle: in the absence of knowledge, violence fills the void.

In 1966, Fred Trump created the blueprint for what Trumps do when they don't get their way. Steeplechase Park was one of the most beloved amusement parks in Coney Island, Brooklyn. After Trump acquired the property (accompanied by nineteen-year-old Donald at the signing ceremony), with plans to demolish it and build residential units, outraged citizens attempted to save it by applying to have it designated as a landmark. Before Steeplechase's landmark status could be certified, however, Fred Trump organized a "demolition party" at which he urged a mob to smash the glass facade of the park's Pavilion of Fun. "Trump sent out engraved invitations and invited people to throw rocks and bricks through the Funny Face—it was a desecration of an icon, it was insane," Charles Denson, the Coney

Island History Project's executive director, told the *Brooklyn Paper*. "Most developers are worried about making a profit, most wouldn't throw a party to desecrate a stained-glass window."

Donald Trump would continue his father's proud tradition of wanton vandalism when he demolished the Bonwit Teller Building on Manhattan's Fifth Avenue to clear the site for Trump Tower. After saying he'd try to preserve the building's priceless Art Deco friezes so that they could be exhibited at the Metropolitan Museum of Art, Trump discovered that it would cost $32,000 to remove them intact. As a clever solution to his problem, he had his workmen smash them to bits.

In 1970, as Trump barred Black renters from his father's buildings in Brooklyn and Queens, white violence exploded in lower Manhattan. On May 8, Mayor John Lindsay ordered the flag at city hall flown at half-staff to commemorate the four students murdered by National Guardsmen during the antiwar protest four days earlier at Kent State University. As young protesters gathered nearby, a mob of angry white construction workers attacked them in a melee that became known as the Hardhat Riot. Not content with their beatdown of the hippies, the rioters launched an assault on city hall. Just as insurrectionists would someday seek to hang Mike Pence, the Hardhat Rioters hunted a quarry of their own: Mayor Lindsay.

In his riveting book, *The Hardhat Riot: Nixon, New York City, and the Dawn of the White Working-Class Revolution*, David Paul Kuhn re-creates the scene: "As the mass coalesced, men's eyes were trained on City Hall. Shouting persisted: 'Where's Lindsay? . . . Lindsay's a rat! . . . We want Lindsay! We want Lindsay!'" The deputy borough president, Leonard Cohen, "saw a 'large mass of men,' about five to six hundred, with yellow hard hats and American flags, pushing against the front of City Hall, 'shouting slogans and chanting angrily.' The men drove forward and reached the foot of the steps.

Suddenly, they surged up the stairs 'as if to storm City Hall itself' . . . Scores of hardhats hopped City Hall's fence, leapt over the hoods of boxy police cars, and toppled iron barricades. Several hardhats ran with flags pointed forward, like soldiers brandishing their colors." A rioter reached the roof of City Hall, where he restored the flag to full staff, to the raucous cheers of his brethren below. By day's end, dozens had been injured.

Prior to these events, Trump's future pen pal Richard M. Nixon had been in a fragile state of mind. Widely vilified for the bombing of Cambodia, he was, according to those close to him, "on the edge of a nervous breakdown." The savagery of the Hardhat Riot seemed to cheer him up. "Last week, a group of construction workers came up Wall Street and beat the living hell out of some demonstrators who were desecrating the American flag," his aide Pat Buchanan wrote to him. "Whether one condones this kind of violence or not, probably half the living rooms in America were in standing applause at the spectacle." There was little doubt whether Nixon and Buchanan condoned this kind of violence; to show his appreciation for the attack, the president invited leaders of the rioters' unions to the White House for a celebratory photo op. Nixon claimed that he was honoring "labor leaders and people from Middle America who still have character and guts and a bit of patriotism." In return, the labor chieftains gave him an honorary hard hat. As Nixon later reminisced, the hardhats "were with us when some of the elitist crowd were running away from us. Thank God for the hardhats!"

Another riot, on November 22, 2000, was orchestrated in part by a Republican operative with ties to both Nixon and Trump: Roger Stone. The seemingly ubiquitous dirty trickster was acting, he said, at the behest of James Baker, the senior Republican official who had served under Ford, Reagan, and George H. W. Bush. Baker was masterminding the party's effort to tip Florida's contested presidential vote in George W. Bush's favor. A recount that could have handed the presidency to Al Gore was underway at the Stephen P. Clark Government Center, in downtown Miami, when a mob of demonstrators, organized by Republicans and dressed in suit jackets and ties, poured into the building to disrupt the process.

Shortly after Joe Geller, the Democratic chairman of Miami-Dade County, arrived at the scene, he was assaulted. "This one guy was tripping me and pushing me and kicking me," Geller told the *Washington Post.* "At one point, I thought if they knocked me over, I could have literally got stomped to death." According to the *New York Times,* "Upstairs in the Clark center, several people were trampled, punched or kicked when protesters tried to rush the doors outside the office of the Miami-Dade supervisor of elections. Sheriff's deputies restored order. When the ruckus was over, the protesters had what they had wanted: a unanimous vote by the board to call off the hand counting." The attack, which became known as the Brooks Brothers Riot, helped secure the presidency for Bush. Citing the halt in the recount, Geller said, "Anybody who says it was unrelated to the intimidation and violence floating around there is not telling the truth. I saw it with my own eyes. Violence, fear and physical intimidation affected the outcome of a lawful elections process." The Republican rioters weren't done, though. They proceeded to Broward County in the hopes of stopping the count there, too.

Sixteen years later, as Donald Trump cruised toward the GOP presidential nomination, he threatened that, if denied his rightful crown at the RNC in July, "I think you'd have riots. I think you'd have riots." Explaining his ominous prediction, he said, "The really big story is how many people are voting in these primaries. The numbers are astronomical. Now if you disenfranchise those people . . . I think you would have problems like you've never seen before. I think bad things would happen, I really do. I believe that. I wouldn't lead it, but I think bad things would happen."

Trump continued making such threats as president, issuing dark warnings about spontaneous eruptions of violence that he "wouldn't lead." In 2019, as the special counsel Robert Mueller investigated his campaign's alleged collusion with Russia during the 2016 election, Trump told Breitbart, "I can tell you I have the support of the police, the support of the military, the support of the Bikers for Trump—I have the tough people, but they don't play it tough—until they go to a certain point, and then it would be very bad, very bad."

In light of Trump and the GOP's long-standing love affair with mob violence, the insurrection at the Capitol seems less like an outlier and more like a sequel. But its predictability makes it no less horrifying. When the history of American infamy is written, Trump might actually read it. So many paragraphs will feature his name.

When Trump first seized control of the GOP, veteran Republicans started reciting what became a familiar refrain: they no longer recognized the party of Ronald Reagan. The March 21, 2016, cover of *Time* offered an early version of this nostalgic take. It featured a black-and-white photo of Ron and Nancy, gazing lovingly at each other and looming like deities over a soft-focus image of a Republican convention, with the headline "What Happened to This Party?" Inside, Peter Wehner, who served under Reagan and both Bushes, wrote an essay titled "The Party of Reagan Is No More," arguing that the "most obvious evidence of this is the rise of Donald Trump, a man who is the antithesis of so much that Ronald Reagan stood for: intellectual depth and philosophical consistency, respect for ideas and elevated rhetoric, civility and personal grace."

The unrecognizability of the "Party of Reagan" has become a

popular talking point for anti-Trump Republicans. "I was a Republican in my youth," Daniel Drezner wrote in the *Washington Post*. "But none of the values that attracted me to the party then are present in Trump's version of the GOP. The party of Reagan is dead. What has emerged in its place is something unspeakable." Before the 2016 California primary, the *San Diego Union-Tribune* took the effort to separate Reagan from Trump into an absurd realm: it shunned the Donald and endorsed the Gipper, who had been dead for twelve years. Apparently the editorial board felt that, much like Frederick Douglass, he'd do an amazing job.

One prominent Republican saw things differently. In 2020, Stuart Stevens, who worked on both of George W. Bush's presidential campaigns, published *It Was All a Lie: How the Republican Party Became Donald Trump*. Stevens points out what few Republicans have acknowledged: the views that people find abhorrent in Trump make him not the antithesis of Reagan but his rightful successor. "What happens if you spend decades focused on appealing to white voters and treating nonwhite voters with, at best, benign neglect?" Stevens asks.

> You get good at doing what it takes to appeal to white voters. That is the truth that led to what is famously called "the southern strategy." That is the path that leads you to becoming what the Republican Party now proudly embraces: a white grievance party. . . . Today, in the age of Donald Trump, the most openly racist president since Andrew Johnson or his hero Andrew Jackson (to the extent a know-nothing narcissist is capable of having a hero), many Republicans who find Trump repulsive or at least consider him abrasive and uncouth hark back to Reagan as the standard compared with whom Trump is woefully inadequate. . . . But in the area of race, there is a direct line from the more genteel prejudice of Ronald Reagan to the white nationalism of Donald Trump.

When the Confederate flag–wavers invaded the Capitol on January 6, it wasn't hard to see them as the descendants of the Confederate flag–wavers Reagan addressed, forty-one years earlier, at the Neshoba County Fair. And, while most people assailed Trump for inciting his mob to overthrow the government, Reaganites still laud their hero for declaring, in his inaugural address, "Government is the problem." Reagan helped stoke the anti-government anger that achieved critical mass with the Tea Party and exploded on January 6. Of course, his followers would argue that he was merely talking about reducing the size of government, not overthrowing it. But making that distinction would require something that Reagan and his successors in the Age of Ignorance have done their best to eliminate: nuance.

Reagan and Trump availed themselves of the same deep bench of sociopathic henchmen, from the corrupt Roy Cohn to the predatory Roger Ailes to the felonious Paul Manafort and Roger Stone. As for Reagan's "civility and personal grace," as Peter Wehner put it, which Reagan, exactly, was he describing? The one who used racist dog whistles like "states' rights" and "welfare queen"? The one who said, of student protesters, "If it takes a bloodbath, let's get it over with"? The one who wished that California's hungry would contract botulism? The one who permitted his press secretary to turn AIDS into a joke? The one who called African leaders cannibals and monkeys? The Party of Reagan seems pretty recognizable to me.

There was no shortage of villains on January 6. But that dark moment also yielded an unlikely hero.

In the days leading up to the insurrection, Trump increasingly pressured his VP, Mike Pence, not to perform the vice president's ceremonial role of certifying the results of the presidential election. Paralyzed with anxiety, a desperate Pence sought advice from a fellow Indianan who had held his office three decades earlier: Dan Quayle.

"Mike, you have no flexibility on this," Quayle informed Pence. "None. Zero. Forget it. Put it away."

"You don't know the position I'm in," Pence said.

"I do know the position you're in," Quayle replied. "I also know what the law is. You listen to the parliamentarian. That's all you do. You have no power."

History doesn't move in a straight line, and the improbable trajectory of Dan Quayle seems to prove that point. After a spell as a national punch line, the hapless veep was consigned to decades of obscurity, only to reemerge, in 2021, as the Republican Party's voice of reason. Quayle's role in saving our democracy might not merit his inclusion on Mount Rushmore, but it's certainly worthy of an exhibit at his vice presidential museum, as well as a question on the museum's Quayle Quiz. At a moment when Mike Pence seemed to be losing his mind, Dan Quayle was there to remind him what a waste it is to lose one's mind, or not to have a mind is being very wasteful.

On March 11, 2020, the day the World Health Organization declared a global pandemic, Americans witnessed an unusual night of television. First, live from the Oval Office, Donald J. Trump spoke robotically from a prepared text. "Smart action today will prevent the spread of the virus tomorrow," he said, referring to one thing that didn't happen and another that unfortunately did.

As strange as his performance was, it wasn't the most bizarre sight American viewers encountered that night. That was over on Fox, during an episode of the reality show *The Masked Singer*. For the culturally deprived among you, here's the show's premise: celebrities disguised in ridiculous outsized costumes sing, and a panel of other celebrities guess their identities. In this episode, the Bear, a female singer wearing a fluffy pink-and-blue bear suit that made her look like a frightening, gargantuan plush toy, pulled off her costume's head, revealing herself to be Sarah Palin. Testing the American people's appetite for surrealism, she had just concluded a caterwauling performance of Sir Mix-a-Lot's rap classic "Baby Got Back." After the show, she told the host, Nick Cannon, that her appearance had been "a walking middle finger to the haters out there in the world." What haters? In 2020, no one was thinking about Sarah Palin. Her appearance seemed more like a walking middle finger to Sir Mix-a-Lot.

Their mouths agape, many Americans saw the juxtaposition of these two televised events as a sign that the End Times were nigh. I, on the other hand, found Palin's appearance on *The Masked Singer* soothing. The sight of the former Alaska governor in a fuzzy bear suit was evidence that the road from reality TV to government also runs in the opposite direction, depositing once-powerful players in a place where they can do considerably less harm. In the Age of Ignorance, I'll take reassurance wherever I can get it.

DEMOCRACY'S
BRAKING SYSTEM

If you were traumatized by how much the ignoramuses I've profiled didn't know, I apologize. But trust me: there's tons more that they didn't know, which, out of kindness, I spared you. Plus, I avoided the whole ugly topic of Newt Gingrich. (Sometimes history must give way to humanitarianism.) So now comes the inevitable question: Did I learn anything by studying people who learned so little?

I did. Just as history is littered with unexpected consequences, so are history projects. As I set out to document how much our politicians didn't know, I stumbled on the inconvenient truth of how much *I* didn't know.

Here's a shining example of my own ignorance. As I stated in the introduction, I have a strong pro-education bias. It's true that education solves a lot of problems. It comes in pretty handy if you're trying to develop a vaccine to wipe out a rampaging pandemic. But my belief in education led me to an erroneous conclusion about how to fix our regrettable habit of electing ignorant leaders. I thought that, if we were better educated as a nation, we'd make smarter choices on Election Day. I wasn't alone: Franklin Delano Roosevelt wrote,

"Democracy cannot succeed unless those who express their choice are prepared to choose wisely. The real safeguard of democracy, therefore, is education."

The only problem with what FDR and I believed is that we were both, well, wrong. Improving our nation's education would yield positive outcomes, like making us more competitive in the global economy, not to mention at trivia night, but there isn't a ton of evidence that it would result in our electing smarter leaders. Why? Because our emotional, not-very-rational engagement with politics renders even the best-educated among us capable of voting like dopes.* This is true no matter where you sit on the political spectrum.

In their book, *The Tea Party and the Remaking of Republican Conservatism*, Theda Skocpol and Vanessa Williamson reported that many Tea Partiers were better educated than the average American, and extremely well-versed in the workings of government. Ironically, though, because their heightened engagement in politics made them avid consumers of Fox News and other right-wing propaganda, they were also extremely well-versed in batshit-crazy fever dreams that overrode their rational faculties.

The same is true on the left. Democrats were justifiably aghast at polling after the 2020 election showing that a huge chunk of Republicans believed Trump's big lie that President Biden's election was illegitimate. But a 2018 YouGov poll revealed that two out of three Democrats believed Russia actually changed the vote tallies of the 2016 election, a baseless conspiracy theory. Similarly, while they were right to assail Trump's attempts to overturn the 2020 election, some liberals—including some well-educated ones—were hoping for a

---

* In his book *Who Voted for Hitler?* (1982), Richard F. Hamilton used voting records to prove that well-educated Germans were among those who supported Donald Trump's favorite author.

similar scenario after 2016. They were counting on an FBI investiga-tion that would result in Trump's immediate imprisonment—despite the decades-old Department of Justice policy against indicting a sitting president. The spectacle of former college radicals who pro-tested the Vietnam War now rooting for the FBI to save democracy vividly demonstrates that education alone isn't the answer.

Liberals and conservatives alike get some of their nuttiest ideas from social media. If we're looking to reverse the ravages of the Age of Ignorance, a good first step might be to stop spending so much of our time on these platforms. During the Trump years, some mem-bers of the "Resistance" thought they were accomplishing something by arguing with their opposite numbers on Facebook and Twitter. Actually, the minute you get into an argument online, the other side automatically wins, because you're expending energy that could have been applied to political activities that are productive and not just symbolic.

What are these productive activities? The political scientist Eitan Hersh, in his book *Politics Is for Power: How to Move Beyond Political Hobbyism, Take Action, and Make Real Change*, offers useful, concrete instructions for political activism. And he correctly identifies a seri-ous problem plaguing today's politics: me.

Okay, maybe not me specifically. But people like me—college-educated white people—are most likely to engage in what Hersh calls "political hobbyism." We think we're participating in politics, but we're often just spectators, following it the way we fol-low sports. Obsessively watching cable news, checking Twitter, and monitoring the latest polls—all of which I've been guilty of—makes us feel like we're staying informed, but to what end? When I do these things, I'm just a passive observer, rooting for my team. There's a difference between going to a Super Bowl party and playing in the Super Bowl; only those who do the latter affect the outcome of the game. Similarly, though it's helpful to know how ignorant our politicians have become over the past fifty years, that knowledge is only valuable if we take action to oust our current crop of dunces. That's not going to be easy. But, in the words of an activist Hersh quotes who was rattled by the 2016 election, "I really started feeling that if we are going to save our democracy, we all really need to work, to do hard things."

Hersh urges us to dial back our day-to-day surveillance of national politics, roll up our sleeves, and get to work on the local level. Organize. Register people to vote. Get out the vote. Go to town meetings. And, maybe the most challenging task of all: try to change people's minds, one voter at a time.

Maybe I convinced myself that I was politically active because I've obediently responded to fundraising appeals from House and Senate candidates across the country. Donating is important, but, as Hersh points out, the way we donate sometimes amounts to little more than hobbyism. Hersh cites the case of Amy McGrath: though an estimable candidate for the U.S. Senate in Kentucky, she had zero chance of beating Mitch McConnell, who wound up winning by twenty points. Nevertheless, well-meaning Democratic donors like me pumped tens of millions of dollars into her campaign, money that could've been allocated more strategically to other, more winnable races. Another downside to this credit-card style of political hobbyism is that it can lull us into believing we don't need to do "hard things," because we've already done our part.

If we follow all of Hersh's advice, how long will it take to repair the wreckage of the Age of Ignorance? Unfortunately, there's no quick fix. We have to be patient. But you know who's been super patient? The Kochs. They've worked for decades to effect change on the local level, with a special emphasis on statehouses and the judiciary. Now we're all living in the Kochs' world, and it's on fire. Hobbyists like me have no choice but to stop checking our phones and get to work.

Now, it would be reasonable for you to ask, would all the arduous effort that Hersh proposes have prevented any of the ignoramuses in this book from being elected? The answer is yes. We probably still would have been stuck with Reagan and Quayle, since their tickets won by landslides. But we might have been spared the devastation wreaked by two of the worst presidents in U.S. history: George W. Bush and Donald J. Trump. Had a few thousand votes in battleground states gone the other way in 2016, Hillary Clinton would've won. A mere 537 votes in one state, Florida, separated George W. Bush and Al Gore in 2000. Still not convinced that organizing on the local level can make a big difference? Well, consider this: I've heard that a community organizer can go really far in politics.

Now that Barack Obama is essentially a superhero in his own cinematic universe, it's easy to forget that, when he first ran for president, his campaign was a long-shot insurgency. In an interview with the *Los Angeles Times* in April 2021, the former president explained how, in 2008, he won the crucial caucuses in Iowa, a "heavily white rural state" with "very few folks who looked like me." A horde of young campaign workers blanketed Iowa and asked voters to share their concerns. By listening to these Iowans, Obama said, the staffers gained their trust, "and it's on the basis of that trust that people started listening to what I stood for."

Listening. Ronald Reagan wasn't great at it. I have to admit, I'm not, either. But it's something I need to work on, because effective activism demands it. Listening is a crucial ingredient of a relatively new campaign technique Hersh advocates called deep canvassing. Unlike traditional canvassing, in which people go from door to door offering prepackaged talking points, deep canvassing goes, well, deeper.

The canvasser might share a personal story that has motivated his or her activism, in the hopes of forging a real connection with the voter, who might wind up sharing a personal story in return. In the best-case scenario, a real conversation will ensue, and the canvasser has a genuine shot at changing the voter's mind. Changing someone's mind is one of the hardest things to do in politics—and in life— which is why so many of us prefer to change our profile pictures. But when you change someone's mind, you start to change the world.

Deep canvassing doesn't always work, but it's produced some impressive victories. In 2018, Question 3 on the Massachusetts ballot asked voters whether they wanted to keep a law protecting transgender people from discrimination. As Brian Resnick reported at Vox, an activist named Vivian Topping used deep canvassing to persuade people to vote yes. "This tactic is the only thing that has been proven to work on nondiscrimination, so without it we wouldn't have been able to win," Topping said. Deep canvassing worked because activists on the ground weren't offering canned talking points. They opened people's minds with the power of personal stories.

No one understands the primacy of storytelling better than Mark Burnett. The story he gave Donald Trump to recite in the opening moments of *The Apprentice* is compelling. "Thirteen years ago, I was seriously in trouble," Trump says. "I was billions of dollars in debt. But I fought back and I won, big league.* I used my brain. I used my negotiating skills. And I worked it all out. Now my company's bigger than it ever was—it's stronger than it ever was." That's a powerful story. It's also a big lie. Trump didn't fight back and win, he didn't work it all out, and his company was neither bigger nor

---

*Trump's frequent use of the phrase "big league" caused many to believe they'd heard him create a new adverb, "bigly." Trump has invented many idiotic neologisms, but it's only fair to strike "bigly" from the list.

stronger than it ever was. He was in a career trough when Burnett threw him a lifeline. But it didn't matter that the story was false. Sometimes false stories are what we want, because they provide our lives with meaning. That's why so many people are drawn to professional wrestling—not to mention folklore and mythology. In the case of Donald Trump, people's hunger for a false story helped elect the worst president in U.S. history.

In an essay published in 2021, James Bernard Murphy, a professor of government at Dartmouth, writes about the essential role that storytelling plays in our lives. Because stories explain the world to us, we'll believe them even if they aren't true. For this reason, Plato realized that stories could be big trouble. Murphy notes, "Plato believed that rational argument could not take hold in a culture until all storytellers were forcibly expelled." (Plato definitely would have banished Mark Burnett.) So if false stories—whether they're about Democrats stealing the election in 2020 or Putin rigging voting machines in 2016—have such power over us, are we doomed to a never-ending Age of Ignorance? Not necessarily. In his conclusion, Murphy suggests a way forward. If we think of our nation as a community, "whoever has the best stories will conjure that community."

I asked Murphy what he meant by "the best stories." He had a perfect example: how, "only in America," a Black man named Barack Hussein Obama was elected president of the United States. Not everyone loved that story—in fact, it drove a lot of people nuts—but Obama's election led to health coverage for millions who'd been uninsured, and protection for those with preexisting conditions. His story saved lives. As a result, Obamacare, which congressional Republicans tried to repeal approximately 900 billion times, keeps getting more popular.

Murphy cited another uplifting story: how, despite the hectoring of Donald Trump, in 2020 local officials across the country—even members of Trump's own party—defended the integrity of a free and fair election. Like Hersh, Murphy believes that some of the best in American democracy happens on the local level. People who must work together every day to keep local government running can't abuse one another the way people do on Twitter or Facebook. You're less likely to act like a raging asshole to someone at a town meeting if tomorrow you might run into him at the gym.*

One of the worst stories in our nation's history happened on January 6, 2021. But one of the best happened a day earlier. On January 5, Georgia voters went to the polls and elected two Democrats to the U.S. Senate. Making the outcome even more improbable, the two winners were an African American, Raphael Warnock, and a Jew, Jon Ossoff. With these two historic victories, Democrats gained just enough votes in the Senate to pass the American Rescue Plan, a $1.9 trillion stimulus bill that lifted millions of American families out of the economic misery caused by the pandemic.

On the day of the runoffs, the *Washington Post* warned that a Democratic victory in Georgia would be a long shot. How did Warnock and Ossoff defy history and win? Donations helped, but it took more than money. It required the organizational genius of Stacey Abrams and the dogged efforts of activists. After witnessing voter suppression in her 2018 Georgia gubernatorial race, Abrams founded an organization called Fair Fight Action to increase voter registration in that state and across the country. On January 5, 2021, Abrams's dedicated volunteers helped Democrats get the unprecedented turnout they needed.†

---

*Of course, we've all seen viral YouTube videos of school board meetings disrupted by raging assholes. But the school board meetings where people are nice to each other don't go viral.
†If we want to do the kind of invaluable work these activists did, getting involved with Fair Fight Action, Michelle Obama's group When We All Vote, or a similar

Predictably, Republicans in Georgia and other states moved to pass restrictive election laws to keep the nasty surprise of January 5 from recurring. The GOP was all for exporting democracy to Iraq and Afghanistan, but it turns out they don't like it much here at home. So what can we do about their attempts to kill democracy? Write angry comments on Facebook? Watch the cable TV host whose sarcastic monologues we always agree with? Or will we fight to save our democracy using the tools of our democracy, and flood the zone with votes? What's the alternative?

I didn't realize it at the time, but, when I was a kid, my fascination with Cleveland mayor Ralph J. Perk's hair-torching mishap probably set me on the road to being a political satirist. In middle school, I spent hours in my bedroom making a Super 8 claymation movie about Nixon and his sleazy henchmen H. R. Haldeman and John Ehrlichman. (Good times.) In high school, I became the editor of the newspaper solely to publish an April Fool's edition full of fake news stories. My writing a satirical news column for the past two decades represents either commitment to a genre or arrested development.

Writing the column and touring as a comedian have given me a platform to raise money for political candidates and causes I believe in. But working on this book has made me aware that I haven't done enough. It's going to take more than money to fix the damage that ignorant politicians have inflicted on our country and the world. I need to join the effort on the ground.

In the introduction to this book, I talked about democracy's braking system, which has kept our nation—just barely, at times—from hurtling off a cliff. On Election Night 2016, it felt like the brakes

---

pro-voting organization (there are many) would be an excellent use of our time and energy.

were shot. The 2020 election told a different story—a better story. It wasn't a better story just because Trump lost, though that alone would have been cause for dancing naked in the streets. Despite unprecedented attacks on our embattled democracy, the brakes worked. The braking system of democracy is in ragged condition right now, but it's still there. The brakes work every time we register to vote and help others do the same. The brakes work when we provide transportation for someone who otherwise wouldn't make it to the polls. The brakes work when we see a long line of people waiting to vote and offer them water. The brakes work when we go to town meetings, make our voices heard, and listen to the voices of others. The brakes work when we organize, fundraise, and canvass. The brakes work when we march, protest, and vote. The brakes work when, against the odds, we change one voter's mind.

We're the brakes.

Acknowledgments

The people I profiled in this book couldn't be more unlike those who helped me publish it. The latter group is highly competent and well-informed—plus, they like to read.

Carlton Cuse, Kyra Darnton, Larry Jacobson, Jonathon Kahn, James Murphy, and Kathryn Schulz contributed essential advice.

Nathan Burstein, my longtime colleague at *The New Yorker*, contributed incisive feedback on an early draft and spectacular copyedits later.

Kyle Paoletta was a dogged and meticulous fact-checker who succeeded in confirming that actual humans really said all those things.

Sloan Harris, my superb agent, read several drafts, gave astute suggestions, and found the book its perfect home.

My publisher and editor, Ben Loehnen, lent his enthusiasm, wit, and intelligence to this project, and made working on it a blast. And Jonathan Karp could not have been more generous with his wisdom and support.

Everyone at Avid Reader Press, Simon & Schuster, and ICM who worked on this book deserves my deep gratitude: Jofie Ferrari-Adler, Meredith Vilarello, Carolyn Kelly, Caroline MacGregor, Alexandra Primiani, Katherine Hernandez, Jonathan Evans, Annie Craig, Alicia Brancato, Alison Forner, Ruth Lee-Mui, Rob Sternitzky, Andrea Johnson, and Julie Flanagan.

My children helped inspire me to write this book. One day, out of the blue, my youngest, Maddie, asked, "Was there ever a president who didn't have a wife?" This led me to a deep dive on James Buchanan, and I soon learned that researching horrible presidents was addictive. Her sister, Lexi, and brother, Max, have entertained me on a daily basis with their hilarious and reliably absurd political hot takes. Despite being a young woman, Lexi does a creepily accurate Trump imitation. As for Max, when he was thirteen and I was recovering from major surgery, he thought the perfect way to hasten my healing was by sending me a YouTube video of Barack Obama's crazy 2004 Illinois senate debate with Alan Keyes. What can I tell you? I've raised these kids well.

And finally, I must give special thanks to the love of my life, Olivia Gentile. I knew when I married Livy that she was a great reporter and writer, but I didn't know what a masterful editor she was until she started marking up my pages. Editing, however, was far from her most amazing contribution. For months she tolerated a husband who went around the house quoting Dan Quayle. That wasn't in our vows.

Notes

INTRODUCTION: THE THREE STAGES OF IGNORANCE

2 *Ralph J. Perk*: Patrick Cooley, "A Historic Look at Former Cleveland Mayor Ralph J. Perk, the 'Hottest Mayor in the Country,'" Cleveland .com, November 2, 2017.

2 *Cuyahoga River*: Lorraine Boissoneault, "The Cuyahoga River Caught Fire at Least a Dozen Times, but No One Cared Until 1969," *Smithsonian Magazine*, June 19, 2019.

2 *Richard Eberling*: Edward P. Whelan, "The Politics of Restoration," *Cleveland Magazine*, November 29, 2007.

3 *H. L. Mencken*: William E. Leuchtenburg, *The American President: From Teddy Roosevelt to Bill Clinton* (New York: Oxford University Press, 2015).

4 *"had done nothing wrong"*: John W. Dean, *Warren G. Harding* (New York: Time Books/Henry Holt, 2004), 160.

4 *anti-lynching law and proposed a commission*: Warren G. Harding's address to a Joint Session of Congress, April 12, 1921; Ronald Radosh and Allis Radosh, "What If Warren Harding Wasn't a Terrible President?" *Slate*, July 16, 2014.

4 *posthumously published diary*: "Mencken Was Pro-Nazi, His Diary Shows," Associated Press, December 5, 1989.

5 *florid passages*: Warren G. Harding–Carrie Fulton Phillips Correspondence, December 24, 1910, Library of Congress.

5 *"I am not fit for this office and should never have been here"*: Darrin Grinder and Steve Shaw, *The Presidents & Their Faith: From George Washington to Barack Obama* (Boise, ID: Elevate Faith, 2012).

5 *more than a hundred men to duels*: Nick Tasler, *The Impulse Factor: Why Some of Us Play It Safe and Others Risk It All* (New York: Fireside, 2008), 55.

6 *first televised presidential debates*: Richard Hofstadter, *Anti-Intellectualism in American Life* (New York: Knopf, 1963), 65–73, 227–28.

6 *dumbing-down process*: Neil Postman, *Amusing Ourselves to Death: Public Discourse in the Age of Show Business* (New York: Viking, 1985), 65–77.

8 *college graduate*: Valerie Strauss, "Which U.S. Presidents Didn't Earn a College Degree? (Two of Them Are on Mount Rushmore)," *Washington Post*, February 12, 2015.

8 *C average*: "The Harvard Grade Cards of Franklin D. Roosevelt and Lathrop Brown," Franklin Delano Roosevelt Foundation.

9 *every library book*: Samuel W. Rushay Jr., "Harry Truman's History Lessons," *Prologue Magazine*, Spring 2009.

CHAPTER 1: THE FIRST STAGE: RIDICULE

14 *doomed to fail*: Will Bunch, "Five Myths About Ronald Reagan's Legacy," *Washington Post*, February 4, 2011.

14 *"Communism would have collapsed anyway"*: Monica Crowley, *Nixon off the Record* (New York: Random House, 1996).

15 *"amiable dunce"*: Marilyn Berger, "Clark Clifford, a Major Adviser to Four Presidents, Is Dead at 91," *New York Times*, October 11, 1998.

15 *misspells Clifford's first name*: David T. Byrne, *Ronald Reagan: An Intellectual Biography* (Dulles, VA: Potomac Books, 2018), xi.

15 *Reagan's big brain*: Ibid., xi–xii.

15 *"do a little arithmetic"*: Ibid., 49–50.

16 *"that we can do without a few freedoms"*: Ronald Reagan, "Are Liberals Really Liberal?" speech, 1963.

16 *"a little intellectual elite in a far-distant capital"*: Ronald Reagan, "A Time for Choosing," speech, October 27, 1964.

16 *In his most damning broadside*: Dan Berrett, "The Day the Purpose of College Changed," *Chronicle of Higher Education*, January 26, 2015.

16 *"dumb as a stump"*: Christopher Hitchens, "Not Even a Hedgehog," *Slate*, June 7, 2004.

16 *"the charm of Ronald Reagan"*: Molly Ivins, *Molly Ivins Can't Say That, Can She?* (New York: Random House, 1991), 104.

17 *"watering the arid desert"*: David S. Broder, "A President Who Flees Information," *Washington Post*, September 1, 1985.

17 *"You could walk through"*: Leuchtenburg, *The American President*, 586.

17　*"not deeply read"*: Haynes Johnson, *Sleepwalking Through History: America in the Reagan Years* (New York: W. W. Norton, 2003), 49.

17　*"never opened a book"*: Lou Cannon, *President Reagan: The Role of a Lifetime* (New York: PublicAffairs, 1991), 138–39.

17　The Law: Ronald E. Merrill, *Ayn Rand Explained: From Tyranny to Tea Party*, revised and updated by Marsha Familaro Enright (Chicago: Open Court, 2013), 39–40; Anne C. Heller, *Ayn Rand and the World She Made* (New York: Nan A. Talese/Doubleday, 2009), 251.

17　*"I urge you not to work for or advocate his nomination"*: Ayn Rand, *The Ayn Rand Letter, Volume IV, Number 2, November–December 1975*.

18　*"voracious reader"*: Dennis Lythgoe, "Reagan Aide Sets the Record Straight," *Deseret News*, May 13, 2001.

18　*"ideas of that kind"*: Rowland Evans and Robert Novak, *The Reagan Revolution: An Inside Look at the Transformation of the U.S. Government* (New York: Dutton, 1981), 230.

18　*"only two chief executives in history that I am aware of who quoted"*: "Two Giants: Steven Hayward Compares Reagan and Churchill," *National Review*, October 19, 2005.

18　*"private library"*: Byrne, *Ronald Reagan*, 72.

18　*"Phi Beta Kappa key"*: James C. Humes, *The Wit & Wisdom of Ronald Reagan* (Washington, DC: Regnery, 2007), 39.

18　*"voracious reader of newspapers and magazines"*: Bill Hogan, "What Reagan Reads," *Washington Journalism Review*, March 1981.

18　*"read the funnies"*: Ibid.

19　Sound of Music: Lou Cannon, *President Reagan: The Role of a Lifetime* (New York: Touchstone, 1991), 56–57.

19　*blocked their release*: Ronnie Dugger, *On Reagan: The Man & His Presidency* (New York: McGraw-Hill, 1983), 19.

19　*"two Vietnams"*: Stephen Prince, *Visions of Empire: Political Imagery in Contemporary American Film* (New York: Praeger, 1992), 119.

19　*"air pollution comes not from chimneys and auto exhaust pipes"*: David E. Rosenbaum, "Opposition Papers for November," *New York Times*, January 8, 1984.

19　*Claremont College*: Lou Cannon, *Governor Reagan: His Rise to Power* (New York: PublicAffairs, 2003), 497.

19　*"A tree's a tree"*: Lou Cannon, "Wrong Facts Revisited," RealClearPolitics, August 3, 2012.

20   *"number one environmentalist"*: Philip Shabecoff, "Watt Softening Attacks on Critics of His Policies," *New York Times*, October 10, 1981.

20   *career-ending boast*: "Foot-in-Mouth Hall of Fame," Associated Press, December 26, 2002.

20   *fictitious patter*: Byrne, *Ronald Reagan*, 10.

20   *played in college*: Francis X. Clines, "The Reagan Play-by-Play Still Plays," *New York Times*, March 31, 1985.

21   *"came up with that one himself"*: Mark J. Green and Gail MacColl, *Reagan's Reign of Error: The Instant Nostalgia Edition* (New York: Pantheon, 1987), 61.

21   *"sugar candy"*: "Remarks at a White House Meeting with Republican Congressmen," Ronald Reagan Presidential Library & Museum, January 27, 1984.

21   *told the Soviet premier*: Larry Speakes, *Speaking Out* (New York: Scribner, 1988), 152, 170.

21   *"he didn't have any specific reaction"*: Donnie Radcliffe, "What Hath Speakes Spoke?" *Washington Post*, April 18, 1988.

22   *unhinged monologue*: Karl E. Meyer, "The Editorial Notebook: The Elusive Lenin," *New York Times*, October 8, 1985.

22   *Welch's loony book*: Robert Welch, *The Blue Book of the John Birch Society* (Belmont, MA: Western Islands, 1959).

22   *"Reagan's talents as a storyteller are legendary"*: Annelise Anderson, Kiron K. Skinner, Martin Anderson, eds., *Stories in His Own Words: The Everyday Wisdom of Ronald Reagan* (New York: Free Press, 2001), ix.

22   *"moral instruction"*: David Gergen, *Eyewitness to Power: The Essence of Leadership: Nixon to Clinton* (New York: Simon & Schuster, 2000), 221.

23   *concentration camps*: Cannon, *President Reagan: The Role of a Lifetime*, 486–88.

23   *"food stamps"*: "Telling Stories," *New York Times*, April 28, 1982.

23   *"I used to get into arguments sometimes with my father"*: The Reagans, Showtime, 2020.

24   *"I certainly hope he hasn't"*: Dugger, *On Reagan*, 21.

24   *"barren terrain"*: William Leuchtenburg, "Behind the Ronald Reagan Myth," *Salon*, December 27, 2015.

25   *Jack Warner*: Joseph Lewis, *What Makes Reagan Run? A Political Profile* (New York: McGraw-Hill, 1968), 19.

25 *love of nukes*: Martin Walker, *The Cold War: A History* (New York: Henry Holt, 1994), 189.

25 *"pave the whole country"*: Jim Cullen, *Democratic Empire: The United States Since 1945* (Hoboken, NJ: Wiley-Blackwell, 2016), 101.

25 *"bloodbath"*: Clara Bingham, "The Battle for People's Park, Berkeley 1969: When Vietnam Came Home," *Guardian*, July 6, 2019.

25 *"blanket waiver"*: Cannon, *President Reagan: The Role of a Lifetime*, 218–19; William L. Bird, *Better Living: Advertising, Media and the New Vocabulary of Business Leadership, 1935–1955* (Evanston, IL: Northwestern University Press, 1999), 201–4.

26 *"never played a governor"*: Roger Simon, "Ronald Reagan, Forever Young," Politico, February 8, 2011.

26 *"provoked ridicule and scorn"*: Gerard DeGroot, *Selling Ronald Reagan: The Emergence of a President* (New York: I. B. Tauris, 2015), 1–2.

26 *"We set out to help 19 countries"*: Ibid., 57–60.

26 *"We set out to help"*: Reagan, "A Time for Choosing."

26 *Stu Spencer and Bill Roberts*: Ibid., 107–26, 224–28.

27 *"baffle 'em with bull"*: James M. Naughton, "Ford's Political Chief," *New York Times*, March 17, 1976.

27 *"never fired anybody in his life"*: DeGroot, *Selling Ronald Reagan*.

27 *"what sources of information he was using"*: Ibid.

28 *"They used 5 x 8 index cards"*: Ibid.

28 *"He left behind the impression"*: Ibid.

28 *"innocent of experience"*: Ibid.

28 *"dramatizes the virtual bankruptcy"*: Ibid.

28 *managing more than four hundred Republican campaigns*: Mark Z. Barabak, "Stuart Spencer Has a Few Zingers Left," *Los Angeles Times*, October 20, 2002.

28 *"A wind is blowing"*: Lewis, *What Makes Reagan Run?*, 139.

29 *California's new governor was unprepared for the role*: Cannon, *President Reagan: The Role of a Lifetime*, 47, 169.

29 *"there are simple answers"*: William E. Gibson, "The Gift of Gaffe," *South Florida Sun-Sentinel*, September 8, 1985.

29 *"a person of the people"*: Colleen J. Shogan, "Anti-Intellectualism in the Modern Presidency: A Republican Populism," *Perspectives on Politics* 5, no. 2 (June 2007), 295–303.

30   *Harry Truman urged him to run for president:* Joseph Epstein, "Adlai Stevenson in Retrospect," *Commentary,* December 1, 1968.

30   Social Register: Michael Beschloss, "How Well-Read Should a President Be?" *New York Times,* June 11, 2000.

30   *had to leave Harvard Law School:* John Bartlow Martin, *Adlai Stevenson of Illinois* (New York: Doubleday, 1976), 528.

30   *egghead:* William Safire, *Safire's Political Dictionary* (New York: Oxford University Press, 2008), 209.

30   *personal motto:* James Reston, "Washington: '*Via Ovicapitum Dura Est,*'" *New York Times,* September 16, 1956.

31   *"portal to the Golden Age":* Adlai Stevenson, "Address Accepting the Presidential Nomination at the Democratic National Convention in Chicago, July 26, 1952," American Presidency Project, UC Santa Barbara.

31   *"I need a majority":* Fredrik Logevall, *JFK: Coming of Age in the American Century, 1917–1956* (New York: Random House, 2020), 527.

31   *"The knuckleheads have beaten the eggheads":* Murray Kempton, "The Sorehead," *New York Post,* November 6, 1952.

31   *"definition of an intellectual":* Dwight D. Eisenhower, "Remarks at a Breakfast Held by Republican Groups of Southern California, September 24, 1954," American Presidency Project, UC Santa Barbara.

31   *"being considered highbrow":* Elvin T. Lim, *The Anti-Intellectual Presidency: The Decline of Presidential Rhetoric from George Washington to George W. Bush* (New York: Oxford University Press, 2008).

31   *he often stayed up until 11:00 p.m.:* Stephen E. Ambrose, *Eisenhower: Soldier and President* (New York: Simon & Schuster, 1990).

32   *"I had failed":* Harry S. Truman, *Mr. Citizen* (New York: Bernhard Geis, 1960).

32   *"The Camera":* Eugene J. McCarthy, *Selected Poems* (Petersham, MA: Lone Oak Press, 1997).

32   *onetime next-door neighbor:* Timothy Stanley and Jonathan Bell, eds., *Making Sense of American Liberalism* (Champaign: University of Illinois Press, 2012), 90.

33   *"God, Jesus, and Adlai Stevenson":* Thomas J. Knock, *The Rise of a Prairie Statesman: The Life and Times of George McGovern* (Princeton, NJ: Princeton University Press, 2016), 144.

33   *"The next guys up will have to be performers":* Joe McGinniss, *The Selling of the President 1968* (New York: Trident Press, 1969), 160.

33   *"I do not think I want the job"*: Leland H. Gregory III, *Presidential Indiscretions* (New York: Dell, 1999), 54.

34   *Stu Spencer was now working for the opposition*: Lois Romano, "Stu Spencer, Quayle's Copilot," *Washington Post*, September 13, 1988.

34   *"Ron is not so qualified to be President"*: James M. Naughton, "Ford's Political Chief," *New York Times*, March 17, 1976.

34   *"The United States has much to offer the Third World War"*: Matthew Parris and Phil Mason, *Read My Lips: A Treasury of the Things Politicians Wished They Hadn't Said* (London: Robson Books, 1996), 35.

34   *"Jerry Ford is so dumb"*: Paul Cook, *Presidential Leadership by Example: A Presidential and First Ladies Report Card for the New Millennium* (Bloomington, IN: Xlibris, 2001), 265.

34   *DKE*: "Growing Up Grand: Fraternity Life," Gerald R. Ford Presidential Library & Museum.

34   *top third of his class*: John Robert Greene, "Gerald Ford: Life Before the Presidency," Miller Center, University of Virginia.

35   *Eureka College Red Devils*: "R. W. Reagan, '32, to Speak to Class of '82," *Chicago Tribune*, May 9, 1982.

35   *"Whip Inflation Now"*: Ronald G. Shafer, "Gerald Ford Responded to an Inflation Crisis with a Voluntary Public Campaign. It Was a Disaster," *Washington Post*, November 16, 2021.

36   *Spencer's survival plan*: Romano, "Stu Spencer, Quayle's Copilot."

36   *Vatican embassy in Panama City*: Reza Rafie, "The Rock 'n' Roll Assault on Noriega: U.S. SOUTHCOM Public Affairs After Action Report Supplement 'Operation Just Cause,' Dec. 20, 1989–Jan. 31, 1990," National Security Archive, February 6, 1996.

36   *"Forgive me, Mr. President"*: Mark Z. Barabak, "Stuart Spencer Has a Few Zingers Left," *Los Angeles Times*, October 20, 2002.

36   *"Ask President Carter"*: *Saturday Night Live*, NBC, March 12, 1977.

37   *"no Soviet domination of Eastern Europe"*: David A. Graham, "The Myth of Gerald Ford's Fatal 'Soviet Domination' Gaffe," *The Atlantic*, August 2, 2016.

37   *"any allegation of domination"*: *Gerald R. Ford: Containing the Public Messages, Speeches, and Statements of the President, 1976–77*, book 2 (Washington, DC: U.S. Government Printing Office, 1979), 2457.

38   *"Ford Library in Ann Arbor"*: "Notes Show Ford Debate Comment Wasn't a Slip," Associated Press, October 6, 1986.

38 *narrow the gap with Carter*: Graham, "The Myth of Gerald Ford's Fatal 'Soviet Domination' Gaffe."

38 *Carter's debate briefing book*: Philip Taubman, "Reagan Aides Say Only One Protested Use of Carter Notes," *New York Times*, July 16, 1983.

39 *"a deft phrase than a technical argument"*: Cannon, *Governor Reagan: His Rise to Power*, 505.

39 *"Facts are stupid things"*: "Remarks at the Republican National Convention in New Orleans, Louisiana, August 15, 1988," American Presidency Project, UC Santa Barbara.

40 *"the leader of the free world is chosen by the people in the Age of Television"*: Postman, *Amusing Ourselves to Death*, 97.

40 *"Politics is just like show business"*: William E. Leuchtenburg, *The American President: From Teddy Roosevelt to Bill Clinton* (New York: Oxford University Press, 2015).

41 *"saw his election as a chance to get some rest"*: Cannon, *President Reagan: The Role of a Lifetime*, 144.

41 *"I'm going to turn over to the secretary of defense"*: Lou Cannon, "Reagan Trusted MX Decision to an 'Inexpert' Weinberger," *Washington Post*, September 16, 1982.

41 *showing him videos and cartoons*: Cannon, *President Reagan: The Role of a Lifetime*, 35, 171.

41 *"grab bag"*: Elizabeth Drew, *Portrait of an Election: The 1980 Presidential Campaign* (New York: Simon & Schuster, 1981), 115.

41 *"Margaret Thatcher"*: Lou Cannon, "Reagan Announces, Urges Strength at Home, Abroad," *Washington Post*, November 14, 1979.

42 *"gravely under-informed"*: Shogan, "Anti-Intellectualism in the Modern Presidency."

42 *"Danny Thomas's"*: Ivins, *Molly Ivins Can't Say That, Can She?*, 105.

42 *"Chairman Moe"*: "Reagan Calls Doe 'Chairman Moe,'" UPI, August 18, 1982.

42 *"Singapore"*: "Remarks at the Welcoming Ceremony for Prime Minister Lee Kuan Yew of Singapore, October 8, 1985," Ronald Reagan Presidential Library & Museum.

42 *"They're all individual countries"*: Lou Cannon, "Latin Trip an Eye-Opener for Reagan," *Washington Post*, December 6, 1982.

42 *"If you look at a map"*: Ibid.

42 *"the people of Bolivia"*: "President Reagan Had a Slip of the Tongue Wednesday . . . ," UPI, December 1, 1982.

43 *unquestioning devotion to the government of apartheid*: David Corn, "Reagan and the Media: A Love Story," *The Nation*, June 10, 2004.

43 *bastion of racial equality*: Lou Cannon, "Reagan Calls South Africa 'Reformist,'" *Washington Post*, August 27, 1985.

43 *"word for freedom"*: "President Reagan Says There Is No Word for Freedom . . . ," UPI, October 31, 1985.

43 *"Nuclear war would be the greatest tragedy"*: "Remarks to Private Sector Leaders During a White House Briefing on the MX Missile, March 6, 1985," Ronald Reagan Presidential Library & Museum.

43 *"stored under a desk"*: Kevin Hillstrom, *Nuclear Energy* (Farmington Hills, MI: Lucent Books, 2013), 34.

43 *"We are trying to get unemployment to go up"*: Thomas J. Craughwell, *Presidential Payola* (Beverly, MA: Fair Winds Press, 2011), 145.

43 *"I'm here to see old foot-in-the-mouth"*: Cannon, *Governor Reagan: His Rise to Power*.

44 *"the Teflon-coated Presidency"*: Pat Schroeder, Remarks to the House of Representatives, August 2, 1983.

44 *the Fourth Estate's wariness about roughing up Reagan*: Mark Hertsgaard, *On Bended Knee: The Press and the Reagan Presidency* (New York: Farrar, Straus and Giroux, 1988), 3, 99, 203.

45 *"add a little circle with an R inside"*: James F. Clarity and Warren Weaver Jr., "Briefing: To Teflon or Not to Teflon," *New York Times*, January 16, 1986.

45 *"a decline in interest by the general public"*: Steven R. Weisman, "Reagan Misstatements Getting Less Attention," *New York Times*, February 15, 1983.

46 Diff'rent Strokes: Joe Reid, "Today in TV History: 'Diff'rent Strokes' Epitomized the Very Special Episode with a Nancy Reagan Cameo," decider.com, April 30, 2015.

46 *Clint Eastwood*: Ira R. Allen, "Reagan to Tax Raisers: 'Go Ahead—Make My Day,'" UPI, March 13, 1985.

46 *approval rating plunged*: E. J. Dionne Jr., "Poll Shows Reagan Approval Rating at 4-Year Low," *New York Times*, March 3, 1987.

47 *Robert Parry*: Robert Pear, "Missing the Iran Arms Story: Did the Press Fail?" *New York Times*, March 4, 1987.

47   *"hard work never killed anybody"*: Cannon, *Governor Reagan: His Rise to Power.*

47   *"sleepless afternoon"*: Leuchtenburg, "Behind the Ronald Reagan Myth."

47   *"'Ronald Reagan slept here'"*: James C. Humes, *The Wit & Wisdom of Ronald Reagan* (Washington, DC: Regnery, 2007), 47.

47   *Joan Quigley*: Donald T. Regan, *For the Record: From Wall Street to Washington* (New York: Harcourt Brace Jovanovich, 1988).

48   *"Would you help us?"*: Mikhail Gorbachev interview, *Charlie Rose*, PBS, April 21, 2009.

48   *"wouldn't we come together to fight that particular threat?"*: "Remarks and a Question-and-Answer Session with Members of the National Strategy Forum in Chicago, Illinois, May 4, 1988," Ronald Reagan Presidential Library & Museum.

48   *"little green men"*: Cannon, *President Reagan: The Role of a Lifetime.*

49   *"The Force is with us"*: "Reagan Presses Call for Antimissile Plan Before Space Group," *New York Times*, March 30, 1985.

49   *added more to the national debt*: Shawn Langlois, "How Much Each U.S. President Has Contributed to the National Debt," MarketWatch, October 29, 2018; Martin Tolchin, "Paradox of Reagan Budgets: Austere Talk vs. Record Debt," *New York Times*, February 16, 1988.

49   *soared from $900 billion to $2.7 trillion*: Sheldon L. Richman, "The Sad Legacy of Ronald Reagan," *The Free Market* 6, no. 10 (October 1988).

50   *"If you are a slum dweller"*: "'Welfare Queen' Becomes Issue in Reagan Campaign," *New York Times*, February 15, 1976.

50   *Black unemployment*: "The President's News Conference, January 19, 1982," Ronald Reagan Presidential Library & Museum.

50   *"There's a woman in Chicago"*: "'Welfare Queen' Becomes Issue in Reagan Campaign."

51   *upgraded the number of her aliases*: Josh Levin, *The Queen: The Forgotten Life Behind an American Myth* (New York: Little, Brown and Company, 2019).

51   *"'picks up her welfare check every week in a Cadillac'"*: Calvin Trillin, *With All Disrespect: More Uncivil Liberties* (New York: Penguin Books, 1985).

51   *"not 80 aliases but four"*: "'Welfare Queen' Becomes Issue in Reagan Campaign."

52   *"all those beautiful white people"*: Dugger, *On Reagan*, 202.

52   *"those monkeys from those African countries"*: Tim Naftali, "Ronald Reagan's Long-Hidden Racist Conversation with Richard Nixon," *The Atlantic*, July 30, 2019.

52   *"the myth that I'm a racist"*: Ronald Reagan, *An American Life* (New York: Simon & Schuster, 1990), 402.

53   *"When they have a man for lunch"*: Dan T. Carter, *From George Wallace to Newt Gingrich: Race in the Conservative Counterrevolution, 1963–1994* (Baton Rouge: Louisiana State University Press, 1996), 64.

53   *"their jungle freedoms"*: "Marianne Mele Hall, the Embattled Chairwoman of the Copyright . . ." UPI, May 8, 1985.

53   *Bill Bennett*: Bob Herbert, "Impossible, Ridiculous, Repugnant," *New York Times*, October 6, 2005.

53   *"I believe in states' rights"*: Ari Berman, *Give Us the Ballot: The Modern Struggle for Voting Rights in America* (New York: Farrar, Straus and Giroux, 2015), 123.

54   *"How are you, Mr. Mayor?"*: Kenneth T. Walsh, *Family of Freedom: Presidents and African Americans in the White House* (Boulder, CO: Paradigm, 2014), 147.

54   *he didn't visit the HUD offices once*: Cannon, *President Reagan: The Role of a Lifetime*.

54   *"I'm your son, Mike"*: Cheryl Lavin, "Family Outcast," *Chicago Tribune*, April 17, 1988.

54   *"Every park bench in America"*: Chris Roberts, "The Great Eliminator: How Ronald Reagan Made Homelessness Permanent," *SF Weekly*, June 29, 2016.

54   *"their own choice for staying out there"*: Steven V. Roberts, "Reagan on Homelessness: Many Choose to Live in the Streets," *New York Times*, December 23, 1988.

54   *"They were all on a diet"*: Reagan, "A Time for Choosing."

55   *"an epidemic of botulism"*: Jack Nelson, "Reagan," *New York Times*, August 15, 1976.

55   *"There's not enough there for a feature movie"*: Richard Brody, "What to Stream: A Blazing Interview with Orson Welles," *The New Yorker*, August 11, 2020.

55   *"refused even to utter the word AIDS"*: Tim Fitzsimons, "LGBTQ History

Month: The Early Days of America's AIDS Crisis," NBC News, October 15, 2018.

55 *"gay plague"*: German Lopez, "The Reagan Administration's Unbelievable Response to the HIV/AIDS Epidemic," Vox, December 1, 2016.

56 *he didn't want to be booed*: Elaine Sciolino, "Reagan, in Switch, Says U.S. Will Pay Some Old U.N. Dues," *New York Times*, September 14, 1988.

56 *"Life has been very good to me"*: Richard E. Meyer and Henry Weinstein, "Campaign Becomes Confrontation with Past: Privilege, Wealth Shaped Quayle," *Los Angeles Times*, August 21, 1988.

57 *"it reminded me of my time in school"*: Maureen Dowd, "The Education of Dan Quayle," *New York Times*, June 25, 1989.

57 *"None of us growing up"*: Gail Sheehy, "Just Danny," *Vanity Fair*, November 1988.

57 *"I might as well have been looking out the window"*: Garry Wills, "Dan Quayle: Late Bloomer," *Time*, April 23, 1990.

57 *"the path of least resistance"*: Gail Sheehy, "Just Danny," *Vanity Fair*, November 1988.

57 *"rumors of plagiarism"*: Richard E. Meyer and Henry Weinstein, "Campaign Becomes Confrontation with Past: Privilege, Wealth Shaped Quayle," *Los Angeles Times*, August 21, 1988.

58 *"there were no private schools around"*: "The Making of the President 1996," *Washington Monthly*, December 1990.

59 *boomers loathed him even more than the general public*: Kent Jenkins Jr., "Quayle Tumult Subsides into Uneasy Normalcy," *Washington Post*, November 4, 1988.

59 *"every woman in the district would want to make love to him"*: Richard F. Fenno Jr., *The Making of a Senator: Dan Quayle* (Washington, DC: CQ Press, 1989), 10.

60 *tear off his cuff links*: Kerwin Swint, *Dark Genius: The Influential Career of Legendary Political Operator and Fox News Founder Roger Ailes* (New York: Union Square Press, 2008), 30.

60 *"more nearly perfect features than Robert Redford"*: Sheehy, "Just Danny."

60 The Candidate: George Lardner Jr. and Dan Morgan, "Quayle Drew on Energy, Affability in Political Rise," *Washington Post*, October 2, 1988.

60 *"Here's a guy who's better-looking"*: Gail Sheehy, "Just Danny," *Vanity Fair*, November 1988.

61 *"I'm not the most articulate emotionalist"*: David Lauter, "The Malta Summit: Bush and Gorbachev Forge Personal Alliance," *Los Angeles Times*, December 4, 1989.

61 *"thanks for the kids"*: "Remarks at a Head Start Center in Catonsville, Maryland, January 21, 1992," American Presidency Project, UC Santa Barbara.

61 *"If a frog had wings"*: Michael S. Rosenwald, "Fragrant Armpits, Napping Aides, Corny Duck Jokes: George H. W. Bush's Wonderful Humor," *Washington Post*, December 4, 2018.

61 *"I turn to country music"*: *Public Papers of the Presidents of the United States: George Bush, 1991*, book II (Washington, DC: United States Government Printing), 1263.

61 *"only less than half full"*: Ibid., 1408.

61 *"the undecideds could go one way or another"*: Bob Herbert, "Political Tongue Twisters," *New York Times*, August 28, 2000.

61 *"big on crematoriums"*: Garry Wills, "The Republicans," *Time*, August 22, 1988.

61 *"For seven and a half years"*: Rosenwald, "Fragrant Armpits, Napping Aides, Corny Duck Jokes: George H. W. Bush's Wonderful Humor."

62 *"get a dog"*: Donald Kaul, "Bushspeak Deciphered," *Baltimore Sun*, May 28, 1992.

62 message: I care: Frank Luntz, *Words That Work: It's Not What You Say, It's What People Hear* (New York: Hachette, 2007).

62 Quayle Quarterly: Evelyn Nieves, "Voters Deny 2nd Term to Quayle Quarterly," *New York Times*, November 5, 1992.

62 *"not to have a mind is being very wasteful"*: Kitty Kelley, *The Family: The Real Story of the Bush Dynasty* (New York: Doubleday, 2004), 483.

62 *"For NASA"*: Lauri Githens, "A Flash of Quayle Brilliance Shines Through the Fog," *Buffalo News*, May 26, 2002.

62 *"Mars is essentially"*: Scott Ross, "Quayle's Advice for Obama . . . Yes, Dan Quayle," nbcwashington.com, November 6, 2008.

63 *"If oxygen, that means we can breathe"*: Kathy Sawyer, "A Quayle Vision of Mars," *Washington Post*, September 1, 1989.

63 *"The western part of Pennsylvania"*: Roger Simon, *Road Show: In America Anyone Can Become President, It's One of the Risks We Take* (New York: Farrar, Straus and Giroux, 1990), 266.

63 *"We are a part of Europe"*: Sharon Millar and John Wilson, eds., *The*

Discourse of Europe: Talk and Text in Everyday Life (Philadelphia: John Benjamins, 2007).

63 *"I practically grew up in Phoenix"*: Leuchtenburg, *The American President.*

63 *"the great state of Chicago"*: Mark Jacob, "The Wrong-Way Guide to Chicago," *Chicago Tribune,* August 18, 2012.

63 *"Hawaii is a unique state"*: Kevin Sack, "Quayle's Working Hard to Give a Better Speech," *New York Times,* October 7, 1992.

64 *"best-educated American people in the world"*: Bahman Dehgan, *America in Quotations* (Jefferson, NC: McFarland & Company, 2003), 78.

64 *"I have made good judgments in the future"*: Michael McQueeney, "The Five Worst Vice Presidential Picks," *History Today,* July 12, 2016.

64 *"The future will be better tomorrow"*: Bruce Kauffmann, "Bruce's History Lessons: Vote Dan Quayle for Veep!," *Tribune-Star,* August 14, 2007.

64 *"The real question for 1988"*: Lesley Stahl, *Reporting Live* (New York: Touchstone, 1999), 325.

64 *"I didn't live in this century"*: McQueeney, "The Five Worst Vice Presidential Picks."

64 *"I stand by all the misstatements that I've made"*: William Boot, "Dan Quayle: The Sequel," *Columbia Journalism Review* 30, no. 3 (September–October 1991).

65 *John Henry Neff Elementary School*: Simon, *Road Show,* 264.

65 *"a cheerleader or a game show contestant"*: Bob Woodward and David S. Broder, *The Man Who Would Be President: Dan Quayle* (New York: Simon & Schuster, 1992), 57.

65 *Quayle had considered making his own bid for the presidency*: Simon, *Road Show,* 278.

65 *"mother hen"*: Lois Romano, "Stu Spencer, Quayle's Copilot," *Washington Post,* September 13, 1988.

66 *"I could see to the back of his head"*: Sidney Blumenthal, *Pledging Allegiance: The Last Campaign of the Cold War* (New York: HarperCollins, 1990), 182.

66 *"I did not know in 1969"*: Timothy J. McNulty, "Candidate Defends VP Choice," *Chicago Tribune,* August 18, 1988.

66 *"he would rather play golf than have sex any day"*: Melinda Henneberger, "Starting Over," *New York Times Magazine,* April 4, 1999.

66 *"'we'd better get a hold of this thing'"*: Woodward and Broder, *The Man Who Would Be President,* 65.

66 *"I didn't think the press conference went that badly"*: Dan Quayle, *Standing Firm: A Vice Presidential Memoir* (New York: HarperCollins, 1994), 33.

67 *"What is he hiding?"*: Anthony Lewis, "What Is Quayle Hiding?" *New York Times*, September 15, 1988.

67 *failed his final exam*: Blumenthal, *Pledging Allegiance*, 273.

67 *affirmative action*: David Lauter and Douglas Jehl, "'Special Factors' Helped Quayle Law School Admission," *Los Angeles Times*, September 10, 1988.

67 *$2.5 million donation to Harvard*: Daniel Golden, "The Story Behind Jared Kushner's Curious Acceptance into Harvard," ProPublica, November 18, 2016.

67 *Indiana University's student leaders*: "Students Criticize Quayle, Ask Him to Show Grades," UPI, September 10, 1988.

68 *"Dan Quayle doesn't know about cities"*: Robert Scheer, "'Making of Quayle': Political Pro Is Pulling All the Strings," *Los Angeles Times*, October 21, 1988.

68 *"the importance of bondage between parent and child"*: Alice Steinbach, "Family Values Are Shrinking into Their Political Value," *Baltimore Sun*, August 30, 1992.

68 *"who's going to be the next president of the United States"*: Mark Crispin Miller, *The Bush Dyslexicon: Observations of a National Disorder* (New York: W. W. Norton, 2001), 39.

68 *"dumber than advertised"*: *Raise Hell: The Life and Times of Molly Ivins*, Janice Engel, dir., 2019.

68 *"didn't burn the American flag"*: Bill Peterson and Laura Parker, "Bush Defends Quayle as War Veterans Cheer," *Washington Post*, August 23, 1988.

68 *"he can't read a speech"*: Bob Woodward and David S. Broder, "Waiting in the Wings for 1996," *Washington Post*, January 12, 1992.

69 *"His eyes would glaze over"*: Jack W. Germond and Jules Witcover, *Whose Broad Stripes and Bright Stars? The Trivial Pursuit of the Presidency, 1988* (New York: Grand Central, 1989), 437.

69 *"He was like a kid"*: Ibid., 441.

69 Nicholas and Alexandra: Hendrik Hertzberg, "Roboflop," *The New Republic*, October 30, 1988.

69 *decided to wing it*: Cathleen Decker, "Quayle Remarks Appear to Bewilder Audience: Sets Aside Prepared Speech to Digress on Not Trusting Soviets," *Los Angeles Times*, September 9, 1988.

70   *"Good basketball always starts with good defense"*: Gary Blair with Rusty Burson, *A Coaching Life* (College Station: Texas A&M University Press, 2017).

70   *"we'll own him again"*: Germond and Witcover, *Whose Broad Stripes and Bright Stars?*, 436.

70   *"President Quayle"*: Marci McDonald, "Open Season on Quayle," *Maclean's*, October 10, 1988.

72   *"the most spontaneous moment of the evening"*: Tom Shales, "On the Air," *Washington Post*, October 6, 1988.

73   *mock debates with Bentsen*: Noah Bierman, " 'Senator, You're No Jack Kennedy' Almost Didn't Happen. How It Became the Biggest VP Debate Moment in History," *Los Angeles Times*, October 4, 2016.

73   *"Does he really do that?"*: Susan Estrich, "90 Seconds Can Define Debates," *Tampa Bay Times*, September 26, 2004.

73   *warned Quayle against hoisting himself up to JFK's pedestal*: Bob Woodward and David S. Broder, "In 1988, 'Control Freak Loses Control,' " *Washington Post*, January 7, 1992.

73   *"I turned to the key supporters"*: Estrich, "90 Seconds Can Define Debates."

73   *"I saw his Adam's apple"*: Germond and Witcover, *Whose Broad Stripes and Bright Stars?*, 440.

74   *"pee-pants performance"*: Hertzberg, "Roboflop."

74   *"even the more serious foreign funerals"*: George F. Will, " 'Never Give a Child a Sword,' " *Washington Post*, October 7, 1988.

74   *Quayle be drug-tested*: Open Phones, C-SPAN, October 6, 1988.

74   *"wounded fawn"*: Tom Sherwood, "Quayle Bolts from Advisers," *Washington Post*, October 12, 1988.

74   *"we have to be pretty happy"*: Tad Devine, "Quayle Can't Lose Tonight," *Washington Post*, October 13, 1992.

74   *"I was convinced we came out on top"*: Simon, *Road Show*, 261.

74   *" 'go out and bury him' "*: Woodward and Broder, "In 1988, 'Control Freak Loses Control.' "

76   *"It was an outrageous question"*: Timothy J. McNulty, " 'Outrageous' Debate Question Angers Kitty Dukakis," *Chicago Tribune*, October 15, 1988.

76   *"I'm not changing anything"*: Simon, *Road Show*, 284.

77   *"wonder whether Willie Horton is Dukakis's running mate"*: Paul Waldman,

"How George H. W. Bush Exploited Racism to Win the Oval Office," *Washington Post*, December 3, 2018.

77   *"Is this your pro-family team for 1988?"*: "George Bush and Willie Horton," *New York Times*, November 4, 1988.

77   *the evolution of racist dog whistles*: Bob Herbert, "Impossible, Ridiculous, Repugnant," *New York Times*, October 6, 2005.

77   *Atwater worked with Bush's son*: David Von Drehle, "Lee Atwater, the Specter of South Carolina," *Washington Post*, February 17, 2000.

78   *"what are you going to do for yourself?"*: Robert Barnes, "Alan Keyes Unknown but Not Anonymous," *Washington Post*, September 11, 1988.

78   *"Quayle's Brain"*: Henry Allen, "Dan Quayle's Gray Matter," *Washington Post*, October 21, 1992.

78   *"Space is almost infinite"*: Ned Sherrin, *Oxford Dictionary of Humorous Quotations* (New York: Oxford University Press, 1995), 313.

79   *"The killers are to blame"*: "Address to the Commonwealth Club of California, May 19, 1992," Dan Quayle online information portal.

79   *"Illegitimacy is something we should talk about in terms of not having it"*: "What We Talk About When We Talk About Quayle," *Esquire*, August 1992.

79   *the most unpopular vice president in modern history*: Megan Thee, "Polls: Cheney Nears Quayle as Least Popular Veep," *New York Times*, July 9, 2007.

79   *"One word sums up probably the responsibility of any vice president"*: Dehgan, *America in Quotations*, 186.

80   *"any unforeseen event that may or may not occur"*: Howard Troxler, "Here's the Scoop for This Year—I Guess," *Tampa Bay Times*, January 2, 1998.

80   *medical malpractice reform*: Kevin Sack, "Quayle's Working Hard to Give a Better Speech," *New York Times*, October 7, 1992.

80   *"Verbosity leads to unclear, inarticulate things"*: "Quayle Says He Won't Be 'Spear Carrier' for Right Wing," Associated Press, November 30, 1988.

80   *"an irreversible trend toward more freedom and democracy"*: Fred R. Shapiro, ed., *The New Yale Book of Quotations* (New Haven, CT: Yale University Press, 2021), 669.

80   *"work toward the elimination of human rights"*: Kenneth Freed, "Last Stop on Latin Tour: Quayle Gives Salvador Ultimatum on Rights," *Los Angeles Times*, February 4, 1989.

81　*"teachers are the only profession that teach our children"*: Tim McDonald, "Send in the Clowns," *News and Tribune*, October 12, 2010.

81　*Quayle was roasted nonstop for his blunder*: Evelyn Nieves, "Spelling by Quayle (That's with an E)," *New York Times*, June 17, 1992.

81　*"Do you have to go to college to be vice president?"*: L. A. Parker, "Sharpton Misspelling Reminds of Trenton's Famous Extra 'E' Incident," *The Trentonian*, August 21, 2018.

81　*"Has anyone checked the cards?"*: Quayle, *Standing Firm*, 331.

83　*the former veep's papers*: Sam Stall, "12 Things We Learned at the Dan Quayle Vice Presidential Learning Center," *Thrillist*, November 6, 2016.

84　*Kellyanne Fitzgerald*: Melinda Henneberger, "Starting Over," *New York Times Magazine*, April 4, 1999.

85　*"There's a time to stay and there's a time to fold"*: David S. Broder, "Quayle Pulls Out of GOP Race," *Washington Post*, September 27, 1999.

CHAPTER 2: THE SECOND STAGE: ACCEPTANCE

86　*"Farewell, once more"*: Calvin Trillin, "Adieu, Dan Quayle," *The Nation*, September 30, 1999.

87　*Fritz Thyssen*: Ben Aris and Duncan Campbell, "How Bush's Grandfather Helped Hitler's Rise to Power," *The Guardian*, September 25, 2004.

88　*Bush's Yale transcript*: Alexandra Robbins and Jane Mayer, "Dept. of Aptitude," *New Yorker*, October 31, 1999.

88　*"president of the fraternity"*: Interview with the author.

89　*"I'm not afraid to make decisions"*: Robert Draper, *Dead Certain: The Presidency of George W. Bush* (New York: Free Press, 2007), 367, 419.

89　*"Ivy League scholar"*: Skip Hollandsworth, "Born to Run," *Texas Monthly*, May 1994.

89　*"I had fun at Yale"*: Hanna Rosin, "The Seeds of a Philosophy," *Washington Post*, July 23, 2000.

89　*"people at Yale felt so intellectually superior"*: Hollandsworth, "Born to Run."

90　*"more intellectual and more cerebral"*: Bill Minutaglio, *First Son: George W. Bush and the Bush Family Dynasty* (New York: Times Books, 1999), 107.

90　*"Conspicuous intelligence"*: David Frum, *The Right Man: An Inside Account of the Bush White House* (New York: Random House, 2003), 20.

90　*stealing a Christmas wreath*: Nicholas D. Kristof, "Ally of an Older Generation Amid the Tumult of the 60's," *New York Times*, June 19, 2000.

90 *looting of Baghdad*: Frank Rich, "And Now: 'Operation Iraqi Looting,'" *New York Times*, April 27, 2003.

90 *applying a hot branding iron to the backs of pledges*: "Branding Rite Laid to Yale Fraternity," *New York Times*, November 8, 1967.

90 *flunked out a few years earlier*: Carly Mallenbaum, "Fact-Checking 'Vice': Did Dick Cheney Really Do All of That?" *USA Today*, December 24, 2018.

90 *"he's not contemplative or reflective"*: Kristof, "Ally of an Older Generation Amid the Tumult of the 60's."

91 *"Champagne Unit"*: Michael Dobbs, "Democrat Says He Helped Bush into Guard to Score Points," *Washington Post*, September 4, 2004.

91 *"one of the great pilots of all time"*: "We Were Soldiers Once?" *Mother Jones*, January/February 2003.

91 *"I'd rather go to war"*: "Bush Compares Raising Twins to War," Associated Press, January 27, 2002.

91 *Chateau Dijon*: Jo Thomas, "After Yale, Bush Ambled Amiably into His Future," *New York Times*, July 22, 2000.

91 *"what's sex like after fifty, anyway?"*: Sam Howe Verhovek, "Is There Room on a Republican Ticket for Another Bush?," *New York Times*, September 13, 1998.

91 *skipping his mandatory physical*: Andrew Glass, "George W. Bush Suspended from Texas Air National Guard, Aug. 1, 1972," Politico, August 1, 2013.

91 *"not at the University of Texas"*: Molly Ivins and Lou Dubose, *Shrub: The Short but Happy Political Life of George W. Bush* (New York: Random House, 2000), xxi.

92 *"sailing paper airplanes around the class"*: Scoop A. Wasserstein, "Big Man on Campus," *Harvard Crimson*, October 21, 2004.

92 *"mano a mano"*: Minutaglio, *First Son*, 6.

92 *racking up a DUI*: Dan Balz, "Bush Acknowledges 1976 DUI Arrest," *Washington Post*, November 3, 2000.

93 *"a deep suspicion of the gratuitous intellectualism of the Ivy League"*: James Moore and Wayne Slater, *Bush's Brain: How Karl Rove Made George W. Bush Presidential* (Hoboken, NJ: John Wiley & Sons, 2003), 106, 140–41.

93 *Arbusto Energy*: George Lardner Jr. and Lois Romano, "Bush Name Helps Fuel Oil Dealings," *Washington Post*, July 30, 1999.

94   *"Today is the first time I've been on a real farm"*: Kristof, "Learning How to
     Run: A West Texas Stumble."

94   *"The only time folks"*: Frank Bruni, *Ambling into History: The Unlikely
     Odyssey of George W. Bush* (New York: HarperCollins, 2002), 122.

94   *"In 1961"*: Kristof, "Learning How to Run: A West Texas Stumble."

95   *"I went to Yale and Harvard"*: *Larry King Live*, CNN, December 30,
     2000.

95   *His fishy maneuvers*: John Dunbar, "A Brief History of Bush, Harken and
     the SEC," Center for Public Integrity, October 16, 2002; Lardner and
     Romano, "Bush Name Helps Fuel Oil Dealings."

96   *"I wouldn't say that patience is one of George's greatest qualities"*: Hollands-
     worth, "Born to Run."

96   *an embarrassing defeat for his son*: Moore and Slater, *Bush's Brain*,
     151–52.

96   *Harry Whittington*: John C. Moritz, "Texan Accidentally Shot by Dick
     Cheney Recalls 2006 Incident," Associated Press, December 14, 2018;
     Paul Farhi, "Since Dick Cheney Shot Him, Harry Whittington's Aim Has
     Been to Move On," *Washington Post*, October 14, 2010.

96   *Rove assumed the task of educating Dubya*: Moore and Slater, *Bush's Brain*,
     162–63.

97   *" 'limit GWB's appearance' "*: Ivins and Dubose, *Shrub*, 48, 52.

97   *Bush prided himself on overseeing the work of his speechwriters*: Moore and
     Slater, *Bush's Brain*, 171, 203, 217.

98   *"some jerk comes along"*: Patricia Kilday Hart, "Little Did We Know . . ."
     Texas Monthly, November 2004.

99   *"I realized that the press"*: Ibid.

99   *well-orchestrated whispering campaign*: Moore and Slater, *Bush's Brain*,
     209–10.

99   *"the Lee Atwater of Texas politics"*: Minutaglio, *First Son*, 329.

99   *push-polling in the 2000 South Carolina primary*: Ann Banks, "Dirty
     Tricks, South Carolina and John McCain," *The Nation*, January 14, 2008.

99   *"an event for Republican governors in Williamsburg"*: Draper, *Dead Cer-
     tain*, 46.

100 *"Tree Man, get up here!"*: Minutaglio, *First Son*, 14.

100 *"doesn't know much, doesn't do much, and doesn't care much"*: Ivins and Du-
     bose, *Shrub*, xvii–xviii.

100   *"I don't like long meetings"*: Alan C. Miller and Judy Pasternak, "Records Show Bush's Focus on Big Picture," *Los Angeles Times*, August 2, 2000.

100   *"reading a 500-page book"*: Tucker Carlson, "Devil May Care," *Talk*, September 1999.

100   *"he or her will be able to pass a literacy test"*: "Caught Read-Handed," Salon, February 21, 2001.

100   *"I highlighted half a page"*: Miller and Pasternak, "Records Show Bush's Focus on Big Picture."

101   *the 152 men and women whose executions he approved*: Bob Ray Sanders, "George W. Bush's Finest Hour as Governor of Texas," *Fort Worth Star-Telegram*, February 22, 2015.

101   *halved the time allotted for considering a death row case*: Jim Yardley, "Bush and the Death Penalty: Texas' Busy Death Chamber Helps Define Bush's Tenure," *New York Times*, January 7, 2000.

101   *"This case has had full analyzation"*: John Connelly, "Bush Bolsters Texas' Justice System," *Seattle Post-Intelligencer*, June 23, 2000.

101   *"one of the reasons I like Texas"*: "10 Questions for Willie Nelson," *Time*, May 24, 2010.

101   *recklessly cutting taxes*: Jim Yardley, "The State Budget: For Bush, Texas Deficit Becomes Issue in Race," *New York Times*, July 14, 2000.

102   *"Wonks are not new to public life"*: Jon Morgan, "The WONK Factor," *Baltimore Sun*, August 13, 1992.

102   *Elvis*: Jill Lawrence, "Don't Be Cruel, Clinton Tells New York Media," Associated Press, April 2, 1992.

102   *"Heartbreak Hotel"*: *The Arsenio Hall Show*, CBS, June 3, 1992.

103   *Presley's increasingly surreal role*: Greil Marcus, "The Elvis Strategy," *New York Times*, October 27, 1992.

103   *the only time the resolutely apolitical King*: David Haven Blake, *Liking Ike: Eisenhower, Advertising, and the Rise of Celebrity Politics* (New York: Oxford University Press, 2016), 148.

103   *Bush Senior's implacable squareness*: Elizabeth Kolbert, "View from the Booth: A Faulty Bush Speech," *New York Times*, August 22, 1992.

103   *sought an audience with Ron and Nancy*: Michael Kelly, "Clinton Chats with Reagan, Then Heads Out to the Mall," *New York Times*, November 28, 1992.

103   *borrowing a tape from the Reagan Library*: Carl M. Cannon, "Clinton Staff

Annoys Republicans by Tapping Successful Reagan Style: '96 Campaign Adapts Its Optimistic Themes," *Baltimore Sun,* June 2, 1996.

104 *"The era of big government is over":* State of the Union address, January 23, 1996.

104 *Rove urged him to buy a ranchette:* Evgenia Peretz, "High Noon in Crawford," *Vanity Fair,* November 2005.

105 *"I will if I'm the president":* Frank Bruni, "Bush Explains His Opposition to Abortion," *New York Times,* November 22, 1999.

105 *"a sense of his soul":* Joint press conference with Vladimir Putin in Ljubljana, Slovenia, June 18, 2001.

105 *"I do need someone to tell me where Kosovo is":* Miller, *The Bush Dyslexicon,* 200.

105 *needed someone to tell him what to call the people:* David Corn, "Bush Gets an F in Foreign Affairs," Salon, November 5, 1999.

105 *"We're a nation in a global world":* Frank Bruni, "In New Hampshire, Bush Is the Image of Scrappiness," *New York Times,* November 4, 1999.

106 *Andy Hiller:* Terry M. Neal, "Bush Falters in Foreign Policy Quiz," *Washington Post,* November 5, 1999.

107 *"the leader of the free world, not a* Jeopardy *contestant":* "Bush Bats .250 in Pop Quiz of Hot Spot Who's Whos," *Los Angeles Times,* November 5, 1999.

107 *they condemned the pop quiz:* NewsHour with Jim Lehrer, PBS, November 5, 1999.

107 *"it makes their man seem like a normal guy":* Jonathan Chait, "Race to the Bottom," *The New Republic,* December 22, 1999.

107 *"he's defiant about it":* "Bush Says He's Smart Enough to be U.S. President," Reuters, November 8, 1999.

107 *"based upon judgment, based upon vision, based upon philosophy":* Scott Shepard, "Gore Chides Bush for Missing Names of Foreign Leaders," *New York Times,* November 5, 1999.

108 *Rick Mercer:* Rally in Canton, Michigan, February 2000.

108 *"What a moron":* "Canadian Official Called Bush 'A Moron,'" CBC News, November 26, 2002.

109 *"He was a little tired":* "22 Minutes Star Pulls Prank on George W. Bush," CBC News, March 22, 2000.

109 *"I took the initiative in creating the Internet":* Late Edition, CNN, March 9, 1999.

109   *wrote a short post about it*: Declan McCullagh, "No Credit Where It's Due," *Wired*, March 11, 1999.

109   *Trent Lott and Dick Armey*: Esther Scott, "Al Gore and the 'Embellishment' Issue: Press Coverage of the Gore Presidential Campaign," Joan Shorenstein Center on the Press, Politics and Public Policy at the John F. Kennedy School of Government, Harvard University, October 2003.

109   *"I created the 'Al Gore created the Internet' story"*: Declan McCullagh, "The Mother of Gore's Invention," *Wired*, October 17, 2000.

110   *Godfrey Sperling questioned Gore's electoral appeal*: Godfrey Sperling, "An Uneasiness with Al Gore?" *Christion Science Monitor*, January 18, 2000.

110   *"susceptible to strange ideas supposedly grounded in science"*: George F. Will, "Candidates Condescending," *Washington Post*, October 26, 2000.

110   *"Is Al Gore destined to be the Adlai Stevenson of our age?"*: Richard Cohen, "Adlai and Ike All Over Again," *Washington Post*, December 5, 2002.

110   *name-checking Reinhold Niebuhr*: Louis Menand, "After Elvis," *The New Yorker*, October 18, 1998.

111   *"One of the great things about books"*: *U.S. News & World Report*, January 3, 2000.

111   *a video diary of her travels with his press entourage*: *Journeys with George*, Alexandra Pelosi and Aaron Lubarsky, dirs., HBO, 2002.

111   *"if you get a C average"*: Margaret Carlson, "In the Name of Their Fathers," *Time*, October 3, 1999.

112   *"I can't remember any specific books"*: Frank Rich, "And the Winner Is . . . George W. Bush," *New York Times*, August 28, 1999.

112   The Very Hungry Caterpillar: Arthur Hoppe, "The Very Hungry George W. Bush," *SF Gate*, November 17, 1999.

112   *at a rally in Albuquerque*: Frank Bruni, "Bush's Odd Pitch: Ignorance Is Bliss," *New York Times*, June 4, 2000.

113   *"And what is Aleppo?"*: Louis Nelson and Daniel Strauss, "Libertarian Candidate Gary Johnson: 'What Is Aleppo?'" *Politico*, September 8, 2016.

113   *"a verbal Rorschach test"*: Elaine Sciolino, "Bush's Foreign Policy Tutor: An Academic in the Public Eye," *New York Times*, June 16, 2000.

113   *"You can buy clever"*: Bruni, "Bush's Odd Pitch: Ignorance Is Bliss."

114   *"Al Gore is the most lethal debater in politics"*: James Fallows, "An Acquired Taste," *The Atlantic*, July 2000.

114   *"[A]ll he had to do was clear a matchbox"*: Molly Ivins and Lou DuBose,

Bushwhacked: Life in George W. Bush's America (New York: Random House, 2003), 249.

115 *the resulting orange hue provided pundits*: Virginia Postrel, "Electoral Beauty Myths," *Reason*, December 11, 2000.

115 *an expert panel of cosmeticians*: Mike Conklin, "It's the Makeup, Stupid," *Chicago Tribune*, October 6, 2000.

116 *"cosmetics has replaced ideology"*: Postman, *Amusing Ourselves to Death*, 4.

116 *"'Hi, I'm George W. Bush'"*: Alison Mitchell, "All Joking Aside, Bush Faces Letterman," *New York Times*, October 20, 2000.

116 *"He's going to be the good old boy next door"*: Kristof, "Learning How to Run: A West Texas Stumble."

116 *as president he would call Africa a nation*: John Cochran, "Bush's Big Trip: Why Africa? Why Now?" ABC News, October 1, 2004.

116 *"This is the first chapter of the twenty-first century"*: Frank Bruni, "Bush Ridicules Gore's Proposals for Tax Cuts," *New York Times*, October 25, 2000.

116 *"we just had some really good news out of Yugoslavia"*: Speech at Al Smith Memorial Dinner, October 19, 2000.

117 *"to the C students, I say"*: "Text: President Bush Speaks at Yale Graduation," *Washington Post*, May 21, 2001.

117 *"Bush often appears with an 'expert'"*: Mark Leibovich, "Don't Stop Him Even If You've Heard This One," *Washington Post*, March 14, 2005.

118 *"You never know what your history is going to be like"*: "Interview with Kai Diekmann of Bilk," American Presidency Project, UC Santa Barbara, May 5, 2006.

118 *9/11 was the day Bush "became president of the United States"*: Adam Sexton, "President Bush Faced Difficult Decisions on 9/11, Former Chief of Staff Says," WMUR Manchester, September 10, 2021.

119 *"a key to foreign policy is to rely on reliance"*: Michael Kelly, "The Democrats' Delusion," *Washington Post*, November 1, 2000.

119 *"There is madmen in the world"*: Dana Milbank, "What's on W's Mind? Hard to Say," *Washington Post*, May 5, 2000.

119 *"we are not so sure who the they are"*: Deborah Orin, "Bush Reflects Crisis That Shaped Him," *New York Post*, September 12, 2002.

119 *Dubya's first phone conversation*: Andrew Rawnsley, *The End of the Party: The Rise and Fall of New Labour* (New York: Viking, 2010).

119 *"Bin Laden Planning Multiple Operations"*: The 9/11 Commission Report (New York: W. W. Norton, 2004), 255.

119 *"Bin Laden Attacks May Be Imminent"*: Senior Executive Intelligence Brief, June 23, 2001.

119 *"Bin Laden Planning High Profile Attacks"*: Senior Executive Intelligence Brief, June 30, 2001.

119 *"UBL [Usama bin Laden] Threats Are Real"*: Michael Morell with Bill Harlow, *The Great War of Our Time, The CIA's Fight Against Terrorism— From al Qa'ida to ISIS* (New York: Twelve, 2015).

120 "OK, Michael. You've covered your ass": Ibid.

120 *"Bin Laden Determined to Strike in US"*: The 9/11 Commission Report, 262; Andrew Glass, "George W. Bush Receives Bin Laden Memo: Aug. 6, 2001," Politico, August 6, 2009; Craig Unger, " 'War President' Bush Has Always Been Soft on Terror," *Guardian*, September 10, 2004.

120 *Bush's allergy to reading*: Cullen Murphy, Todd S. Purdum, and Philippe Sands, "Farewell to All That: An Oral History of the Bush White House," *Vanity Fair*, February 2009.

120 *"the sense of purpose that he had previously lacked"*: Paul Burka, "The Man Who Isn't There," *Texas Monthly*, February 2004.

120 *"[I]t transformed him"*: "Sept 11 Brought US into Age of Terrorism," Associated Press, September 7, 2008.

120 *"9/11 seized the American with the sense of purpose"*: Rawnsley, *The End of the Party*.

120 *Barbara Bush*: Daniel S. Lucks, *Reconsidering Reagan: Racism, Republicans, and the Road to Trump* (Boston: Beacon Press, 2020), 250.

121 *we'd very much been with the terrorists*: Hannah Bloch, "A Look at Afghanistan's 40 Years of Crisis—From the Soviet War to Taliban Recapture," NPR, August 19, 2021.

121 *David Frum had borrowed the term "axis"*: Frum, *The Right Man*, 235–40; Elisabeth Bumiller, "A New Washington Whodunit: The Speechwriter Vanishes," *New York Times*, March 4, 2002.

121 *"Freedom isn't America's gift to the world"*: Kevin Peraino, "Everything's Coming Up . . ." *Newsweek*, January 25, 2006.

123 *" 'the reality-based community' "*: Ron Suskind, "Faith, Certainty and the Presidency of George W. Bush," *New York Times Magazine*, October 17, 2004.

123 *"I don't do nuance"*: Richard Cohen, "Bush's War Against Nuance," *Washington Post*, February 17, 2004.

123 *"nuancing him to death"*: Moore and Slater, *Bush's Brain*, 317.

123 *"Fuck Saddam. We're taking him out"*: George Packer, *The Assassins' Gate: America in Iraq* (New York: Farrar, Straus & Giroux, 2005), 45.

123 *$2 trillion war*: Daniel Trotta, "Iraq War Costs U.S. More Than $2 Trillion: Study," Reuters, March 14, 2013.

124 *"I thought the Iraqis were Muslims!"*: Diane E. Dees, "Sunnis and Shiites and Muslims, Oh My!" *Mother Jones*, August 4, 2006.

124 *The year the U.S. invaded Iraq*: Michael E. O'Hanlon and Ian Livingston, "Iraq Index: Tracking Variables of Reconstruction & Security in Post-Saddam Iraq," Brookings Institution, January 31, 2011.

124 *narrating slides of himself*: Speech at the Radio and Television Correspondents' Association of Washington, DC, Dinner, March 24, 2004.

124 *Dick Cheney's prediction*: Hendrik Hertzberg, "Cakewalk," *The New Yorker*, April 6, 2003.

124 *"it was not a peaceful welcome"*: Brian Williams, "President Bush on Iraq, Katrina, the Economy," NBC News, December 12, 2005.

124 *high-tech whoopee cushion*: Bob Woodward, *State of Denial: Bush at War, Part III* (New York: Simon & Schuster, 2006), 402.

125 *Max Mayfield*: "Hurricane Katrina: A Nation Still Unprepared," Report prepared by the Senate Committee on Homeland Security and Governmental Affairs, 2006.

125 *"I don't think anybody anticipated the breach of the levees"*: Margaret Ebrahim, "Videos Prompt Calls for New Katrina Probe," Associated Press, March 2, 2006.

125 *"The president seemed to be thinking of his memoirs"*: Matthew Latimer, *Speech-Less: Tales of a White House Survivor* (New York: Crown, 2009), 256–60.

126 *a poll famously asked voters*: "Bush Gets 'Beer Vote,'" Realbeer.com, October 17, 2000.

126 *"Zogby, an allegedly reputable polling company"*: Richard Benedetto, "Who's More Likeable, Bush or Kerry?" *USA Today*, September 17, 2004.

126 *"You break it, you own it"*: Bob Woodward, *Plan of Attack* (New York: Simon & Schuster, 2004), 150.

127 "4 dollar a gallon gasoline?": White House Press Conference, February 28, 2008.

127 *He was a Black man in a country*: Robert McNamara, "US Presidents Who Were Enslavers," ThoughtCo, December 15, 2020.

128 *"that great and famous political figure"*: Peggy Noonan, "Hillary Reveals Her Inner Self," *Wall Street Journal*, November 3, 2007.

128 *"Barack Obama is running an Adlai Stevenson campaign"*: Steve Clemons, "Obama Must Shed Adlai Stevenson to Give Hillary a Race," *Huffington Post*, November 4, 2007.

128 *"that his 'Adlai problem' is no laughing matter"*: Ned Temko, "All About Adlai," *Guardian*, September 8, 2008.

128 *"a vitamin-deficient Adlai Stevenson"*: Karl Rove, "Memo to Obama: Win Iowa or Lose the Race," *Financial Times*, December 2, 2007.

128 *"I've found as I say all across this land"*: Speech in La Crosse, Wisconsin, October 13, 1980.

129 *Yuengling*: Carrie Budoff Brown, "Pennsylvania, Meet Barack Obama," Politico, March 29, 2008; Daniel Nasaw, "Obama's Bid for the Bowling Alley Set," *Guardian*, March 31, 2008.

129 *"Be fucking presidential"*: Michael Fleming, "*Playboy* Interview: Samuel L. Jackson," *Playboy* (October 2013), 133–34.

130 *"I love Tina Fey!"*: Michael Joseph Gross, "Sarah Palin: The Sound and the Fury," *Vanity Fair*, October 2010.

131 *"I'm a fuckin' redneck"*: Geoffrey Dunn, *The Lies of Sarah Palin: The Untold Story Behind Her Relentless Quest for Power* (New York: St. Martin's Press, 2011), 184.

131 *"Was this woman—who, at home"*: Levi Johnston, "Me and Mrs. Palin," *Vanity Fair*, October 2009.

132 *"reminiscent of former President George Bush's selection"*: Michael Cooper and Elisabeth Bumiller, "McCain Chooses Palin as Running Mate," *New York Times*, August 29, 2008.

132 *"Who's Sarah Palin?"*: Dan Balz and Haynes Johnson, *The Battle for America: The Story of an Extraordinary Election* (New York: Viking, 2009).

132 *a luxury Alaskan cruise*: Jane Mayer, "The Insiders," *The New Yorker*, October 27, 2008.

133 *"Am I allowed to say that?"*: Jay Nordlinger, "Babes Left and Right, &c.," *National Review*, March 19, 2012.

134 *Vetting a running mate traditionally takes months*: Marisa M. Kashino, "A. B. Culvahouse: The Man Who Vetted Sarah Palin," *Washingtonian*, April 21, 2011.

134 *"I have been more diligent tracking a moose"*: Levi Johnston, *Deer in the Headlights: My Life in Sarah Palin's Crosshairs* (New York: Touchstone, 2011).

134 *"a certain aura about her"*: Kashino, "A. B. Culvahouse: The Man Who Vetted Sarah Palin."

134 *"Why do you want to be vice president?"*: Andy Barr, "McCain Vetter: Palin Nailed Interview," Politico, April 17, 2009.

134 *The tangled tale of Palin's education*: "Palin Well Traveled During Her College Years," Associated Press, September 5, 2008.

135 *"interviews with a dozen professors"*: Robin Abcarian, "She Graduated with Anonymity," *Los Angeles Times*, October 21, 2008.

136 *"She has a remarkably short attention span"*: Dunn, *The Lies of Sarah Palin*, 129.

136 *" 'What's the flavor of the day?' "*: Michael Joseph Gross, "Sarah Palin: The Sound and the Fury," *Vanity Fair*, October 2010.

136 *Troopergate*: Stephen Branchflower report to the Alaska Legislative Council, October 10, 2008.

137 *she unleashed this torrent*: *Charlie Rose*, PBS, October 12, 2007.

137 *"She's a star!"*: John Heilemann and Mark Halperin, *Game Change: Obama and the Clintons, McCain and Palin, and the Race of a Lifetime* (New York: HarperCollins, 2010), 359.

138 *"She will not be ready on January 20"*: Kashino, "A. B. Culvahouse: The Man Who Vetted Sarah Palin."

138 *"I've been a risk taker all of my life"*: Balz and Johnson, *The Battle for America*.

138 *"John was the decider"*: Marisa McQuilken, "A. B. Culvahouse Praises Sarah Palin," *Legal Times*, April 17, 2009.

138 *"It's God's plan"*: Heilemann and Halperin, *Game Change*, 364.

138 *"It would be the first time I had ever heard her mention the fella"*: Johnston, *Deer in the Headlights*, 92.

139 *tapped to vet running mates*: Isaac Arnsdorf, "Could the Trump VP Vetting Process Go off the Rails?" Politico, July 14, 2016.

139 *"She doesn't know anything"*: Heilemann and Halperin, *Game Change*, 370.

139 *under the command of the Queen*: Raf Sanchez, "Sarah Palin 'Believed Queen was in Charge of British Forces in Iraq,' " *Telegraph*, February 20, 2012.

139 *the difference between England and the United Kingdom*: Dunn, *The Lies of Sarah Palin*, 202.

139 *she sought a meeting with Thatcher*: Patt Morrison, "Thatcher and Palin? Out of Frame, Out of Bounds," *Los Angeles Times*, June 15, 2010.

139 *Pledge of Allegiance*: Mark C. Toulouse, "Pledging Allegiance to the Pledge," *Religion & Ethics Newsweekly*, PBS, September 26, 2008.

140 *"He has a strong sense of character"*: Patricia Kilday Hart, "His Fantastic Four," *Texas Monthly*, August 1999.

140 *"Dan Quayle, as I've said before, is a very quick study"*: Cathleen Decker, "Quayle Welcomed by GOP Senators but Dole Is Tepid," *Los Angeles Times*, September 8, 1988.

140 *"I think he had to learn, but he was a quick study"*: "Michael Deaver Oral History," Miller Center, University of Virginia, September 12, 2002.

140 *"He was a quick study," Baker said*: "Howard H. Baker Jr. Oral History," Miller Center, University of Virginia, August 24, 2004.

140 *Palin's tutors treated her like a tabula rasa*: Heilemann and Halperin, *Game Change*, 370–71.

140 *fill-in sports reporter*: Elizabeth Holmes, "Sarah Palin, Sports Reporter," *Wall Street Journal*, August 31, 2008; Rick Chandler, "Sarah Palin's Former Sports Director Tells All," *Deadspin*, September 3, 2008.

141 *"[S]he didn't know what countries formed NAFTA"*: Dunn, *The Lies of Sarah Palin*, 201–2.

141 *"[H]er grasp of rudimentary facts and concepts was minimal"*: Heilemann and Halperin, *Game Change*, 397.

141 *"she preferred People magazine"*: Dunn, *The Lies of Sarah Palin*, 217.

141 *"I love C. S. Lewis"*: "Charlie Rose Green Room," October 12, 2007.

142 *she was a news junkie*: Kaylene Johnson, *Sarah: How a Hockey Mom Turned the Political Establishment Upside Down* (Epicenter Press, 2008), 21–22, 53.

142 *"I sure never saw her read a book"*: Johnston, *Deer in the Headlights*, 128.

142 *interview with Charlie Gibson*: *World News Tonight with Charles Gibson*, ABC, September 11, 2008.

143 *at least seven Bush Doctrines*: Michael Abramowitz, "Many Versions of 'Bush Doctrine,'" NBC News, September 13, 2008.

143 *Wasilla Assembly of God*: "Palin Says Iraq War Is 'Task from God,'" UPI, September 3, 2008.

143 *"would never presume to know God's will"*: *World News Tonight with Charles Gibson*, September 11, 2008.

143 *"I believe God wants me to be president"*: Alan Cooperman, "Bush Leaves Specifics of His Faith to Speculation," NBC News, September 16, 2004.

143 *"I've heard the call"*: Stephen Mansfield, *The Faith of George W. Bush* (Lake Mary, FL: Charisma House, 2003).

144 *"chosen by the grace of God to lead at that moment"*: Michael Duffy, "The President: Marching Alone," *Time*, September 9, 2002.

144 *"I think the Lord works in mysterious ways"*: Steven Waldman, "Heaven Sent," *Slate*, September 13, 2004.

144 *"I got lost in a blizzard of words there"*: *World News Tonight with Charles Gibson*, September 11, 2008.

144 *infamous grilling by CBS's Katie Couric*: *CBS Evening News*, CBS, September 24–30, 2008.

146 *"'Does any of this really matter?'"*: Andrew Halcro, "What It's Like to Debate Sarah Palin," *Christian Science Monitor*, October 1, 2008.

146 *they focused on Palin's strength: glittering generalities*: Heilemann and Halperin, *Game Change*, 404.

148 *a CNN poll showed Biden besting Palin in the debate*: "Debate Poll Says Biden Won, Palin Beat Expectations," CNN Politics, October 3, 2008.

150 *"shouldn't the public get the benefit of another Biden-Palin debate"*: William Kristol, "The Wright Stuff," *New York Times*, October 5, 2008.

150 *"our neighboring country of Afghanistan"*: "In Slip-Up Palin Calls Afghanistan 'Our Neighboring Country,'" Reuters, October 5, 2008.

150 *"not a man who sees America as you see America"*: Haroon Siddique, "Palin Makes Obama Terrorist Claim," *Guardian*, October 5, 2008.

151 *McCain was unprepared for what Palin had wrought*: Heilemann and Halperin, *Game Change*, 422.

151 *Masked Avengers*: "Palin's Staff Didn't Know French President's Name," *New Zealand Herald*, November 3, 2008.

152 *Obama and McCain both conferred with Fed chief Ben Bernanke*: Heilemann and Halperin, *Game Change*, 380–81.

153 *"I think that she helped usher in an era of know-nothingness"*: "The Big Story: Can They Beat Obama?" Event held by the *New Yorker*, November 14, 2011.

154 *"Life is too short to compromise time and resources"*: Speech in Wasilla, Alaska, July 3, 2009.

154 *"Sarah was sad for a while"*: Johnston, "Me and Mrs. Palin."

154 *$1.25 million advance*: Daniel Nasaw, "Sarah Palin Earned $1.25m Advance for Going Rogue Memoir," *Guardian*, October 27, 2009.

155 *this nugget of wisdom*: Sarah Palin, *Going Rogue: An American Life* (New York: HarperCollins, 2009), 105; John Wooden Legs, "Back on the War Ponies," in *We Are the People: Voices from the Other Side of American History*, eds. Nathaniel May, Clint Willis, and James W. Loewen (Boston: De Capo Press, 2003).

155 *Palin was nothing if not prolific*: Sarah Palin, *America by Heart: Reflections on Family, Faith, and Flag* (New York: Harper, 2010), 26–27, 189, 222–23.

156 *Palin here turns her attention to the Bible*: Sarah Palin, *Sweet Freedom: A Devotional* (Washington, DC: Regnery, 2015).

157 *gave her a multiyear deal at $1 million per annum*: Gabriel Sherman, "The Elephant in the Green Room," *New York*, May 20, 2011.

157 *"It's wonderful to be part of a place"*: "Palin to Join Fox News as Contributor," Fox News, January 11, 2010.

157 *"the wonder and majesty of Alaska"*: "Discovery Communications Acquires 'Sarah Palin's Alaska,'" Discovery, March 25, 2010.

157 *"She's a Great Shot"*: *Sarah Palin's Alaska*, TLC, December 5, 2010.

157 *"She once pulled it out, shook some bullets out of their box"*: Johnston, *Deer in the Headlights*.

158 *signature snippy style*: Bob Woodward and David S. Broder, "Quayle's Reputation vs. the Record," *Washington Post*, January 7, 1992.

158 *"Take Sarah Palin seriously"*: David S. Broder, "Sarah Palin Displays Her Pitch-Perfect Populism," *Washington Post*, February 11, 2010.

159 *The Tea Party had emerged*: Theda Skocpol and Vanessa Williamson, *The Tea Party and the Remaking of Republican Conservatism* (New York: Oxford University Press, 2012), 45–82, 104.

160 *"How can I make sure that I, that you"*: Speech at National Tea Party Convention, Nashville, Tennessee, February 6, 2010.

160 *"the government that governs least governs best"*: Speech at Tea Party Express Launch Rally, Searchlight, Nevada, March 27, 2010.

160 *endorsing as many candidates as she could*: Shira Toeplitz, "Palin Endorsement a Shock to Some," Politico, August 3, 2010.

161 *"Linda is running her own race"*: Mark Pazniokas, "Palin Says McMahon's a 'Mama Grizzly,'" *Connecticut Mirror*, October 7, 2010.

161 *"Sarah Palin is a giant in American politics"*: Brian Montopoli, "Rand Paul Claims Sarah Palin Endorsement," CBS News, February 1, 2010.

161 *"[D]on't give me the power in Washington to be making rules"*: Nick Baumann, "2010's Most Important Senate Race?" *Mother Jones*, August 3, 2010.

162 *"I'm gonna pass on the age of the Earth"*: Dan Amira, "Five Other Embarrassing Answers to the 'Age of the Earth' Question," *New York*, November 19, 2012.

162 *"just sunspot activity or just something in the geologic eons of time"*: Steve Schultze, "Sunspots Are Behind Climate Change, Johnson Says," *Milwaukee Journal Sentinel*, August 16, 2010.

162 *"Standard gargle"*: Andrew Jeong, "A GOP senator suggested gargling mouthwash to kill the coronavirus. Doctors and Listerine are skeptical," *Washington Post*, December 9, 2021.

163 *"those dumbasses at the Tea Party"*: Allison Sherry, "Senate Hopeful Buck Regrets Criticism of Tea Party Birthers," *Denver Post*, July 25, 2010.

163 *fellow mama grizzlies*: Paul Harris, "Mama Grizzlies Lead Republican Hunt for Angry Women's Votes," *Guardian*, October 23, 2010.

163 *"they would bring a chicken to the doctor"*: Richard Adams, "Pay Medical Bills with a Chicken, Says Republican Candidate," *Guardian*, April 21, 2010.

163 *"I have bartered with patients"*: Ben Smith, "Barter Background," Politico, April 21, 2010.

163 *"man-caused climate change mantra"*: Evan Lehmann, "Reid, in Fistfight, Could Take More Punches from Climate Bill," *New York Times*, May 26, 2010.

163 *science linking abortion to breast cancer*: Emily Richmond, "Little Chance Seen on Measure Calling for Abortion Warnings," *Las Vegas Sun*, April 10, 2001.

163 *separation of church and state*: Anjeanette Damon, "Sharron Angle's Take on Separation of Church and State," *Las Vegas Sun*, July 18, 2010.

164 *"Second Amendment remedies"*: Anjeanette Damon and David McGrath Schwartz, "Armed Revolt Part of Sharron Angle's Rhetoric," *Las Vegas Sun*, June 17, 2010.

164 *eliminating the IRS and auditing the Fed*: J. Patrick Coolican, "How the Candidates for Senate Would Fix, Not Fix, Wall Street," *Las Vegas Sun*, April 28, 2010.

164 *Sharia law*: Don Amira, "Sharron Angle Is Saying More Things That People Don't Understand," *New York*, October 8, 2010.

164 *"Sometimes dictators have good ideas"*: "Ensign Played Reid in Angle Debate Prep; Angle Once Said Dictators Have 'Good Ideas,'" *Las Vegas Sun*, November 17, 2010.

164 *O'Donnell outdid every other evangelical Christian*: Brian Montopoli, "Christine O'Donnell Wanted to Stop 'Whole Country from Having [Premarital] Sex,'" CBS News, September 24, 2010; Devin Dwyer, "Christine O'Donnell: Homosexuality an 'Identity Disorder,'" ABC News, September 18, 2010; Tim Grieve and Andy Barr, "Meet Christine O'Donnell . . . ," Politico, September 15, 2010.

164 *"Why aren't monkeys still evolving into humans?"*: *Politically Incorrect with Bill Maher*, HBO, October 15, 1998.

165 *"mice with fully functioning human brains"*: *The O'Reilly Factor*, Fox News, 2007.

165 *"the most egregious abuses of medical research"*: State of the Union address, January 31, 2006.

165 *"History does not look kindly on those"*: Steve Benen, "Conservatives Push for 'Human-Animal Hybrid' Ban," *Washington Monthly*, July 11, 2009.

165 *"The mixing of Human Embryos with Jellyfish cells"*: Kate Sheppard, "Georgia Lawmaker Wants to Make Sure Embryos Don't Glow in the Dark," *Huffington Post*, February 19, 2015.

166 *"I dabbled in witchcraft"*: *Politically Incorrect with Bill Maher*, HBO, October 29, 1999.

167 *"legitimate rape"*: Amy Davidson Sorkin, "What Does Todd Akin Think 'Legitimate Rape' Is?" *The New Yorker*, August 19, 2012.

167 *"Hand the mantle to someone else"*: Mollie Reilly, "Sarah Palin: Todd Akin Should 'Take One for the Team,'" *Huffington Post*, August 21, 2012.

167 *"even if life begins in that horrible situation of rape"*: Kim Geiger, "Indiana Senate Candidate Mourdock Calls Rape Pregnancy God's Will," *Los Angeles Times*, October 23, 2012.

168 *"the reason that the slaves were eventually freed"*: Vocal Point, Truth in Action Ministries, April 3, 2014.

168 *"Ground Zero Mosque supporters"*: Stephanie Condon, "Palin's 'Refudiate' Tweet on Mosque Near Ground Zero Draws Fire (For Substance and Style)," CBS News, July 20, 2010.

168 *"English is a living language"*: Tweet on July 18, 2010.

169   *"Word of the Year"*: "Refudiate Named New Oxford American Diction-
      ary's 2010 Word of the Year," Oxford University Press, November 16,
      2010.

169   *retell the story of Paul Revere's Midnight Ride*: Richard Adams, "Sarah Palin
      on Paul Revere's Ride: 'Hey British, We're Coming,'" *Guardian*, June 6,
      2011.

170   *"You're the state where the shot was heard around the world"*: Kendra Marr,
      "Bachmann Fails U.S. History 101," Politico, March 12, 2011.

170   *"worked tirelessly until slavery was no more in the United States"*: Speech to
      Iowans for Tax Relief in Des Moines, Iowa, January 21, 2011.

170   *Bachmann later defended her statement*: "Bachmann Defends 'Slavery' Re-
      marks," *Good Morning America*, June 28, 2011.

170   *"the thinking man's Sarah Palin"*: "Meghan McCain: Michele Bachmann
      'Smarter' Than Sarah Palin," *Huffington Post*, December 1, 2011.

171   *she boasted that she shared a birthplace*: Richard Adams, "Michele Bach-
      mann Gets Her John Waynes Mixed Up," *Guardian*, June 27, 2011.

171   *the U.S. would not have an embassy in Iran*: Molly Hunter, "US Embassy
      in Iran? Michele Bachmann's 'Oops' Moment," ABC News, December 1,
      2011.

171   *linking Obama to the 2009 swine flu epidemic*: Glenn Thrush, "Dems in
      Power During Flu, Bachmann Notes," Politico, April 28, 2009.

171   *"the rise of the Soviet Union"*: James Oliphant, "Michele Bachmann: Be-
      ware 'the Soviet Union,'" *Los Angeles Times*, August 19, 2011.

171   *"He is now putting us in Africa"*: Amanda Terkel, "Michele Bachmann:
      Obama 'Put Us in Libya. He Is Now Putting Us in Africa,'" *Huffington
      Post*, October 18, 2011.

171   *"Hoot Smalley"*: Speech on the floor of the House of Representatives,
      April 27, 2009.

172   *"Before we get started"*: Maggie Haberman, "Bachmann gives Elvis birth-
      day wishes on the anniversary of his death," *Politico*, August 16, 2011.

172   *"you know how I feel about guns!"*: Kelley Shannon, "Palin Endorses Perry
      for Governor," NBC DFW, February 3, 2009.

172   *"Oops"*: Republican Primary Debate, Oakland University, Rochester,
      Michigan, November 9, 2011.

173   *"the dangers of contraception in this country"*: Michael Scherer, "Rick San-
      torum Wants to Fight 'The Dangers of Contraception,'" *Time*, Febru-
      ary 14, 2012.

173   *"I can call this napkin a paper towel"*: The Last Word with Lawrence
       O'Donnell, MSNBC, August 9, 2011.

174   *"man on child, man on dog"*: Deena Zaru, "Rick Santorum 'Absolutely'
       Regrets Comparing Homosexuality to Bestiality," CNN Politics, July 23,
       2015.

174   *"he wants you to go to college"*: Felicia Sonmez, "Santorum: Obama Is 'a
       Snob' Because He Wants 'Everybody in America to Go to College,'"
       Washington Post, February 25, 2012.

174   *"If you were Satan"*: Speech at Ave Maria University in Ave Maria, Florida,
       August 29, 2008.

174   *"infielders for the Detroit Tigers"*: Katrina Trinko, "Romney Calls Himself
       a 'Severely Conservative Republican Governor,'" *National Review*, Febru-
       ary 10, 2012.

175   *$36,511 in campaign funds*: Jonathan D. Salant and Joshua Green, "Cain
       Used Campaign Funds to Buy Autobiography from His Company,"
       Bloomberg, October 18, 2011.

175   *"Who's the president of Uzbekistan?"*: Interview with David Brody, Chris-
       tian Broadcasting Network, October 8, 2011.

176   *first-person narration, lifted from the* Going Rogue *audiobook*: Robert
       Abele, "Movie Review: 'The Undefeated,'" *Los Angeles Times*, July 15,
       2011.

176   *it cost a reported million dollars to produce*: Scott Conroy, "Palin's Secret
       Weapon: New Film to Premiere in June," RealClearPolitics, May 25,
       2011; *"The Undefeated*: Grosses," Box Office Mojo.

176   *significantly less than the Republican National Committee paid in 2008*:
       Patrick Healy and Michael Luo, "$150,000 Wardrobe for Palin May Alter
       Tailor-Made Image," *New York Times*, October 22, 2008.

CHAPTER 3: THE THIRD STAGE: CELEBRATION

177   *"7-Eleven"*: Theodore Schleifer, "Donald Trump Mixes Up '9/11' with
       '7/11,'" CNN Politics, April 19, 2016.

178   *"I'm intelligent"*: Jerry Useem, "What Does Donald Trump Really Want?"
       Fortune, April 3, 2000.

178   *"I got very good marks"*: Late Edition with Wolf Blitzer, CNN, March 19,
       2004.

178   *"I was a really good student at the best school in the country"*: Good Morning
       America, ABC, March 17, 2011.

178   *"I'm, like, a really smart person"*: Kurtis Lee, "Donald Trump's Immigration Stance Divides, Inflames and Inspires," *Los Angeles Times*, July 12, 2015.

178   *"probably the hardest school to get into"*: *Meet the Press*, NBC, August 17, 2015.

178   *"my IQ is one of the highest"*: Tweet from May 8, 2013, as recorded in the Trump Twitter Archive.

178   *"I went to an Ivy League college"*: Callum Borchers, "Trump Says the Media Unfairly Portrays Him as Uncivil, Which He's Not Because He 'Went to an Ivy League College,'" *Washington Post*, October 25, 2017.

179   *"never release his grades or SAT scores"*: Grace Ashford, "Michael Cohen Says Trump Told Him to Threaten Schools Not to Release Grades," *New York Times*, February 27, 2019.

179   *"I have a very good brain and I've said a lot of things"*: *Morning Joe*, MSNBC, March 16, 2016.

179   *"I know more about ISIS than the generals do"*: Speech in Fort Dodge, Iowa, on November 12, 2015.

179   *"It would take an hour-and-a-half to learn everything"*: Lois Romano, "Donald Trump, Holding All the Cards: The Tower! The Team! The Money! The Future!" *Washington Post*, November 15, 1984.

179   *"I know more about courts than any human being on Earth"*: Speech in Beaumont, Texas, on November 14, 2015.

179   *"I know more about renewables than any human being on Earth"*: *Hannity*, Fox News, April 13, 2016.

180   *"I think nobody knows more about taxes than I do"*: *Good Morning America*, ABC, May 13, 2016.

180   *"Technology—nobody knows more about technology than me"*: Interview with Pete Hegseth, Fox News, December 31, 2018.

180   *"I know more about Cory than he knows about himself"*: Tweet from July 25, 2016, as recorded in the Trump Twitter Archive.

180   *"Nobody knows debt better than me"*: *CBS This Morning*, CBS, June 22, 2016.

180   *"stunningly uninformed"*: John Bolton, *The Room Where It Happened: A White House Memoir* (New York: Simon & Schuster, 2020).

180   called him an *"idiot"*: Eli Watkins, "Former Trump Aide Says He's Refusing Mueller Subpoena: 'Screw That,'" CNN Politics, March 5, 2018; Michael Wolff, *Fire and Fury: Inside the Trump White House* (New York:

Henry Holt, 2018); Carol E. Lee, Courtney Kube, Kristen Welker, and Stephanie Ruhle, "Kelly Thinks He's Saving U.S. from Disaster, Calls Trump 'Idiot,' Say White House Staffers," NBC News, April 30, 2018.

180 *H. R. McMaster, the national security adviser*: Joseph Bernstein, "Sources: McMaster Mocked Trump's Intelligence at a Private Dinner," BuzzFeed, November 20, 2017.

180 *"fucking moron"*: Carol E. Lee, Kristen Welker, Stephanie Ruhle, and Dafna Linzer, "Tillerson's Fury at Trump Required an Intervention from Pence," NBC News, October 4, 2017.

181 *According to the Flesch-Kincaid grade-level test*: Bill Frischling, "'Stable Genius'—Let's Go to the Data," Factba.se, January 8, 2018.

181 *"I have the best words"*: Speech in Hilton Head, South Carolina, on December 20, 2015.

181 *misspelled a word every five days on Twitter*: Marina di Marzo, "How Often Does Trump Misspell Words on Twitter? These Researchers Have an Answer," CNN Business, November 3, 2019.

182 *"Prince of Whales"*: Tweet from June 13, 2019, as recorded in the Trump Twitter Archive.

182 *"Rupublicans"*: Tweet from October 30, 2019, as recorded in the Trump Twitter Archive.

182 *"hamberders"*: Tweet from January 14, 2019, as recorded in the Trump Twitter Archive.

182 *"leightweight chocker"*: Harper Neidig, "Trump Stumbles Over Spelling in Twitter Rant About Debate," The Hill, February 26, 2016.

182 *"Melanie"*: Tweet from May 19, 2018, as recorded in the Trump Twitter Archive.

182 *The list goes on*: Tweets from June 8, 2019, May 3, 2017, and December 19, 2019, as recorded in the Trump Twitter Archive; Deena Zaru and Tal Kopan, "Marco Rubio Teases Donald Trump over Twitter Spelling," CNN Politics, February 26, 2016; Martin Pengelly, "Donald Trump Accuses China of 'Unpresidented' Act over US Navy Drone," *Guardian*, December 17, 2016.

182 *His favorite words*: Tweets from February 15, 2020, August 19, 2017, and March 4, 2017, as recorded in the Trump Twitter Archive; Aidan Quigley, "Make America Spell Again? 25 of Donald Trump's Twitter Spelling Errors," *Newsweek*, June 25, 2017.

182 *he typed "lose" and "unfair" as "loose" and "infair"*: Tweets from January 31, 2016, and October 30, 2019, as recorded in the Trump Twitter Archive.

182 *his habit of randomly capitalizing*: Tweets from October 26, 2020, and December 30, 2020, as recorded in the Trump Twitter Archive.

182 *he believes an apostrophe is called a hyphen*: Tweet from September 27, 2019, as recorded in the Trump Twitter Archive.

183 *"I read passages"*: *Megyn Kelly Presents*, Fox News, May 27, 2016.

183 *"I seriously doubt that Trump has ever read a book"*: Jane Mayer, "Donald Trump's Ghostwriter Tells All," *The New Yorker*, July 18, 2016.

183 *he kept a collection of Hitler's speeches*: Marie Brenner, "After the Gold Rush," *Vanity Fair*, September 1990.

183 *according to an email attributed to his chief economic adviser*: Wolff, *Fire and Fury*.

183 *National Security Council staffers tried to trick him*: Steve Hollands and Jeff Mason, "Embroiled in Controversies, Trump Seeks Boost on Foreign Trip," Reuters, May 17, 2017.

184 *"I like bullets or I like as little as possible"*: Jim VandeHei and Mike Allen, "Reality Bites: Trump's Wake-Up Call," Axios, January 18, 2017.

184 *he had to file for bankruptcy six times*: Tom Winter, "Trump Bankruptcy Math Doesn't Add Up," NBC News, June 24, 2016.

184 *"What's seventeen times six?"*: *The Howard Stern Show*, February 27, 2006.

184 *"I know South Korea better than anyone"*: White House Coronavirus Task Force briefing, March 30, 2020.

184 *His biggest math mistake*: Ryan Teague Beckwith, "President Trump's Budget Includes a $2 Trillion Math Mistake," *Time*, May 23, 2017.

184 *"global warming"*: Tweet from January 28, 2019, as recorded in the Trump Twitter Archive.

184 *"created by and for the Chinese"*: Tweet from November 6, 2012, as recorded in the Trump Twitter Archive.

185 *"lightbulbs can cause cancer"*: Tweet from October 17, 2012, as recorded in the Trump Twitter Archive.

185 *"Not only are wind farms disgusting looking"*: Tweet from April 3, 2012, as recorded in the Trump Twitter Archive.

185 *"The fumes coming up to make these massive windmills"*: Presidential Debate at Belmont University in Nashville, Tennessee, October 22, 2020.

185 *"the noise causes cancer"*: Speech at a National Republican Congressional Committee event, April 2, 2019.

185 *"kills all the birds"*: Presidential Debate at Belmont University in Nashville, Tennessee, October 22, 2020.

186 *"the Kansas Poison Control Center"*: "Kansas Official Says Man Drank Cleaner After Trump Floated Dangerous Disinfectant Remedy," *Wichita Eagle*, April 28, 2020.

186 *"The closest thing is in 1917"*: White House Press Conference, August 10, 2020.

187 *"Frederick Douglass is an example of somebody who's done an amazing job"*: White House event, February 1, 2017.

187 *"he saw what was happening with regard to the Civil War"*: Jessica Estepa, "Note to President Trump: Andrew Jackson Wasn't Alive for the Civil War," *USA Today*, May 1, 2017.

187 *He claimed repeatedly that he'd been named*: Tara Subramaniam, Daniel Dale, and Holmes Lybrand, "Fact Check: Former Michigan Congressman Sheds Light on Trump's Claim to Be Michigan's 'Man of the Year,'" CNN Politics, August 16, 2019.

188 *Veterans Choice*: Daniel Dale, "Trump Walks Out of News Conference After Reporter Asks Him About Veterans Choice Lie He's Told More Than 150 Times," CNN Politics, August 9, 2020.

188 *"You know how famous Concord is?"*: Speech in Manchester, New Hampshire, February 10, 2020.

188 *"I never knew we had so many countries"*: Remarks at a White House banquet with Japanese prime minister Shinzo Abe, November 6, 2017.

188 *He didn't know the difference between England and Great Britain*: Piers Morgan, "Up Close and VERY Personal with The Donald on Air Force One," *Daily Mail*, July 14, 2018.

188 *He didn't know that the Republic of Ireland wasn't part of the UK*: Kate Lyons, "'Embarrassing' Trump Told Ireland Is Not Part of UK," *Irish Times*, July 13, 2018.

188 *he didn't know that Britain possessed nuclear weapons*: Bolton, *The Room Where It Happened*.

188 *"Teresa"*: Jane Onyanga-Omara, "White House Misspells Theresa May's Name Three Times Ahead of Trump Meeting," *USA Today*, January 27, 2017.

188 *thought Colorado bordered Mexico*: Kevin Liptak and Caroline Kelly, "Trump Says US Is Building a Wall in Colorado—a State That Doesn't Border Mexico," CNN Politics, October 24, 2019.

188   *Finland was a part of Russia*: Bolton, *The Room Where It Happened*.

188   *"Nambia"*: "Where Is 'Nambia'? President Trump 'Invents' African Country," BBC, September 21, 2017.

188   *"Thighland"*: Speech in Clyde, Ohio, August 6, 2020.

188   *"Nipple" and "Button"*: John Walcott, " 'Willful Ignorance.' Inside President Trump's Troubled Intelligence Briefings," *Time*, February 2, 2019; Daniel Lippman, "Trump's Diplomatic Learning Curve: Time Zones, 'Nambia' and 'Nipple,' " Politico, August 13, 2018.

188   *"Ah, I think I can set him up"*: Ibid.

189   *a 2018 meeting with the leaders of Latvia*: Tom Porter, "Trump Confused the Baltics with Balkans—and Accused Confused Leaders of Starting Yugoslav Wars," *Newsweek*, November 11, 2018.

189   *he seemed confused about whether Presbyterians were Christians*: M. J. Lee, "God and the Don," CNN Politics, June 2017.

190   *"The success of professional wrestling"*: Chris Hedges, *Empire of Illusion: The End of Literacy and the Triumph of Spectacle* (New York: Nation Books, 2009), 5–6.

190   *an almost uninterrupted string of failures*: Ben Terris, "And Then There Was the Time Donald Trump Bought a Football Team . . . ," *Washington Post*, October 19, 2015; Tom Winter and Dartunorro Clark, "Federal Court Approves $25 Million Trump University Settlement," NBC News, February 6, 2018; Dylan Matthews, "I Bought Donald Trump's Board Game. You Should Not," Vox, August 19, 2015.

190   *"islands of competence"*: Robert Brooks and Sam Goldstein, *Raising Resilient Children: Fostering Strength, Hope, and Optimism in Your Child* (New York: McGraw-Hill, 2001).

191   *"the enemy of the people"*: Tweet from October 29, 2018, as recorded in the Trump Twitter Archive.

191   *Friedrich Trump*: Gwenda Blair, *The Trumps: Three Generations That Built an Empire* (New York: Touchstone, 2000), 61–90.

191   *building thousands of apartments and refusing to rent them to Black applicants*: Tracie Rozhon, "Fred C. Trump, Postwar Master Builder of Housing for Middle Class, Dies at 93," *New York Times*, June 26, 1999; Jonathan Mahler and Steve Eder, " 'No Vacancies' for Blacks: How Donald Trump Got His Start, and Was First Accused of Bias," *New York Times*, August 27, 2016.

191   *"My father taught me everything I know"*: Jason Horowitz, "Fred Trump Taught His Son the Essentials of Showboating Self-Promotion," *New York Times*, August 12, 2016.

191   *Kew-Forest*: Michael D'Antonio, *Never Enough: Donald Trump and the Pursuit of Success* (New York: Thomas Dunne, 2015), 40.

192   *"I punched my music teacher"*: Donald Trump with Tony Schwartz, *Trump: The Art of the Deal* (New York: Random House, 1987), 71–72.

192   *New York Military Academy*: Paul Schwartzman and Michael E. Miller, "Confident. Incorrigible. Bully: Little Donny Was a Lot Like Candidate Donald Trump," *Washington Post*, June 22, 2016; Brent Johnson, "Trump's Military School Roommate: Our Goal Was 'to Lead America,'" NJ.com, September 13, 2015.

192   *"When I look at myself in the first grade"*: D'Antonio, *Never Enough*.

192   *"You're a king"*: Harry Hurt III, *Lost Tycoon: The Many Lives of Donald J. Trump* (New York: W. W. Norton, 1993).

192   *Trump's admission to Penn*: Mary L. Trump, *Too Much and Never Enough: How My Family Created the World's Most Dangerous Man* (New York: Simon & Schuster, 2020), 72.

193   *In 1973, the U.S. Department of Justice sued Trump Management*: David W. Dunlap, "1973: Meet Donald Trump," *New York Times*, July 30, 2015.

193   *A judge dismissed the Trumps' countersuit*: Michael Kranish and Robert O'Harrow Jr., "Inside the Government's Racial Bias Case Against Donald Trump's Company, and How He Fought It," *Washington Post*, January 23, 2016.

193   *a glowing and not-very-fact-checked profile*: Judy Klemesrud, "Donald Trump, Real Estate Promoter, Builds Image as He Buys Buildings," *New York Times*, November 1, 1976.

194   *A 1984* Times *article belatedly corrected this whopper*: William E. Geist, "The Expanding Empire of Donald Trump," *New York Times Magazine*, April 8, 1984.

194   *Schwartz did far more than ghostwrite* The Art of the Deal: Jane Mayer, "Donald Trump's Ghostwriter Tells All," *The New Yorker*, July 18, 2016.

195   *"Perhaps the most important thing I learned at Wharton"*: Trump with Schwartz, *The Art of the Deal*, 77.

195   *For anyone interested in a book that translates* The Art of the Deal *into reality*: Barbara A. Res, *Tower of Lies: What My Eighteen Years of Working*

with Donald Trump Reveals About Him (Los Angeles: Graymalkin Media, 2020), 7–15, 81–83.

196 *a speech for Trump in Portsmouth, New Hampshire*: Michael Kruse, "Roger Stone's Last Dirty Trick," Politico, January 25, 2019; Frank Clifford, "Non-Candidate Trump Talks Tough on Political Issues," *Los Angeles Times*, October 23, 1987.

197 *teased the trip in September*: Michael Oreskes, "Trump Gives a Vague Hint of Candidacy," *New York Times*, September 2, 1987; Fox Butterfield, "New Hampshire Speech Earns Praise for Trump," *New York Times*, October 23, 1987.

197 *"We have countries out there that are our so-called allies"*: *The Phil Donahue Show*, November 30, 1987.

197 *"Mrs. Nixon told me you were great"*: Charley Lanyon, "This 1987 Letter from Nixon to Future Candidate Trump Predicted His Win," *New York*, November 10, 2016.

197 *Trump reached out to Roger Stone's business partner, Lee Atwater*: Jane Mayer, "The Secret Papers of Lee Atwater, Who Invented the Scurrilous Tactics That Trump Normalized," *The New Yorker*, May 6, 2021.

198 *"strange and unbelievable"*: Jon Meacham, "Nostalgia for the Grace of George H. W. Bush," *New York Times*, October 15, 2016.

198 *had purchased in bulk to cement its best-seller status*: Alex Shepherd, "Art of the Steal," *The New Republic*, September 18, 2017.

198 *"he's conservative, and he's rich"*: Interview with Larry King, CNN, August 17, 1988.

199 *place ads in the* New York Times, *the* Washington Post: Ilan Ben-Meir, "That Time Trump Spent Nearly $100,000 on an Ad Criticizing U.S. Foreign Policy in 1987," BuzzFeed, July 10, 2015; "Real Estate Developer Donald J. Trump Bought . . ." Associated Press, 1987.

199 *the Associated Press reported that U.S. oil imports*: "Imports of Oil at 6-Year High," Associated Press, September 18, 1986.

199 *he would move homeless people into vacant units*: Jonathan Mahler, "Tenants Thwarted Donald Trump's Central Park Real Estate Ambitions," *New York Times*, April 18, 2016; Jose Pagliery, "Donald Trump Was a Nightmare Landlord in the 1980s," CNN Money, March 28, 2016.

199 *"a phenomenon that started two years ago"*: *Tucker Carlson Tonight*, Fox News, July 1, 2019.

199 *Trump's most notorious work in the full-page-ad art form*: Jan Ransom, "Trump Will Not Apologize for Calling for Death Penalty Over Central Park Five," *New York Times*, June 18, 2019; James Queally, "$41-Million Settlement in 'Central Park Five' Case Gets Final Approval," *Los Angeles Times*, September 5, 2014.

200 *a colt named Alibi*: Will Hobson, "The Sad Saga of Thoroughbred D.J. Trump, Donald Trump's Lone Foray into Horse Racing," *Washington Post*, May 19, 2017.

201 *jumping into professional boxing*: Hurt, *Lost Tycoon*.

201 *Having insanely overspent*: Matt Viser, "Donald Trump's Airline Went from Opulence in the Air to Crash Landing," *Boston Globe*, May 27, 2016; "Trump Boat Was Sunk by Hotel Debts," *Times* (London), February 13, 2017.

201 *a downcast Donald with the headline "Trump: The Fall"*: *Newsweek*, June 18, 1990.

202 Home Alone 2: Kevin Polowy, "Donald Trump Forced His Way into 'Home Alone 2,' and Audiences Ate It Up," Yahoo!, November 13, 2020; "CBC Edit of Trump Scene from Home Alone 2 Was Done in 2014," CBC News, December 26, 2019.

202 *"If there is one word to describe Atlantic City"*: Priscilla Painton, "Atlantic City, New Jersey: Boardwalk of Broken Dreams," *Time*, September 25, 1989.

202 *"I don't have any experience"*: Presidential Debate in St. Louis, Missouri, October 11, 1992.

203 *Whenever someone criticized him*: Susan Baer, "Ross Speak: Perot Tosses Homey Homilies Around Faster Than Snow Melts on a Hot July Day," *Baltimore Sun*, October 23, 1992.

203 *he claimed that Republican operatives were wiretapping his office*: Richard L. Berke, "Perot Says He Quit in July to Thwart G.O.P. 'Dirty Tricks,'" *New York Times*, October 26, 1992.

203 *"We got the safety valve"*: Concession speech, Dallas, Texas, November 3, 1992.

203 *Patsy Cline's "Crazy"*: John M. Broder, "Perot Winds Up Campaign with a New Theme: 'Crazy,'" *Los Angeles Times*, November 3, 1992.

203 *"My governor can beat up your governor"*: Pam Belluck, "A Tough Match: 'Jesse the Gov.' vs. Daily Grind," *New York Times*, January 4, 1999.

204   *"I'll be on television a lot"*: Geraldine Baum, "The Donald Erases Line Between Politics, Comedy," *Los Angeles Times*, December 6, 1999.

204   *"probably sounded better in the original German"*: Katharine Q. Seelye, "Molly Ivins, Columnist, Dies at 62," *New York Times*, February 1, 2007.

204   *"He's a Hitler lover"*: *Meet the Press*, NBC, October 24, 1999.

204   *Stone pitted Trump against Buchanan*: David Freedlander, "An Oral History of Donald Trump's Almost-Run for President in 2000," *New York*, October 11, 2018.

205   *"I may have played some role in derailing them as a party"*: *Get Me Roger Stone*, Dylan Bank, Daniel DiMauro, and Morgan Pehme, dirs., Netflix, 2017.

205   *A 60* Minutes *segment filmed in 1999*: *60 Minutes II*, CBS, January 1, 2000.

205   *body-slammed Minnesota's $3 billion budget surplus*: "In Grim Forecast, Minnesota Predicts $4.56 Billion Deficit," *Minnesota Daily*, December 5, 2002.

206   The Apprentice *was an exquisite work of video chicanery*: Patrick Radden Keefe, "How Mark Burnett Resurrected Donald Trump as an Icon of American Success," *The New Yorker*, December 27, 2018.

208   *"I knew everyone in my class except Donald Trump"*: Rebecca Tan and Alex Rabin, "Many of Trump's Wharton Classmates Don't Remember Him," *Daily Pennsylvanian*, February 20, 2017.

209   *"This all dates back to when we were growing up together in Kenya"*: *The Tonight Show with Jay Leno*, NBC, October 24, 2012.

209   *"more power to him"*: *Justice with Judge Jeanine Pirro*, Fox News, April 9, 2011.

209   *"pseudo-events"*: Daniel J. Boorstin, *The Image, or What Happened to the American Dream* (New York: Atheneum, 1961), 12.

211   *He didn't mention Poland*: Massimo Calabresi, "What Donald Trump Knew About Undocumented Workers at His Signature Tower," *Time*, August 25, 2016.

212   *Know-Nothings*: Mathieu Billings, "Nativist Riots and the Know-Nothing Party," Bill of Rights Institute; *Catholic Historical Review* 11, no. 2 (July 1925), 217–51.

212   *filing a trademark application*: Katherine Kerrick, "(Trade)mark America Great Again: Should Political Slogans Be Able to Receive Trademark

Protection?" *University of New Hampshire Law Review* 18, no. 2 (March 2020), 309–42.

212 *Jabberwocky-like endorsement speech*: Speech at Iowa State University, Ames, Iowa, January 19, 2016.

213 *"How many Palestinians were on those airplanes on September 9?"*: *Hardball with Chris Matthews*, MSNBC, April 30, 2002.

213 *"They want an outsider this time"*: *Today*, NBC, May 12, 2016.

213 *"flooding the zone with shit"*: Michael Lewis, "Has Anyone Seen the President?" Bloomberg, February 9, 2018.

214 *the easily refutable claim that Trump's inauguration crowd*: White House Press Briefing, January 21, 2017.

214 *"alternative facts"*: *Meet the Press*, NBC, January 22, 2017.

215 *"Bowling Green Massacre"*: *Hardball with Chris Matthews*, MSNBC, February 2, 2017.

215 *Trump bemoaned a terror attack in Sweden*: Speech in Melbourne, Florida, February 18, 2017.

215 *"What has he been smoking?"*: Tweet on February 19, 2017.

215 *Sehwan*: Alexandra Topping, " 'Sweden, Who Would Believe This?': Trump Cites Non-Existent Terror Attack," *Guardian*, February 19, 2017.

216 *"Every time you see a Caravan"*: Tweet on October 22, 2018, as recorded in the Trump Twitter Archive.

216 *"In addition to stopping all payments to these countries"*: Tweet on October 18, 2018, as recorded in the Trump Twitter Archive.

216 *Family America Project*: David Corn, "Marjorie Taylor Greene Was a Moderator of a Facebook Group Featuring Death Threats and Racist Memes," *Mother Jones*, February 3, 2021.

216 *California wildfires were caused by lasers*: Jonathan Chait, "GOP Congresswoman Blamed Wildfires on Secret Jewish Space Laser," *New York*, January 28, 2021.

217 *Anglo-Saxon caucus*: Alan Fram, "New Conservative Group Would Save 'Anglo-Saxon' Traditions," Associated Press, April 17, 2021.

217 *Boebert said that she started open-carrying a firearm*: Daniel Dale, "Fact-Checking Lauren Boebert's Story About a Man Getting Beaten to Death Outside Her Restaurant," CNN Politics, March 13, 2021.

217 *"Protecting and defending the Constitution"*: Tweet on February 19, 2021.

217 *House Speaker Nancy Pelosi proposed fining members*: "Pelosi Wants Fines

for U.S. Lawmakers Who Don't Comply with Firearms Screening," Reuters, January 13, 2021.

218   *"How did we get here? A lot of these kids don't know"*: Paul Gattis, "Tuberville Says Alabama Schools Don't Teach 'Good and Bad' of Country's History," AL.com, October 28, 2020.

218   *A quick way to improve education*: Todd Stacy, "In the Weeds w/ Tommy Tuberville, Alabama's Next Senator," *Alabama Daily News*, November 12, 2020.

218   *"[T]here is one person that changes climate in this country"*: Ed Howell, "Tuberville Talks on Issues During DME Interview," *Daily Mountain Eagle*, October 30, 2019.

218   *"change the course of the moon's orbit"*: Virtual Hearing of the Subcommittee on National Parks, Forests, and Public Lands, June 8, 2021.

218   *"[W]hen they want to go on a date"*: Emily Heil, "Louie Gohmert: Best Caribou Wingman Ever," *Washington Post*, February 7, 2012.

219   *"The caribou love it"*: Zachary Coile, "The Last Refuge," *San Francisco Chronicle*, August 28, 2005.

219   the ocean floor is rising: Eli Watkins, "GOP Congressman Asks If Rocks Are Causing Sea Levels to Rise," CNN Politics, May 18, 2018.

219   *"I'm not a scientist"*: Scott Maxwell, "Rick Scott on Climate Change: 'I'm Not a Scientist . . . I'm Not a Scientist . . . Well, I'm Not a Scientist,'" *Orlando Sentinel*, May 28, 2014; Michael Hainey, "All Eyez on Him," *GQ*, November 19, 2012.

220   *cease using the terms "climate change" and "global warming"*: Tristram Korten, "In Florida, Officials Ban Term 'Climate Change,'" *Miami Herald*, March 8, 2015.

220   *Gaetz demonstrated his fealty to Donald Trump*: Lia Eustachewich, "Florida Rep. Matt Gaetz Is Engaged to Ginger Luckey," *New York Post*, December 31, 2020.

220   *"Hitler was right on one thing"*: "Republican Congresswoman Mary Miller Quotes Hitler During Rally," *Guardian*, January 10, 2021.

221   *"Hitler did a lot of good things"*: Michael C. Bender, *Frankly, We Did Win This Election: The Inside Story of How Trump Lost* (New York: Grand Central, 2021).

221   *cartoonish gas mask*: Caroline Kelly, "Rep. Matt Gaetz Wore a Gas Mask on House Floor During Vote on Coronavirus Response Package," CNN Politics, March 9, 2020.

221 *casting doubt on both climate change and the theory of evolution*: Alan Yuhas, "How Republican Presidential Candidates Are Getting Away with Denying Evolution," *Guardian*, May 5, 2015; "Scientific Evidence Doesn't Support Global Warming, Sen. Ted Cruz Says," *Morning Edition*, NPR, December 9, 2015.

221 *slammed the* Sesame Street *legend*: Tweet on November 6, 2021.

222 *"throwing their lives into potential disarray"*: Zac Anderson, "Coronavirus Florida: DeSantis Says No to Stay-at-Home Order as Pressure Builds," *Florida Times-Union*, March 23, 2020.

222 *"That is the dumbest shit I have heard in a long time"*: Matt Dixon, "'Dumbest S—': DeSantis Takes Heat as He Goes His Own Way on Coronavirus," Politico, March 24, 2020.

222 *"suppressed unfavorable facts"*: Mario Ariza, David Fleshler, and Cindy Krischer Goodman, "Secrecy and Spin: How Florida's Governor Misled the Public on the COVID-19 Pandemic," *South Florida Sun Sentinel*, December 3, 2020.

223 *"the worst mistake I ever made in my life"*: Tony Messenger, "Danforth Calls His Support of Hawley the 'Worst Mistake' of His Life," *St. Louis Post-Dispatch*, January 7, 2021.

223 *Fred Trump created the blueprint for what Trumps do*: Dennis Lynch, "Remembering the Day Trump's Dad Destroyed a Coney Icon," *Brooklyn Paper*, May 23, 2016; "10 Secrets of Fred Trump's Coney Island Revealed in History Project Exhibit," Coney Island History Project, May 26, 2016.

224 *Bonwit Teller Building*: Robert D. McFadden, "Developer Scraps Bonwit Sculptures," *New York Times*, June 6, 1980.

224 Hardhat Riot: David Paul Kuhn, *The Hardhat Riot: Nixon, New York City, and the Dawn of the White Working-Class Revolution* (New York: Oxford University Press, 2020), 176, 179–80, 198–99, 223, 252.

225 *"Whether one condones this kind of violence or not"*: Media Memorandum for the President from Patrick J. Buchanan, May 21, 1970.

226 *Brooks Brothers Riot*: Michael E. Miller, "'It's Insanity!': How the 'Brooks Brothers Riot' Killed the 2000 Recount in Miami," *Washington Post*, November 15, 2018; Dexter Filkins and Dana Canedy, "Protest Influenced Miami-Dade's Decision to Stop Recount," *New York Times*, November 24, 2000.

226 *They proceeded to Broward County*: Nicholas Kulish and Jim VandeHei,

"GOP Protest in Miami-Dade Is a Well-Organized Effort," *Wall Street Journal*, November 27, 2000.

226   *"I think you'd have riots"*: Eugene Scott, "Donald Trump on Brokered Convention: 'I Think You'd Have Riots,'" CNN Politics, March 17, 2016.

226   *"I think bad things would happen"*: *New Day*, CNN, March 16, 2016.

227   *"I can tell you I have the support of the police"*: Alexander Marlow, Matthew Boyle, Amanda House, and Charlie Spierling, "President Donald Trump: Paul Ryan Blocked Subpoenas of Democrats," Breitbart, March 13, 2019.

228   *"I was a Republican in my youth"*: Daniel W. Drezner, "What Do Republicans Stand For in 2019?" *Washington Post*, July 16, 2019.

228   *One prominent Republican saw things differently*: Stuart Stevens, *It Was All a Lie: How the Republican Party Became Donald Trump* (New York: Knopf, 2020), 11, 17–18.

229   *a desperate Pence sought advice from a fellow Indianan*: Bob Woodward and Robert Costa, *Peril* (New York: Simon & Schuster, 2021), 198–200.

CONCLUSION: DEMOCRACY'S BRAKING SYSTEM

234   *"The real safeguard of democracy, therefore, is education"*: Message for American Education Week, September 27, 1938.

234   *many Tea Partiers were better educated*: Theda Skocpol and Vanessa Williamson, *The Tea Party and the Remaking of Republican Conservatism* (New York: Oxford University Press, 2012), 23–44.

234   *polling after the 2020 election*: "Ipsos/Reuters Poll: The Big Lie," Ipsos, May 21, 2021.

234   *two out of three Democrats*: Kelly Frankovic, "Russia's Impact on the Election Seen Through Partisan Eyes," YouGov America, March 9, 2018.

235   *What are these productive activities?*: Eitan Hersh, *Politics Is for Power: How to Move Beyond Political Hobbyism, Take Action, and Make Real Change* (New York: Scribner, 2020), 21–28, 94–105.

236   *Hersh cites the case of Amy McGrath*: Eitan Hersh, "Rage-Donating Only Made Democrats Feel Better," *The Atlantic*, November 12, 2020.

237   *"very few folks who looked like me"*: Dorany Pineda, "Barack Obama Has Some Advice for Young Activists: 'Be Clear and Strategic,'" *Los Angeles Times*, April 21, 2021.

238   *Question 3 on the Massachusetts ballot*: Brian Resnick, "How to Talk Someone Out of Bigotry," Vox, January 29, 2020.

238 *"big league"*: Liam Stack, "Yes, Trump Really Is Saying 'Big League,' Not 'Bigly,' Linguists Say," *New York Times*, October 24, 2016.

239 *In an essay published in 2021*: James Bernard Murphy, "Meaning and Knowledge: Why Stories Beat Facts," *Valley News*, April 17, 2021.

240 *a Democratic victory in Georgia would be a long shot*: Aaron Blake, "Democrats Are Fighting History in the Georgia Runoffs," *Washington Post*, January 5, 2021.

240 *unprecedented turnout*: Bernard L. Fraga, Zachary Peskowitz, and James Szewczyk, "New Georgia Runoffs Data Finds That More Black Voters Than Usual Came Out. Trump Voters Stayed Home," *Washington Post*, January 29, 2021.

Index

About the Author

ANDY BOROWITZ is an award-winning comedian and *New York Times* bestselling author. He grew up in Cleveland, Ohio, and graduated from Harvard College, where he was president of the *Harvard Lampoon*. In 1998, he began contributing humor to *The New Yorker*'s "Shouts & Murmurs" and "Talk of the Town" departments, and in 2001, he created The Borowitz Report, a satirical news column, which has millions of readers around the world. In 2012, *The New Yorker* began publishing The Borowitz Report. As a storyteller, he hosted "Stories at the Moth" from 1999 to 2009. As a comedian, he has played to sold-out venues around the world, including during his national tour, "Make America Not Embarrassing Again," from 2018 to 2020. He is the first-ever winner of the National Press Club's humor award. He lives with his family in New Hampshire.